Programming in CoffeeScript

Developer's Library

ESSENTIAL REFERENCES FOR PROGRAMMING PROFESSIONALS

Developer's Library books are designed to provide practicing programmers with unique, high-quality references and tutorials on the programming languages and technologies they use in their daily work.

All books in the *Developer's Library* are written by expert technology practitioners who are especially skilled at organizing and presenting information in a way that's useful for other programmers.

Key titles include some of the best, most widely acclaimed books within their topic areas:

PHP & MySQL Web Development
Luke Welling & Laura Thomson
ISBN 978-0-672-32916-6

MySQL
Paul DuBois
ISBN-13: 978-0-672-32938-8

Linux Kernel Development
Robert Love
ISBN-13: 978-0-672-32946-3

Python Essential Reference
David Beazley
ISBN-13: 978-0-672-32862-6

Programming in Objective-C
Stephen G. Kochan
ISBN-13: 978-0-321-56615-7

PostgreSQL
Korry Douglas
ISBN-13: 978-0-672-33015-5

Developer's Library books are available at most retail and online bookstores, as well as by subscription from Safari Books Online at **safari.informit.com**

Developer's Library
informit.com/devlibrary

Programming in CoffeeScript

Mark Bates

Addison-Wesley

Upper Saddle River, NJ • Boston • Indianapolis • San Francisco
New York • Toronto • Montreal • London • Munich • Paris • Madrid
Cape Town • Sydney • Tokyo • Singapore • Mexico City

Programming in CoffeeScript

ISBN-13: 978-0-32-182010-5
ISBN-10: 0-32-182010-X

Library of Congress Cataloging-in-Publication Data is on file

Trademarks

Warning and Disclaimer

Bulk Sales

Pearson offers excellent discounts on this book when ordered in quantity for bulk purchases or special sales. For more information, please contact

U.S. Corporate and Government Sales
1-800-382-3419
corpsales@pearsontechgroup.com

For sales outside of the U.S., please contact

International Sales
international@pearsoned.com

Text printed in the United States on recycled paper at R.R. Donnelley in Crawfordsville, Indiana

First printing May 2012

Editor-in-Chief
Mark Taub

Acquisitions Editor
Debra Williams Cauley

Senior Development Editor
Chris Zahn

Managing Editor
Kristy Hart

Project Editor
Andy Beaster

Copy Editor
Barbara Hacha

Indexer
Tim Wright

Proofreader
Debbie Williams

Technical Editors
Stuart Garner
Dan Pickett

Publishing Coordinator
Olivia Basegio

Book Designer
Gary Adair

Compositor
Nonie Ratcliff

❖

Rachel, Dylan, and Leo: My life for you.

❖

Contents at a Glance

Preface xv

Part I: Core CoffeeScript

1 Getting Started 3

2 The Basics 13

3 Control Structures 33

4 Functions and Arguments 65

5 Collections and Iterations 81

6 Classes 123

Part II: CoffeeScript in Practice

7 Cake and Cakefiles 161

8 Testing with Jasmine 171

9 Intro to Node.js 193

10 Example: Todo List Part 1 (Server-side) 217

11 Example: Todo List Part 2 (Client-side w/ jQuery) 237

12 Example: Todo List Part 3 (Client-side w/ Backbone.js) 255

Index 277

Table of Contents

Dedication v

Acknowledgments xii

About the Author xiv

Preface xv

What Is CoffeeScript? xvii
Who Is This Book For? xix
How to Read This Book xix
How This Book Is Organized xxi
  Part I: Core CoffeeScript xxii
  Part II: CoffeeScript in Practice xxii
Installing CoffeeScript xxiii
How to Run the Examples xxiii
Notes xxiv

Part I: Core CoffeeScript

1 Getting Started 3

The CoffeeScript REPL 3
In-Browser Compilation 6
Caveats 7
Command-Line Compilation 7
  The `compile` Flag 7
The CoffeeScript CLI 8
  The `output` Flag 9
  The `bare` Flag 9
  The `print` Flag 10
  The `watch` Flag 10
  Executing CoffeeScript Files 11
  Other Options 11
Wrapping Up 12
Notes 12

2 The Basics 13

Syntax 13
  Significant Whitespace 14
  Function Keyword 16
  Parentheses 16

Scope and Variables 18
    Variable Scope in JavaScript 18
    Variable Scope in CoffeeScript 19
    The Anonymous Wrapper Function 20
Interpolation 23
    String Interpolation 23
    Interpolated Strings 23
    Literal Strings 25
    Heredocs 28
    Comments 29
    Inline Comments 29
    Block Comments 30
Extended Regular Expressions 31
Wrapping Up 31
Notes 32

3 Control Structures 33
Operators and Aliases 33
    Arithmetic 33
    Assignment 35
    Comparison 39
    String 42
    The Existential Operator 43
    Aliases 46
    The `is` and `isnt` Aliases 47
    The `not` Alias 48
    The `and` and `or` Aliases 49
    The Boolean Aliases 50
    The `@` Alias 51
If/Unless 52
    The `if` Statement 53
    The `if/else` Statement 54
    The `if/else if` Statement 56
    The `unless` Statement 58
    Inline Conditionals 60
Switch/Case Statements 60
Wrapping Up 63
Notes 63

4 Functions and Arguments 65
Function Basics 68
Arguments 70
Default Arguments 72
Splats... 75
Wrapping Up 79
Notes 79

5 Collections and Iterations 81
Arrays 81
Testing Inclusion 83
Swapping Assignment 85
Multiple Assignment aka Destructing Assignment 86
Ranges 90
Slicing Arrays 92
Replacing Array Values 94
Injecting Values 95
Objects/Hashes 96
Getting/Setting Attributes 101
Destructuring Assignment 103
Loops and Iteration 105
Iterating Arrays 105
The `by` Keyword 106
The `when` Keyword 107
Iterating Objects 108
The `by` Keyword 109
The `when` Keyword 109
The `own` Keyword 110
`while` Loops 113
`until` Loops 114
Comprehensions 116
The `do` Keyword 119
Wrapping Up 120
Notes 121

6 Classes 123
Defining Classes 123
Defining Functions 125
The `constructor` Function 126

Scope in Classes 127
Extending Classes 137
Class-Level Functions 145
Prototype Functions 150
Binding (-> Versus =>) 151
Wrapping Up 158
Notes 158

Part II: CoffeeScript in Practice

7 Cake and Cakefiles 161
Getting Started 161
Creating Cake Tasks 162
Running Cake Tasks 163
Using Options 163
Invoking Other Tasks 167
Wrapping Up 169
Notes 170

8 Testing with Jasmine 171
Installing Jasmine 172
Setting Up Jasmine 172
Introduction to Jasmine 175
Unit Testing 176
Before and After 181
Custom Matchers 187
Wrapping Up 190
Notes 191

9 Intro to Node.js 193
What Is Node.js? 193
Installing Node 194
Getting Started 195
Streaming Responses 197
Building a CoffeeScript Server 199
Trying Out the Server 214
Wrapping Up 215
Notes 215

10 Example: Todo List Part 1 (Server-side) 217
Installing and Setting Up Express 218
Setting Up MongoDB Using Mongoose 222
Writing the Todo API 225
Querying with Mongoose 226
Finding All Todos 227
Creating New Todos 228
Getting, Updating, and Destroying a Todo 230
Cleaning Up the Controller 232
Wrapping Up 236
Notes 236

11 Example: Todo List Part 2 (Client-side w/ jQuery) 237
Priming the HTML with Twitter Bootstrap 237
Interacting with jQuery 240
Hooking Up the New Todo Form 242
Cleaning Up the Todo List with Underscore.js Templates 244
Listing Existing Todos 247
Updating Todos 248
Deleting Todos 252
Wrapping Up 253
Notes 253

12 Example: Todo List Part 3 (Client-side w/ Backbone.js) 255
What Is Backbone.js? 255
Cleaning Up 256
Setting Up Backbone.js 256
Writing our Todo Model and Collection 260
Listing Todos Using a View 263
Creating New Todos 265
A View per Todo 268
Updating and Validating Models from Views 270
Validation 272
Deleting Models from Views 273
Wrapping Up 275
Notes 275

Index 277

Acknowledgments[1]

I said it in my first book, and I'll say it again here: Writing a book is incredibly hard work! Please make sure no one ever tells you differently. If they do, they are either an incredible liar or Stephen King. Fortunately for me I fall somewhere in the middle.

Writing a book is simultaneously a very independent and solitary activity, as well as a team effort. After I put the kids to bed, I head down to my office, crack open a few Guinesses (is the plural Guinei?), crank up the tunes, and work, by myself, into the wee hours of the morning. When I finish a chapter, I send it off to my editor, who then sends it off to a bunch of people who take what I have written and improve it in ways that I didn't know possible. Whether it's as simple as correcting grammar or spelling mistakes, to something more complex such as helping to improve the flow of the book, or point out where example code could be improved to further clarify a point. So, while the writing may be done alone in a dark room by yours truly, the final product is the culmination of many people's hard work.

In this section of the book, I get the chance to say thank you to those who help shape, define, and otherwise ensure that the book you are currently holding (or downloading) is of the highest quality it can be. So without further adieu I'm going to thank people Academy Awards style, knowing that I'm sure I've left someone off the list, for which I am incredibly sorry.

First and foremost I have to thank my beautiful wife, Rachel. Rachel is one of the most supportive and strong people I have ever met. Each night I get to crawl into bed beside her and each morning I get the joy of waking up next to her. I have the pleasure of staring into her eyes and seeing unconditional love there. I also get the encouragement to write books, start my own business, and to do whatever it is that will make me happiest in life. She gave me two handsome sons and in return I've given her bad jokes and my used cell phones. I clearly got the better end of the bargain in this marriage, and for that I am eternally grateful.

Next, I would like to thank my sons, Dylan and Leo. While neither of them directly contributed to this book, they do make life worth living and they give my life an energy and excitement that only children can. I love you boys both so very much.

Before moving off the subject of my family, I would like to thank my parents (especially you Mom!) and the rest of my family for always being there to both simultaneously support me and cut me down to size. I love you all.

Next I have to thank Debra Williams Cauley. Debra was my editor, handler, and psychiatrist on my first book, *Distributed Programming with Ruby*. I can only hope that other authors have the fortune to work with an editor as good as Debra. She truly has the patience of a saint.

[1] Many at my publishing house thought that my acknowledgments section, as well as other parts of this book, were a bit risqué, so the original has been edited down to what you see here. I apologize if you are offended by anything I wrote, that was never my intention. Apparently, I've been told, my sense of humor is not appreciated by all. If you do like bad fart jokes, then please follow me on Twitter @markbates.

I hope that should I ever write another book, Debra will be right there with me. I can't imagine writing a book without her. Thank you, Debra.

When writing a technical book, there are people that are very important to the process; they are the technical reviewers. A technical reviewer's job is to read each chapter and critique it from a technical standpoint, as well as answer the question, "Does it make sense to learn this here?" These reviewers are there to act as your audience. They are technically minded and know their subject. Therefore, the feedback that you get from them is incredibly important. On this book there have a been a few technical reviewers. But the two I really want to call out are Stuart Garner and Dan Pickett. Stuart and Dan went way above the call of duty on this book and were by no means afraid of telling me when I did or said something boneheaded. They received frantic phone calls and emails from me at all hours of the day and night and responded with amazing feedback. If I didn't want all those sweet royalty checks all to myself I might've been tempted to cut them in. (Don't worry, they got paid for their work. They each received a coupon for one free hour of "Mark" time.) Thank you Dan and Stuart, and the rest of the technical reviewers, for all of your hard work.

There are people who contribute to a book like this in different ways. Someone has to design the cover, index the book, write the language (CoffeeScript), or do any of the other countless jobs involved in something like this. Here is a list of some of those people (that I know about), in no particular order: Jeremey Ashkenas, Trevor Burnham, Dan Fishman, Chris Zahn, Gregg Pollack, Gary Adair, Sandra Schroeder, Obie Fernandez, Kristy Hart, Andy Beaster, Barbara Hacha, Tim Wright, Debbie Williams, Brian France, Vanessa Evans, Dan Scherf, Gary Adair, Nonie Ratcliff, and Kim Boedigheimer.

I would also like to thank everyone I have seen since I first starting writing this book who have heard me blather on for hours about it. I know it's not that interesting to most people, but damn, do I love to hear the sound of my voice. Thank you all for not punching me in the mouth, like I probably deserve.

Finally, I would like to say thank you to you, the reader. Thank you for purchasing this book and helping to support people such as myself who, at the end of the day, really just want to help out our fellow developers by sharing the knowledge we have with the rest of the world. It's for you that I have put the countless hours of work and toil into this book. I hope that by the time you close the cover, you will have gained a better understanding of CoffeeScript and how it can impact your development. Good luck.

About the Author

Mark Bates is the founder and chief architect of the Boston-based consulting company Meta42 Labs. Mark spends his days focusing on new application development and consulting for his clients. At night he writes books, raises kids, and occasionally he forms a band and "tries to make it."

Mark has been writing web applications, in one form or another, since 1996. His career started as a UI developer writing HTML and JavaScript applications before moving toward the middle(ware) with Java and Ruby. Nowadays, Mark spends his days cheating on Ruby with his new mistress, CoffeeScript.

Always wanting to share his wisdom, or more correctly just wanting to hear the sound of his own voice, Mark has spoken at several high-profile conferences, including RubyConf, RailsConf, and jQueryConf. Mark has also taught classes on Ruby and Ruby on Rails. In 2009 Mark's first (surprisingly not his last!) book, *Distributed Programming with Ruby*, was published by Addison-Wesley.

Mark lives just outside of Boston with his wife, Rachel, and their two sons, Dylan and Leo. Mark can be found on the web at: http://www.markbates.com, http://twitter.com/markbates, and http://github.com/markbates.

Preface

I started my professional development career in 1999, when I first was paid a salary to be a developer. (I don't count the few years before that when I was just having fun playing around on the Web.) In 1999 the Web was a scary place. HTML files were loaded down with `font` and `table` tags. CSS was just coming on the scene. JavaScript[1] was only a few years old, and a battlefield of various implementations existed across the major browsers. Sure, you could write some JavaScript to do something in one browser, but would it work in another browser? Probably not. Because of that, JavaScript got a bad name in the early 2000s.

In the middle of the 2000s two important things happened that helped improve JavaScript in the eyes of web developers. The first was AJAX.[2] AJAX enabled developers to make web pages more interactive, and faster, by making remote calls back to the server in the background without end users having to refresh their browsers.

The second was the popularity of JavaScript libraries, such as Prototype,[3] that made writing cross-browser JavaScript much simpler. You could use AJAX to make your applications more responsive and easier to use and a library like Prototype to make sure it worked across major browsers.

In 2010, and certainly in 2011, the Web started evolving into "single page" applications. These applications were driven through the use of JavaScript frameworks, such as Backbone.js.[4] These frameworks allowed the use of an MVC[5] design pattern using JavaScript. Whole applications would be built in JavaScript and then downloaded and executed in the end user's browser. This all made for incredibly responsive and rich client-side applications.

On the developer's side, however, things weren't all roses. Although the frameworks and tools made writing these sorts of applications easier, JavaScript itself proved to be the pain point. JavaScript is at times both an incredibly powerful language and an incredibly frustrating one. It is full of paradoxes and design traps that can quickly make your code unmanageable and bug ridden.

So what were developers to do? They want to build these great new applications, but the only universally accepted browser language is JavaScript. They could certainly write these applications in Flash,[6] but that would require plug-ins, and it won't work on some platforms, such as iOS[7] devices.

I first discovered CoffeeScript[8] in October 2010. CoffeeScript promised to help tame JavaScript and to expose the best parts of the quirky language that is JavaScript. It presented a cleaner syntax, like forgoing most punctuation in favor of significant whitespace and protection from those design traps that awaited JavaScript developers at every turn, such as poor scoping and misuse of the comparison operators. Best of all, it did all this while compiling to standard JavaScript that could then be executed in any browser or other JavaScript runtime environment.

When I first used CoffeeScript, the language was still very rough around the edges, even at version 0.9.4. I used it on a project for a client to try it out to see whether it was worth the little bit of hype I was hearing. Unfortunately, at the time two things caused me to push it aside. The first was that it was still not quite ready for prime time. There were too many bugs and missing features.

The second reason why I didn't use CoffeeScript was because the app I was trying it out on wasn't a very JavaScript-heavy application. I was mostly doing a few validation checks and an occasional bit of AJAX, which Ruby on Rails[9] helped me do with very little, if any, JavaScript code.

So what made me come back to CoffeeScript? Some six months after I had tried out CoffeeScript for the first time, it was announced[10] that Rails 3.1 would ship with CoffeeScript as the default JavaScript engine. Like most developers I was taken aback by this. I had tried CoffeeScript and didn't think it was that great. What were they thinking?

Unlike a lot of my fellow developers, I took the time to have another look at CoffeeScript. Six months is a very long time in the development of any project. CoffeeScript had come a long, long way. I decided to try it again, this time on an application that had some pretty heavy JavaScript. Within a few days of using CoffeeScript again, I became not just a convert but an advocate of the language.

I'm not going to tell you exactly what it was that converted me, or try to tell you why I love it. I want you to form your own opinion. Over the course of this book I hope to both convert you and make you an advocate of this wonderful little language for reasons that are all your own. But I will give you a little sneak peak at what's to come. Here's a bit of CoffeeScript, from an actual application, followed by its equivalent JavaScript. Enjoy!

Example: **(source: sneak_peak.coffee)**

```
@updateAvatars = ->
  names = $('.avatar[data-name]').map -> $(this).data('name')
  Utils.findAvatar(name) for name in $.unique(names)
```

Example: **(source: sneak_peak.js)**

```
(function() {

  this.updateAvatars = function() {
    var name, names, _i, _len, _ref, _results;
    names = $('.avatar[data-name]').map(function() {
      return $(this).data('name');
    });
    _ref = $.unique(names);
    _results = [];
    for (_i = 0, _len = _ref.length; _i < _len; _i++) {
      name = _ref[_i];
      _results.push(Utils.findAvatar(name));
```

```
    }
    return _results;
  };

}).call(this);
```

What Is CoffeeScript?

CoffeeScript is a language that compiles down to JavaScript. Not very informative, I know, but it's what it does. CoffeeScript was developed to closely resemble languages such as Ruby[11] and Python.[12] It was designed to help developers write their JavaScript more efficiently. By removing unnecessary punctuation like braces, semicolons, and so on, and by using significant whitespace to replace those characters, you can quickly focus on the code at hand—and not on making sure you have all your curly braces closed.

Chances are you would write the following JavaScript like this:

Example: **(source: punctuation.js)**

```
(function() {

  if (something === something_else) {
    console.log('do something');
  } else {
    console.log('do something else');
  }

}).call(this);
```

So why not write it like this:

Example: **(source: punctuation.coffee)**

```
if something is something_else
  console.log 'do something'
else
  console.log 'do something else'
```

CoffeeScript also gives you several shortcuts to write rather complicated sections of JavaScript with just a short code snippet. Take, for example, this code that lets you loop through the values in an array, without worrying about their indices:

Example: **(source: array.coffee)**

```
for name in array
  console.log name
```

Example: **(source: array.js)**

```
(function() {
  var name, _i, _len;

  for (_i = 0, _len = array.length; _i < _len; _i++) {
    name = array[_i];
    console.log(name);
  }

}).call(this);
```

In addition to the sugary sweet syntax improvements CoffeeScript gives you, it also helps you write better JavaScript code by doing things such as helping you scope your variables and classes appropriately, making sure you use the appropriate comparison operators, and much more, as you'll see during the course of reading this book.

CoffeeScript, Ruby, and Python often get mentioned together in the same breath, and for good reason. CoffeeScript was directly modeled on the terseness and the simple syntax that these languages have to offer. Because of this, CoffeeScript has a much more modern "feel" than JavaScript does, which was modeled on languages such as Java[13] and C++.[14] Like JavaScript, CoffeeScript can be used in any programming environment. Whether you are writing your application using Ruby, Python, PHP,[15] Java, or .Net,[16] it doesn't matter. The compiled JavaScript will work with them all.

Because CoffeeScript compiles down to JavaScript, you can still use any and all of the JavaScript libraries you currently use. You can use jQuery,[17] Zepto,[18] Backbone,[19] Jasmine,[20] and the like, and they'll all just work. You don't hear that too often when talking about new languages.

This all sounds great, I hear you saying, but what are the downsides of using CoffeeScript over just plain old JavaScript? This is a great question. The answer is, not much. First, although CoffeeScript is a really nice way to write your JavaScript, it does not let you do anything you couldn't already do with JavaScript. I still can't, for example, create a JavaScript version of Ruby's famous *method_missing*.[21] The biggest downside would have to be that it's another language for you or the members of your team to learn. Fortunately, this is easily rectified. As you'll see, CoffeeScript is incredibly easy to learn.

Finally, should CoffeeScript, for whatever reason, not be right for you or your project, you can take the generated JavaScript and work from there. So really, you have nothing to lose by giving CoffeeScript a try in your next project, or even in your current project (CoffeeScript and JavaScript play very well with each other).

Who Is This Book For?

This book is for intermediate- to advanced-level JavaScript developers. There are several reasons why I don't think this book is good for those unfamiliar with JavaScript, or for those who only have a passing acquaintance.

First, this book is not going to teach you about JavaScript. This is a book about CoffeeScript. Along the way you are certainly going to learn a few bits and bobs about JavaScript (and CoffeeScript has a knack for making you learn more about JavaScript), but we are not going to start at the beginning of JavaScript and work our way up.

Example: **What does this code do? (source: example.js)**

```
(function() {
  var array, index, _i, _len;

  array = [1, 2, 3, 4, 5, 6, 7, 8, 9, 10];

  for (_i = 0, _len = array.length; _i < _len; _i++) {
    index = array[_i];
    console.log(index);
  }

}).call(this);
```

If you don't know what the preceding code example does, I recommend that you stop reading here. Don't worry, I really want you to come back and keep reading. I just think that you will get the most out of this book if you already have a good understanding of JavaScript. I will be covering certain basic areas of JavaScript as we go along, usually to help illustrate a point or help you to better understand what CoffeeScript is doing. Despite covering certain areas of JavaScript for clarity, it really is important that you have a fundamental grasp of JavaScript before we continue. So please, go find a good book on JavaScript (there are plenty out there), read it, and then join me along our journey to become CoffeeScript gurus.

For those of you who are already JavaScript rock stars, let's step up your game. This book is going to teach you how to write cleaner, more succinct, and better JavaScript using the sweet sugary goodness that is CoffeeScript.

How to Read This Book

I have to tried to present the material in this book to help you form building blocks to learning CoffeeScript. The chapters, in Part I, should be read in order because each chapter will build on the concepts that we have learned in previous chapters—so please, no jumping around.

As we go through each chapter, you'll notice a few things at work.

First, whenever I introduce some outside library, idea, or concept, I include a footnote to a website where you can learn further information about that subject. Although I would love to be able to talk your ear off about things like Ruby, there is not enough space in this book to do that. So if I mention something and you want to find out more about it before continuing, go to the bookmarked site, quench your thirst for knowledge, and come back to the book.

Second, as we go through each chapter I will sometimes walk you through the wrong solution to a problem first. After you see the wrong way to do something, we can then examine it, understand it, and then work out the correct solution to the problem at hand. A great example of this is in Chapter 1, "Getting Started," when we talk about the different ways to compile your CoffeeScript to JavaScript.

At some points in the book you will come across something like this:

> **Tip Some helpful tip here.**
>
> These are little tips and tricks that I think might be of value to you.

Finally, throughout the book I will present you with two or three code blocks at a time. I will first give you the CoffeeScript example followed by the compiled (JavaScript) version of the same example. If there is any output from the example (and if I think it's worth showing) I will include the output from the example, as well. Here's what that looks like:

Example: **(source: example.coffee)**

```
array = [1..10]

for index in array
  console.log index
```

Example: **(source: example.js)**

```
(function() {
  var array, index, _i, _len;

  array = [1, 2, 3, 4, 5, 6, 7, 8, 9, 10];

  for (_i = 0, _len = array.length; _i < _len; _i++) {
    index = array[_i];
    console.log(index);
  }

}).call(this);
```

Output: **(source: example.coffee)**

```
1
2
3
4
5
6
7
8
9
10
```

Sometimes there are errors that I want to show you. Here is an example:

Example: **(source: oops.coffee)**

```
array = [1..10]

oops! index in array
  console.log index
```

Output: **(source: oops.coffee)**

```
Error: In content/preface/oops.coffee, Parse error on line 3: Unexpected 'UNARY'
    at Object.parseError (/usr/local/lib/node_modules/coffee-script/lib/coffee-script/
➥parser.js:470:11)
    at Object.parse (/usr/local/lib/node_modules/coffee-script/lib/coffee-script/
➥parser.js:546:22)
    at /usr/local/lib/node_modules/coffee-script/lib/coffee-script/coffee-script.
➥js:40:22
    at Object.run (/usr/local/lib/node_modules/coffee-script/lib/coffee-script/
➥coffee-script.js:68:34)
    at /usr/local/lib/node_modules/coffee-script/lib/coffee-script/command.js:135:29
    at /usr/local/lib/node_modules/coffee-script/lib/coffee-script/command.js:110:18
    at [object Object].<anonymous> (fs.js:114:5)
    at [object Object].emit (events.js:64:17)
    at afterRead (fs.js:1081:12)
    at Object.wrapper [as oncomplete] (fs.js:252:17)
```

How This Book Is Organized

In an effort to help you get the most from this book, I have split it into two distinct parts.

Part I: Core CoffeeScript

The first part of this book is designed to cover the entire CoffeeScript language from top to bottom. By the end of this part of the book, you should be fully armed to attack any CoffeeScript project that comes your way, including those in the second part of this book.

Chapter 1, "Getting Started," introduces the various ways CoffeeScript can be compiled and run. It also introduces the powerful coffee command-line utility and REPL that ships with CoffeeScript.

In Chapter 2, "The Basics," we start to explore what makes CoffeeScript different from JavaScript. Talk of syntax, variables, scope, and more will lay a strong foundation for the rest of the book.

Chapter 3, "Control Structures," focuses on an important part of any language, control structures such as `if` and `else`. You will also learn the differences between some operators in CoffeeScript and those in JavaScript.

Chapter 4, "Functions and Arguments," covers the ins and outs of functions in CoffeeScript. We'll talk about defining functions, calling functions, and a few extras such as default arguments and splats.

From arrays to objects, Chapter 5, "Collections and Iterations," shows you how to use, manipulate, and iterate over collection objects in CoffeeScript.

Chapter 6, "Classes," ends the first part of the book by covering classes in CoffeeScript. Define new classes, extend existing classes, override functions in super classes, and more.

Part II: CoffeeScript in Practice

The second part of this book focuses on using CoffeeScript in practical examples. Through learning about some of the ecosystem that surrounds CoffeeScript, as well as building a full application, by the end of Part II your CoffeeScript skills should be well honed.

Chapter 7, "Cake and Cakefiles," covers the Cake tool that ships with CoffeeScript. You can use this little tool for creating build scripts, test scripts, and more. We'll cover all that it has to offer.

Testing is a very important part of software development, and Chapter 8, "Testing with Jasmine," gives a quick tour through one of the more popular CoffeeScript/JavaScript testing libraries, Jasmine. This chapter will exercise the popular pattern of test-driven development by writing tests first for a calculator class.

Chapter 9, "Intro to Node.js," is a quick introduction to the event-driven server-side framework, Node.js. In this chapter we will use CoffeeScript to build a simple HTTP server that will automatically compile CoffeeScript files into JavaScript files as they are requested by the web browser.

In Chapter 10, "Example: Todo List Part 1 (Server-side)," we will be building the server-side part of a todo list application. Building on Chapter 9, we will build an API using the Express.js web framework and the Mongoose ORM for MongoDB.

In Chapter 11, "Example: Todo List Part 2 (Client-side w/ jQuery)," we will build a client for the todo list API we built in Chapter 10 using the popular jQuery libary.

Finally, in Chapter 12, "Example: Todo List Part 3 (Client-side w/ Backbone.js)," we will rebuild the client for the todo list application, this time forsaking jQuery in favor of the client-side framework, Backbone.js.

Installing CoffeeScript

I am not a big fan of having installation instructions in books, mostly because by the time the book hits the shelf, the installation instructions are out of date. However, people—and by people, I mean those who publish books—believe that there should be an installation section for books. So this is mine.

Installing CoffeeScript is pretty easy. The easiest way to install it is to go to http://www.coffeescript.org and look at the installation instructions there.

I believe the maintainers of projects like CoffeeScript and Node[22] are the best people to keep the installation instructions up to date for their projects, and their websites are a great place to find those instructions.

At the time of writing, CoffeeScript was at version: 1.2.0. All examples in this book should work on that version.

How to Run the Examples

You will be able to find and download all the original source code for this book at https://github.com/markbates/Programming-In-CoffeeScript. As you'll see, all the examples tell you which example file to look to. The example files will be in a folder relevant to their respective chapter.

Unless otherwise indicated, you should be able to run the examples in your terminal, like so:

```
> coffee example.coffee
```

So now that you know how to run the examples in this book, as soon as you have CoffeeScript installed, why don't you meet me at Chapter 1 and we can get started? See you there.

Notes

1. http://en.wikipedia.org/wiki/JavaScript
2. http://en.wikipedia.org/wiki/Ajax_(programming)
3. http://www.prototypejs.org/
4. http://documentcloud.github.com/backbone/
5. http://en.wikipedia.org/wiki/Model–view–controller
6. http://www.adobe.com/
7. http://www.apple.com/ios/
8. http://www.coffeescript.org
9. http://www.rubyonrails.org
10. http://www.rubyinside.com/rails-3-1-adopts-coffeescript-jquery-sass-and-controversy-4669.html
11. http://en.wikipedia.org/wiki/Ruby_(programming_language)
12. http://en.wikipedia.org/wiki/Python_(programming_language)
13. http://en.wikipedia.org/wiki/Java_(programming_language)
14. http://en.wikipedia.org/wiki/C%2B%2B
15. http://en.wikipedia.org/wiki/Php
16. http://en.wikipedia.org/wiki/.NET_Framework
17. http://www.jquery.com
18. https://github.com/madrobby/zepto
19. http://documentcloud.github.com/backbone
20. http://pivotal.github.com/jasmine/
21. http://ruby-doc.org/docs/ProgrammingRuby/html/ref_c_object.html#Object.method_missing
22. http://nodejs.org

Part I

Core CoffeeScript

In this first half of the book we are going to cover everything you've ever wanted to know, and everything you'll ever need to know, about CoffeeScript. By the end of this part of the book, you should be ready to code in CoffeeScript, be comfortable with the toolset it provides, and understand the ins and outs of the language itself.

We'll start at the very beginning with the basics, such as learning how to run and compile a CoffeeScript file; then we'll move on to learn the syntax of CoffeeScript. After we feel comfortable with syntax, we'll cover control structures, functions, collections, and, finally, classes.

Each chapter will build on what we've learned in previous chapters. Along the way you'll learn about all the great tricks that CoffeeScript has for helping you write fantastic JavaScript-based applications. So come on, we've got a lot to cover—let's get started!

1

Getting Started

Now that you've read the Preface and have CoffeeScript installed, what do you say we actually start using it? In this chapter we walk through a few ways that CoffeeScript can be executed and compiled.

I'm going to cover some good ways and some not so good ways to compile and execute your code. Although we won't be covering the inner workings of CoffeeScript in this chapter, it is definitely an invaluable read as you start to work with CoffeeScript. Knowing the ins and outs of the command-line tools that ship with CoffeeScript will make your life easier, not only as you read this book, but as you start developing your first CoffeeScript applications.

Even if you have played around already with the CoffeeScript command-line tools, there is a good chance you might learn something new in this chapter, so please take a few minutes to read it before jumping straight to Chapter 2, "The Basics."

The CoffeeScript REPL

CoffeeScript ships with a really powerful REPL[1], otherwise known as an interactive console, ready to go so you can start playing with CoffeeScript immediately.

Getting started with the REPL is incredibly easy. Simply type the following into your favorite Terminal window:

```
> coffee
```

Then you should see a prompt that looks something like the following:

```
coffee>
```

If you see the `coffee` prompt, we are ready to start playing around with some CoffeeScript.

The alternative for starting the REPL is this:

```
> coffee -i
```

or if you really like typing a lot:

```
> coffee --interactive
```

Let's start with a basic example. Type the following into the console:

```
coffee> 2 + 2
```

You should be presented with the following answer:

```
coffee> 4
```

Congratulations, you've just written your very first piece of CoffeeScript!

Okay, let's try something a little more interesting—something more CoffeeScript-esque. We won't worry too much about what is happening in the following code (we'll cover it all in greater length later); let's just get it to run.

Example: **(source: repl1.coffee)**

```
a = [1..10]
b = (x * x for x in a)
console.log b
```

Output: **(source: repl1.coffee)**

```
[ 1, 4, 9, 16, 25, 36, 49, 64, 81, 100 ]
```

Now that is a lot nicer chunk of CoffeeScript, isn't it? Briefly, we created a new array and filled it with the integers 1 to 10. Then we looped through the numbers in the array, `a`, multiplied them by themselves and created a second array, `b`, containing those new values. Wow, eh? Like I said, I'll happily explain how all that works later; for now, simply bask in the glory of all the lines of JavaScript you didn't have to write. But in case you are curious as to what the JavaScript would look like, here it is:

Example: **(source: repl1.js)**

```
(function() {
  var a, b, x;

  a = [1, 2, 3, 4, 5, 6, 7, 8, 9, 10];

  b = (function() {
    var _i, _len, _results;
    _results = [];
    for (_i = 0, _len = a.length; _i < _len; _i++) {
      x = a[_i];
      _results.push(x * x);
```

```
    }
    return _results;
  })();

  console.log(b);

}).call(this);
```

As you can see, the REPL can be a fun way to play around and experiment with different ideas. However, not everything is roses in the land of the CoffeeScript REPL. CoffeeScript, as you'll see, is designed around the concept of whitespace being significant. That leaves us with a bit of a problem when trying to write multiline CoffeeScript in the REPL. The answer comes to us in the form of the \ character.

Let's try to write a simple function, `add`, that takes in two numbers and returns the sum of those numbers. Enter the following code into the REPL line by line:

Example: **(source: repl2.coffee)**

```
add = (x, y)->\
  x + y
console.log add(1, 2)
```

Output: **(source: repl2.coffee)**

```
3
```

Notice how at the end of the first line we added a \. That tells the REPL that we want to add more lines to that expression. It's important that you keep adding the \ for every line you want to add to the expression. The first line that doesn't end with \ will be considered the end of the expression, and the REPL will attempt to execute that expression.

It is also important to notice that we still had to indent the line after the \ so that CoffeeScript was able to properly interpret that line of the expression and put it into its proper place.

Finally, to quit the REPL, simply press `ctrl-C` and the process will end.

The REPL is a powerful and quick way to try out a few ideas, but as we've seen it can get a bit hard to use when dealing with more complex code. Later in this chapter, in the section "Executing CoffeeScript Files," we'll discuss how to execute files containing CoffeeScript, which is a more appropriate way of running complex code.

In-Browser Compilation

When developing web applications, a time will come when you want to write some CoffeeScript directly inline in your HTML[2] file. CoffeeScript does allow you to do this, and I will show you how. However, I want to caution you against doing such a thing. First, there is a very good reason why practices such as Unobtrusive JavaScript[3] have become so popular recently. Although being able to execute CoffeeScript in the browser is nifty, it really is not the best compilation option available to us. By keeping your JavaScript in separate files and out of the HTML layer, you are able to keep your code cleaner and degrade more gracefully in environments that don't support JavaScript.

At first, writing Unobtrusive JavaScript can be a bit confusing and difficult, but after a while it becomes easier to write, more reusable, and more logical to do so. Using tools like jQuery, you can wait for the page to load and attach all the appropriate JavaScript to the correct objects on the page. However, sometimes you do have to prime the pump, so to speak. Usually this means calling an `init` method, perhaps passing in some JSON[4] to do so. I would encourage you to write this tiny amount of code using pure JavaScript. However, should you really want to write it in CoffeeScript, there is a way to let the browser compile it for you.

Let's take a look at an HTML file with a bit of CoffeeScript embedded in it.

Example: **(source: hello_world.html)**

```
<html>
  <head>
    <title>Hello World</title>
    <script src='http://jashkenas.github.com/coffee-script/extras/coffee-script.js'
➥type='text/javascript'></script>
  </head>
  <body>
    <script type='text/coffeescript'>
      name = prompt "What is your name?"
      alert "Hello, #{name}"
    </script>
  </body>
</html>
```

Because browsers, at least at the time of this writing, don't contain native support for CoffeeScript compilation, you will need to include a compiler in your page to use. Fortunately, the CoffeeScript team has one ready and waiting. To include it in your HTML file, add the following line to the head of your HTML file:

```
<script src='http://jashkenas.github.com/coffee-script/extras/coffee-script.js'
type='text/javascript'></script>
```

You can, of course, pull down the contents of the `coffee-script.js` file and store it locally in your project, should you wish.

The only other step in getting our inline CoffeeScript to compile in the browser is to make sure that we set the appropriate `type` on our `script` tags, like so:

```
<script type='text/coffeescript'></script>
```

When the page loads, the CoffeeScript compiler in `coffee-script.js` will search your HTML document for any `script` tags with a `type` of `text/coffeescript`, compile them into the equivalent JavaScript form, and then execute the compiled JavaScript code.

Caveats

Now that you know how to compile CoffeeScript inline in your HTML document, I would like to point out a few things. First, everything that we discuss in this book, in terms of scope, anonymous function wrappers, and so on, all holds true when compiling CoffeeScript in this fashion. So it's important to keep this in mind when writing your code like this.

Second, and this is probably the big one to take away here, is that this is not a particularly fast way of compiling your CoffeeScript. When deploying this to production, it means all your users will have to download an extra 162.26KB file to compile your CoffeeScript. Then after the page loads, the compiler has to go through the page looking for the `text/coffeescript` tags, compile them, and then execute them. That's not a very good user experience.

Armed with this knowledge, I'm hoping you choose the right path and compile your CoffeeScript offline before deploying to production.

Command-Line Compilation

Although being able to execute CoffeeScript in the browser is useful and fairly easy, it really is not the best compilation option available to us. We should be compiling our CoffeeScript before we serve it up the on the Web. However, it is entirely possible that you are writing a Node application or some other server-side application that won't be in a browser, so browser compilation won't work there.

So how best should we compile our CoffeeScript? Great question. You will find a lot of third-party libraries that will compile your CoffeeScript files for you (in different languages and on various platforms), but it is important to understand how to do it yourself, so you can write your own compilation scripts, should you need to.

The `compile` Flag

Let's start with the most important flag to the `coffee` command, `-c`. The `-c` flag will take the CoffeeScript file you pass to it and compile it out to a JavaScript file for you in the same location. This is how I compiled the source code examples in this book.

Let's go ahead and create a simple file called `hello_world.coffee` and make it look like this:

```
greeting = "Hello, World!"
console.log greeting
```

Now we can compile that file like so:

```
> coffee -c hello_world.coffee
```

That should compile our CoffeeScript file into a new JavaScript file in the same directory called `hello_world.js`. The contents of `hello_world.js` should look like this:

```
(function() {
  var greeting;

  greeting = "Hello, World!";

  console.log(greeting);

}).call(this);
```

Our `hello_world.js` JavaScript file is ready for production! Time for a cup of tea.

The CoffeeScript CLI

We've played with the REPL and have learned how to compile our CoffeeScript using the command line `coffee` tool, but the `coffee` command offers a few other interesting options that we should quickly look at. To see a full list of what the `coffee` command has to offer, enter the following into your terminal:

```
> coffee --help
```

You should see output similar to the following:

```
Usage: coffee [options] path/to/script.coffee

  -c, --compile      compile to JavaScript and save as .js files
  -i, --interactive  run an interactive CoffeeScript REPL
  -o, --output       set the directory for compiled JavaScript
  -j, --join         concatenate the scripts before compiling
  -w, --watch        watch scripts for changes, and recompile
  -p, --print        print the compiled JavaScript to stdout
  -l, --lint         pipe the compiled JavaScript through JavaScript Lint
  -s, --stdio        listen for and compile scripts over stdio
  -e, --eval         compile a string from the command line
  -r, --require      require a library before executing your script
  -b, --bare         compile without the top-level function wrapper
  -t, --tokens       print the tokens that the lexer produces
```

```
  -n, --nodes         print the parse tree that Jison produces
      --nodejs        pass options through to the "node" binary
  -v, --version       display CoffeeScript version
  -h, --help          display this help message
```

Let's take a look at some of those options now.

The `output` Flag

Although compiling the JavaScript file in the same directory as the CoffeeScript is all right when you are just playing around, chances are you probably want to keep the files in separate directories. So how do we compile our `hello_world.coffee` file into, for instance, `public/javascripts`?

The answer is simple: we need to add the `-o` to our terminal command:

```
> coffee -o public/javascripts -c hello_world.coffee
```

If you check your `public/javascripts` directory, you'll find your newly compiled `hello_world.js` file waiting there for you.

One thing that the `-o` flag does not let you do is change the name of the file. The compiled JavaScript file will have the same name as the original CoffeeScript file, except with the `.js` extension instead of the `.coffee` extension. Because you cannot rename the file using the `coffee` command, you'll either want to rename your original file or write a script that does both the compilation of your CoffeeScript file and then renames them to something more to your liking.

The `bare` Flag

As you'll see later in the book, when CoffeeScript compiles, it wraps the generated JavaScript in an anonymous function. Because we'll cover this topic in more detail in Chapter 2, I won't go into it here. What follows is an example of that anonymous function being wrapped in the generated JavaScript code:

Example: **(source: hello_world.js)**

```
(function() {
  var greeting;

  greeting = "Hello, World!";

  console.log(greeting);

}).call(this);
```

Now, at times, for whatever your reasons, you may not want that anonymous function wrapper. In those cases we can pass the CoffeeScript compiler the `-b` flag.

```
> coffee -b -c hello_world.coffee
```

That will compile our CoffeeScript into the following JavaScript:

Example: **(source: hello_world_bare.js)**

```
var greeting;

greeting = "Hello, World!";

console.log(greeting);
```

Now that you know how to remove the anonymous wrapper, I want to caution you about doing so. There are a lot of *very* good reasons as to why it is being generated in the first place. If you'd like to find out more about this anonymous function, see Chapter 2.

The `print` Flag

Sometimes when you're compiling your CoffeeScript files, what you really want is to see the output of the file. Fortunately, the `coffee` command has you covered with the `-p` flag:

```
> coffee -p hello_world.coffee
```

This will print out to your terminal something like the following:

```
(function() {
  var greeting;

  greeting = "Hello, World!";

  console.log(greeting);

}).call(this);
```

This can be incredibly useful for debugging purposes or as a great learning tool with CoffeeScript. By comparing your CoffeeScript against the compiled JavaScript (as we do in this book), you can start to understand what CoffeeScript is doing under the covers. This was a huge help for me when I was originally learning CoffeeScript. It has also helped me to become a better JavaScript developer by investigating some of the choices that the complier has made.

The `watch` Flag

As you are developing your CoffeeScript projects, you're not going to want to keep going to the command line to keep compiling. To make this a little easier for you, CoffeeScript gives you the optional -w parameter to the `coffee` command. With this parameter you can tell the `coffee` command to keep watching your CoffeeScript files and if they change to recompile them. Here is an example:

```
> coffee -w -c app/assets/coffeescript
```

With this command, anytime a `.coffee` file is touched[5] in the `app/assets/coffeescript` directory, or any subdirectories, it is automatically compiled.

As of CoffeeScript 1.2.0, the -w will watch for new files that have been added to a watched directory. In my experience, however, it can be quite buggy because of some underlying Node issues. Hopefully, these issues will be worked out by the time you read this. However, plenty of third-party tools exist that are designed to listen to file system events, such as files being added and removed. My personal favorite, as of the time of writing, is Guard.[6] It's a Ruby gem that lets you listen for these types of events and execute some custom code, such as compiling CoffeeScript files, when these events occur.

> **Tip**
>
> In addition to Guard, you might also want to check out Jitter[7] by Trevor Burham. It accomplishes a similar goal of watching and compiling all your CoffeeScript files. It is also written using CoffeeScript, so that's not a bad thing.

Executing CoffeeScript Files

We've covered various ways to compile our CoffeeScript and have discussed some of the options we can pass into the `coffee` command when compiling CoffeeScript, but what about just executing the CoffeeScript file in question? Perhaps you are writing a web server using CoffeeScript or even a simple script that does some basic number crunching. You could compile our scripts using the tools you've already learned about, then link to them in an HTML file, and finally, run them in a browser. That would work for a simple script, but not for something more complex like a web server. Nor is it a practical idea.

To help with this situation, the `coffee` command lets us execute our CoffeeScript files like this:

```
> coffee hello_world.coffee
```

Most of the examples that we look at throughout this book can be run in just this fashion (unless otherwise noted).

Other Options

There are a few other options such as -n and -t. Although these options can give you some really interesting output and insight into how CoffeeScript compiles your code, they won't really be of help to us during the course of this book so I won't be covering them here. I do, however, encourage you to take some time to run the extra options to see what they produce. You can find out more about these options by reading the annotated source[8] for CoffeeScript online.

Wrapping Up

In this chapter we've taken a tour of the different ways that we can compile and execute our CoffeeScript code. We've looked at the pros and cons of the ways that CoffeeScript can be compiled and are now armed with the knowledge we need to be able to play with the examples in the rest of this book. Finally, we dug into the `coffee` command to learn the most important options and parameters we can pass to it.

Notes

1. Read-eval-print loop - http://en.wikipedia.org/wiki/Read-eval-print_loop
2. http://en.wikipedia.org/wiki/Html
3. http://en.wikipedia.org/wiki/Unobtrusive_JavaScript
4. http://en.wikipedia.org/wiki/Json
5. Touching a file means lots of different things on different operating systems, but usually just saving the file is enough of a "touch" to trigger the `-w` into doing its magic.
6. https://github.com/guard/guard
7. https://github.com/TrevorBurnham/jitter
8. http://jashkenas.github.com/coffee-script/documentation/docs/command.html

2

The Basics

Now that we've covered the boring stuff, like compiling and executing your CoffeeScript, we will start covering how to actually write it. Let's dive right in.

In this chapter we are going to examine the syntax of CoffeeScript. We'll look at punctuation, scope, variables, and a few other choice bits.

Syntax

Much of CoffeeScript's press has been due to its syntax, in particular its lack of punctuation. Punctuation such as curly braces and semicolons are extinct in the world of CoffeeScript, and parentheses are an endangered species.

To illustrate this point, let's take a look at a bit of JavaScript that most of you might be familiar with. Here is a piece of jQuery code to make a remote AJAX request and do some work with the results:

Example: **(source: jquery_example.js)**

```
$(function() {
  $.get('example.php', function(data) {
    if (data.errors != null) {
      alert("There was an error!");
    } else {
      $("#content").text(data.message);
    }
  }, 'json')
})
```

CoffeeScript allows us to strip out a lot of the extra punctuation in that example. Here is what the same code written in CoffeeScript would look like:

Example: **(source: jquery_as_coffee.coffee)**

```
$ ->
  $.get 'example.php', (data) ->
      if data.errors?
        alert "There was an error!"
      else
        $("#content").text data.message
    , 'json'
```

Later in this book we are going to get into greater detail on what most of the parts of that example are doing, but for now let's examine what we took out of the JavaScript example when writing our CoffeeScript example.

Significant Whitespace

The first thing we did was to remove all curly braces and semicolons.

Example: **(source: jquery.js)**

```
$(function()
  $.get('example.php', function(data)
    if (data.errors != null)
      alert("There was an error!")
    else
      $("#content").text(data.message)
  , 'json')
)
```

How does this work? How does CoffeeScript know how to parse the code to make sense of it? The answer is quite simple, and chances are it is something you are already doing every day: whitespace! CoffeeScript, like Python, uses the concept of significant whitespace to tell it how to parse expressions.

I've heard people grumble about significant whitespace before saying they don't like it. I find that to be an unusual argument. Would you write the same JavaScript example like the following?

Example: **(source: jquery.js)**

```
$(function() {
$.get('example.php', function(data) {
if (data.errors != null) {
```

```
alert("There was an error!");
} else {
$("#content").text(data.message);
}
}, 'json')
})
```

I should hope not! If you are writing JavaScript this way, I beg you to do your fellow developers a favor and take the extra second to make sure your code is properly indented. Readability is key to maintenance. It is also the key to helping you convert your existing JavaScript to CoffeeScript.

With significant whitespace, CoffeeScript knows that when you indent a line below your `if` statement the compiler should position that line inside of the `if` block. The next time the compiler sees indentation at the same level as that `if` statement, it knows that you are finished writing your `if` statement and executes that line at the same level as the `if` statement.

Here is a brief example of the type of error you would get if you did not properly format your CoffeeScript code:

Example: **(source: whitespace.coffee)**

```
for num in [1..3]
    if num is 1
      console.log num
       console.log num * 2
  if num is 2
        console.log num
        console.log num * 2
```

Output: **(source: whitespace.coffee)**

```
Error: In content/the_basics/whitespace.coffee, Parse error on line 4: Unexpected
➥'INDENT'
    at Object.parseError (/usr/local/lib/node_modules/coffee-script/lib/coffee-script/
➥parser.js:470:11)
    at Object.parse (/usr/local/lib/node_modules/coffee-script/lib/coffee-script/
➥parser.js:546:22)
    at /usr/local/lib/node_modules/coffee-script/lib/coffee-script/coffee-script.
➥js:40:22
    at Object.run (/usr/local/lib/node_modules/coffee-script/lib/coffee-script/
➥coffee-script.js:68:34)
    at /usr/local/lib/node_modules/coffee-script/lib/coffee-script/command.js:135:29
    at /usr/local/lib/node_modules/coffee-script/lib/coffee-script/command.js:110:18
    at [object Object].<anonymous> (fs.js:114:5)
```

```
    at [object Object].emit (events.js:64:17)
    at afterRead (fs.js:1081:12)
    at Object.wrapper [as oncomplete] (fs.js:252:17)
```

Function Keyword

The next thing we did was eliminate that old `function` keyword. None of the CoffeeScript code we will write will ever use the `function` keyword.

Example: **(source: jquery.js)**

```
$( ()->
  $.get('example.php', (data)->
    if (data.errors != null)
      alert("There was an error!")
    else
      $("#content").text(data.message)
  , 'json')
)
```

Instead of the `function` keyword we can use an arrow, ->, to the right of the arguments list. This is a little difficult to remember and get straight at first, I know, but it actually makes a lot of sense if you think about the flow of the code and where the arguments are "pointing."

Parentheses

Next we removed some, but not all, of our parentheses in the example code.

Example: **(source: jquery.js)**

```
$ ->
  $.get 'example.php', (data)->
    if data.errors != null
      alert "There was an error!"
    else
      $("#content").text data.message
  , 'json'
```

Why didn't we remove all parentheses? In almost all cases, removing parentheses is optional. The rules about when to use the parentheses can be a bit confusing, especially when we talk about functions. Let's take a look at our code to see why we left some in and took some out.

When we went to call the `alert` function, like this:

```
alert "There was an error!"
```

we were able to remove the parentheses. The reason is that if a function is being passed arguments, we can omit the parentheses. However, if a function is not being passed any arguments, we need to supply the parentheses so that JavaScript knows that we are calling a function and not a variable. Like I said: a bit confusing.

> **Tip**
>
> When in doubt, you can use the parentheses all the time if you feel it helps to make your code cleaner and easier to read.

So, if we don't need the parentheses when calling a function with arguments, why did we use parentheses on this line?

```
$("#content").text data.message
```

Why didn't we write it like this instead?

```
$ "#content" .text data.message
```

If we had done that, the compiled JavaScript would look like this for that line:

```
$("#content".text(data.message));
```

As you can see, CoffeeScript isn't sure what you are calling the `text` function on, so it assumes it is the string `"#content"`. By leaving the parentheses in there, we are telling CoffeeScript where exactly it needs to call the `text` method; in this case it's on the jQuery object returned by `$("#content")`.

Before we move away from the subject of parentheses (don't worry we'll be talking about them again when we talk about functions), I want to point out that parentheses can still be used for logical grouping.

Example: **(source: grouping.coffee)**

```
if x is true and (y is true or z is true)
  console.log 'hello, world'
```

Example: **(source: grouping.js)**

```
(function() {

  if (x === true && (y === true || z === true)) console.log('hello, world');

}).call(this);
```

Scope and Variables

In this section we talk about how scope and variables work and are defined in CoffeeScript. In JavaScript this can be a tricky subject, often the source of confusion and bugs. In this section we see how CoffeeScript tries to make bugs related to scope a thing of the past.

Variable Scope in JavaScript

When declaring variables in JavaScript, a lot of people, both experienced and beginner, do not realize that there are two ways to declare variables. If they do know the two ways to declare variables, they may not know the difference between the two. Because of that, let's take a brief second to look at the two ways and understand, at least on a basic level, what they do.

Look at the following code snippet:

Example: **(source: js_variable_scope.js)**

```
a = 'A';
myFunc = function() {
  a = 'AAA';
  var b = 'B';
}
```

If we were to run that code in a browser or another JavaScript engine, we would get the following:

Output:

```
> console.log(a)
A
> myFunc();
> console.log(a)
AAA
> console.log(b)
ReferenceError: b is not defined
```

Chances are you probably were expecting that when trying to reference variable `b` it would raise an error. However, you were probably not expecting variable `a` to return the value defined in the `myFunc` function, were you? So why is that?

The answer is simple and goes to the heart of the difference between the way those two variables were defined.

When we defined variable `a` without using the `var` keyword, we were telling JavaScript to create that variable in the global namespace. Because a variable called `a` already existed in the global namespace, we clobbered our original variable and replaced it with the new one we defined inside of `myFunc`. Oops.

The variable `b` was defined inside of the `myFunc` function using the keyword `var`, which told JavaScript to create a variable named `b` and scope it to inside the function `myFunc`. Because the variable `b` is scoped inside the function when we tried to access the variable outside of the function, we got an error because JavaScript couldn't find a variable named `b` defined in the global namespace.

> **Tip**
>
> The example shown in the section "Variable Scope in JavaScript" demonstrates why you should always use the keyword `var` when defining variables. This is definitely a best practice, and CoffeeScript wants to help make sure you always do that.

Variable Scope in CoffeeScript

Now that we understand a little something about how variable scoping works in JavaScript, let's take a quick look at our example again, this time written in CoffeeScript:

Example: **(source: coffeescript_variable_scope.coffee)**

```
a = 'A'
myFunc = ->
  a = 'AAA'
  b = 'B'
```

Example: **(source: coffeescript_variable_scope.js)**

```
(function() {
  var a, myFunc;

  a = 'A';

  myFunc = function() {
    var b;
    a = 'AAA';
    return b = 'B';
  };

}).call(this);
```

Ignoring for a moment the anonymous wrapper function around our code (we will be talking about that shortly), let's look at the way CoffeeScript has declared our variables. Notice that each of our variables, including the variable pointing to our `myFunc` function, is declared with the `var` keyword. CoffeeScript has our back to ensure sure we do the right thing in terms of variable declaration.

One rather interesting thing to point out about this code is that although CoffeeScript helps us with proper variable declaration, it still doesn't prevent us from clobbering our original `a` variable. The reason for this is that when CoffeeScript is compiling the JavaScript, it sees that there was a previously defined variable named `a` and assumes that you intended to use that variable inside of your function.

The Anonymous Wrapper Function

As you've seen, and should have noticed, all of our compiled JavaScript has been wrapped in an anonymous, self-executing function. I know by now that you are wondering what that function is doing there. Let me tell you.

As we saw with our JavaScript variable scope examples, we were able to easily access variables that were defined without the `var` keyword. When we defined those variables, they ended up in a global namespace that is easily accessible by everyone.

When we defined our `a` variable, even using the `var` keyword, we were still defining it in the global namespace. Why is that, you ask? The reason is quite simple—we defined it outside of any functions. Because the variable was defined outside of a function scope, it is available to the global namespace. That means that if another library you are using also defines `a`, then one of the two variables will be clobbered by the one that was last to be defined. This, of course, is true of any namespace, not just the global one.

So how do you define variables, and functions, outside of the global namespace so they are accessible to your program and no one else's? You do that by wrapping your code in an anonymous wrapper function. This is exactly what CoffeeScript is doing for you when it compiles your code to JavaScript.

Now, this is the point where you should be thinking two things. The first is, "That's clever, I can do whatever I want in there and not have to worry about polluting the global namespace." The second thing you should be asking yourself is, "Wait, how do I expose the variables and functions I want to the global namespace so I and others can access them?" Those are two very important thoughts. Let's address the second, because it's the one that needs to be addressed.

If you were to write your entire program or library within the confines of an anonymous function, as CoffeeScript forces you to do, no other libraries or code in your application could access your code. That might be just what you want to happen. However, if it is not what you want, there are a few ways we can remedy this problem.

Here's an example of one way we could share a function with the outside world:

Example: **Exposing with `window` (source: expose_with_window.coffee)**

```
window.sayHi = ->
  console.log "Hello, World!"
```

Example: **Exposing with `window` (source: expose_with_window.js)**

```
(function() {

  window.sayHi = function() {
    return console.log("Hello, World!");
  };

}).call(this);
```

In that example we are using the `window` object to expose our function. In a world where all our code is being executed in the browser, this is a perfectly good way to expose the function. However, with the success of Node.JS and other server-side JavaScript technologies, it is becoming more and more popular to run JavaScript in environments other than that of the browser. If we were to try to run this using the `coffee` command, we would get the following output:

Example: **Exposing with `window` (source: expose_with_window.coffee.output)**

```
ReferenceError: window is not defined
    at Object.<anonymous> (.../the_basics/expose_with_window.coffee:3:3)
    at Object.<anonymous> (.../the_basics/expose_with_window.coffee:7:4)
    at Module._compile (module.js:432:26)
    at Object.run (/usr/local/lib/node_modules/coffee-script/lib/coffee-script/
➥coffee-script.js:68:25)
    at /usr/local/lib/node_modules/coffee-script/lib/coffee-script/command.js:135:29
    at /usr/local/lib/node_modules/coffee-script/lib/coffee-script/command.js:110:18
    at [object Object].<anonymous> (fs.js:114:5)
    at [object Object].emit (events.js:64:17)
    at afterRead (fs.js:1081:12)
    at Object.wrapper [as oncomplete] (fs.js:252:17)
```

When running the `coffee` command, there is no `window` object to expose our function through. So how do we solve this problem? The answer is very simple. When CoffeeScript creates the anonymous function wrapper for us, it conveniently passes in `this`. We can easily attach our function to `this` and expose it that way. Let's look:

Example: **Exposing with `this` (source: expose_with_this.coffee)**

```
this.sayHi = ->
  console.log "Hello, World!"
```

Example: **Exposing with `this` (source: expose_with_this.js)**

```
(function() {

  this.sayHi = function() {
    return console.log("Hello, World!");
  };

}).call(this);
```

If we were to execute that code in a browser, our function would be exposed to other JavaScript code because `this` in the browser refers to the `window` object. In the `coffee` command or in a Node.JS application `this` refers to the `global` object. By using `this` to expose your functions and variables, you make your code both future and platform proof.

Now for the sake of completeness, there is an even simpler and, I think, cleaner way of exposing your code, and that is like this:

Example: **Exposing with `@` (source: expose_with_at.coffee)**

```
@sayHi = ->
  console.log "Hello, World!"
```

Example: **Exposing with `@` (source: expose_with_at.js)**

```
(function() {

  this.sayHi = function() {
    return console.log("Hello, World!");
  };

}).call(this);
```

As you can see in the compiled JavaScript, the `@` symbol in CoffeeScript got compiled out to `this.`. In CoffeeScript, wherever you would use `this.` you can replace it with `@` and expect it to work the same way. Although using `@` is optional, it is the preferred way in CoffeeScript, so I will be using it exclusively throughout the book.

Interpolation

In this section we talk about string interpolation, heredocs, and comments in CoffeeScript. String interpolation will let us easily build dynamic strings without having to worry about annoying and error-prone concatenation syntax. Heredocs allow us to easily build nicely formatted multiline strings. Comments, well, should be self-explanatory.

String Interpolation

One of my personal pet peeves in JavaScript is trying to build a dynamic string. Let me give you an example. Let's build an HTML text field in JavaScript that is using a few dynamic attributes:

Example: **(source: javascript_concatenation.js)**

```
var field, someId, someName, someValue;
someName = 'user[firstName]';
someId = 'firstName';
someValue = 'Bob Example';
field = "<input type='text' name='" + someName + "' id='" + someId + "' value='" +
➥(escape(someValue)) + "'>";
console.log(field);
```

Output: **(source: javascript_concatenation.js)**

```
<input type='text' name='user[firstName]' id='firstName' value='Bob%20Example'>
```

See how ugly, confusing, and potentially buggy that code is? Did I remember to properly close all the `'` around my tag attributes? Did I add the correct number of `"`? I think so, but it certainly isn't easy to see at a glance.

CoffeeScript has followed the lead of some of the more modern languages, like Ruby, and gives us two different types of strings, interpolated and literal. Let's look at them.

Interpolated Strings

To get rid of all the nasty concatenation we saw in our HTML text field example, CoffeeScript lets us, instead, use string interpolation to solve the problem.

What is string interpolation? String interpolation is a way for us to inject arbitrary CoffeeScript code inside of a string and have it executed at runtime. In our example, we want to stick a few variables into our HTML string, and CoffeeScript lets us do that. Here's how you could write the same example, this time using CoffeeScript's string interpolation:

Example: **(source: html_string_interpolation.coffee)**

```
someName = 'user[firstName]'
someId = 'firstName'
someValue = 'Bob Example'

field = "<input type='text' name='#{someName}' id='#{someId}' value='#{escape
➥someValue}'>"

console.log field
```

Example: **(source: html_string_interpolation.js)**

```
(function() {
  var field, someId, someName, someValue;

  someName = 'user[firstName]';

  someId = 'firstName';

  someValue = 'Bob Example';

  field = "<input type='text' name='" + someName + "' id='" + someId + "' value='" +
➥(escape(someValue)) + "'>";

  console.log(field);

}).call(this);
```

Output: **(source: html_string_interpolation.coffee)**

```
<input type='text' name='user[firstName]' id='firstName' value='Bob%20Example'>
```

Doesn't that code look better? That code is easier to read, write, and maintain.

In JavaScript, as you know, there is no such thing as interpolated strings. All strings are considered equal. In CoffeeScript, all strings are not created equal. Double-quoted strings, such as the one we just used, tell the CoffeeScript compiler to process the string and turn it into a concatenated JavaScript string, if necessary. Single-quoted strings are called literal strings in CoffeeScript, and we'll look at them in just a minute.

When we want to inject some CoffeeScript into a double-quoted string, we use the `#{}` syntax. Everything between the two curly braces will be separated out by the compiler and then concatenated to the string we are building. The code we put inside the curly braces can be any valid CoffeeScript we would like:

Example: **(source: string_interpolation_extra.coffee)**

```
text = "Add numbers: #{1 + 1}"
console.log text

text = "Call a function: #{escape "Hello, World!"}"
console.log text

day = 'Sunday'
console.log  "It's a beautiful #{if day is 'Sunday' then day else "Day"}"
```

Example: **(source: string_interpolation_extra.js)**

```
(function() {
  var day, text;

  text = "Add numbers: " + (1 + 1);

  console.log(text);

  text = "Call a function: " + (escape("Hello, World!"));

  console.log(text);

  day = 'Sunday';

  console.log("It's a beautiful " + (day === 'Sunday' ? day : "Day"));

}).call(this);
```

Output: **(source: string_interpolation_extra.coffee)**

```
Add numbers: 2
Call a function: Hello%2C%20World%21
It's a beautiful Sunday
```

Literal Strings

Literal strings are just what their name suggests, literal strings. That means that whatever you put into the string is exactly what you get back from the string; this is how JavaScript behaves.

To build a literal string in CoffeeScript you need to use single quotes, `'`. Let's revisit our previous example of building an HTML text field. This time, instead of using double quotes around our string, let's use single quotes and see what happens:

Example: **(source: html_string_literal.coffee)**

```
someName = 'user[firstName]'
someId = 'firstName'
someValue = 'Bob Example'

field = '<input type=\'text\' name=\'#{someName}\'
➥id=\'#{someId}\' value=\'#{escape(someValue)}\'>'

console.log field
```

Example: **(source: html_string_literal.js)**

```
(function() {
  var field, someId, someName, someValue;

  someName = 'user[firstName]';

  someId = 'firstName';

  someValue = 'Bob Example';

  field = '<input type=\'text\' name=\'#{someName}\'
➥id=\'#{someId}\' value=\'#{escape(someValue)}\'>';

  console.log(field);

}).call(this);
```

Output: **(source: html_string_literal.coffee)**

```
<input type='text' name='#{someName}' id='#{someId}' value='#{escape(someValue)}'>
```

As we can tell by our output, we are not getting the desired outcome. This is because literal strings do not support string interpolation. Instead of seeing our dynamic content mixed into the string, we are just seeing the placeholders for that dynamic content. There are certainly times when this would be the desired outcome; however, those times are few and far between.

Although literal strings won't let you inject any dynamic content into them, they still do a little bit of parsing and manipulation, the same as JavaScript. Literal strings in CoffeeScript still let you use common escape characters. Take, for example, the following:

Example: **(source: literal_string_with_escapes.coffee)**

```
text = "Header\n\tIndented Text"
console.log text
```

Example: **(source: literal_string_with_escapes.js)**

```
(function() {
  var text;

  text = "Header\n\tIndented Text";

  console.log(text);

}).call(this);
```

Output: **(source: literal_string_with_escapes.coffee)**

```
Header
        Indented Text
```

As you can see, our newline character, `\n`, and our tab character, `\t`, were properly interrupted and handled correctly in the output. CoffeeScript, like JavaScript, allows us to use double backslashes to escape a single backslash, as seen here:

Example: **(source: literal_string_with_backslash.coffee)**

```
text = "Insert \\some\\ slashes!"
console.log text
```

Example: **(source: literal_string_with_backslash.js)**

```
(function() {
  var text;

  text = "Insert \\some\\ slashes!";

  console.log(text);

}).call(this);
```

Output: **(source: literal_string_with_backslash.coffee)**

```
Insert \some\ slashes!
```

In languages like Ruby a performance improvement can be had by using literal strings. The runtime environment doesn't need to parse the string and do the required manipulation on it as the program is executing. However, because CoffeeScript compiles down to JavaScript, the performance gain moves from runtime to compilation time.

Tip

The performance gain found by using literal strings instead of interpolated strings is found only at compilation time. I see no downside to using double-quoted, interpolated strings all the time. Even if you are not using the power of interpolated strings right now, you make it easy to use at a later date by making all your strings interpolated.

Heredocs

A heredoc[1], or here document, lets you build a multiline string easily in CoffeeScript, while preserving all the spaces and newlines of the multiline string. Heredoc strings follow the same rules as interpolated and literal strings do. To build an interpolated heredoc string in CoffeeScript, you use three double quotes at each end of the string. To build a literal heredoc string, you would use three single quotes at each end of the string.

Let's look at a simple example. Let's take our previous HTML text field and add some more HTML around it:

Example: **(source: heredoc.coffee)**

```
someName = 'user[firstName]'
someId = 'firstName'
someValue = 'Bob Example'

field = """
        <ul>
          <li>
            <input type='text' name='#{someName}' id='#{someId}'
value='#{escape(someValue)}'>
          </li>
        </ul>
        """

console.log field
```

Example: **(source: heredoc.js)**

```
(function() {
  var field, someId, someName, someValue;

  someName = 'user[firstName]';

  someId = 'firstName';

  someValue = 'Bob Example';
```

```
  field = "<ul>\n  <li>\n    <input type='text' name='" + someName + "' id='" + someId
➥+ "' value='" + (escape(someValue)) + "'>\n  </li>\n</ul>";

  console.log(field);

}).call(this);
```

Output: **(source: heredoc.coffee)**

```
<ul>
  <li>
    <input type='text' name='user[firstName]' id='firstName' value='Bob%20Example'>
  </li>
</ul>
```

As you can see, our final output was nicely formatted, just like our original text. You can also see that the original indentation level the heredoc begins with is maintained throughout, making it easy to keep the code well formatted.

Comments

Every good language needs to supply more than one way to add comments, and CoffeeScript is no different. There are two ways to write comments in CoffeeScript, and both ways have different effects on the compiled JavaScript.

Inline Comments

The first type of comment is the inline comment. Inline comments are very simple. To create an inline comment, you simply use a # symbol. Everything after the # symbol to the end of the line will be ignored by the CoffeeScript compiler.

Example: **(source: inline_comment.coffee)**

```
# Calculate the company payroll
calcPayroll()

payBils() # Pay the company's bills
```

Example: **(source: inline_comment.js)**

```
(function() {

  calcPayroll();
```

```
  payBils();

}).call(this);
```

You can see that our comments do not make their way into the final JavaScript source. There is some debate as to whether this is a good thing or a bad thing. It would be nice to have the comment next to the JavaScript code. However, because there is not always a nice, direct mapping from CoffeeScript to JavaScript, it makes it difficult for the compiler to always know where the comment should go. On the plus side, our compiled JavaScript is lighter because it is not peppered with comments, leaving us to comment our code fully without fear of bloating the JavaScript.

Block Comments

The other type of comment that CoffeeScript gives us is a block comment. Block comments are great for writing lengthy, multiline comments. Such comments can include license and versioning information, documentation of API usage, and so on. Unlike inline comments, CoffeeScript does include block comments in the compiled JavaScript code.

Example: **(source: block_comment.coffee)**

```
###
My Awesome Library v1.0
Copyright: Me!
Released under the MIT License
###
```

Example: **(source: block_comment.js)**

```
/*
My Awesome Library v1.0
Copyright: Me!
Released under the MIT License
*/

(function() {



}).call(this);
```

Defining block comments, as you can see, is very similar to defining heredocs. Block comments are defined by using three # symbols on both sides of the comment.

Extended Regular Expressions

CoffeeScript and JavaScript are identical in how you define, use, and execute regular expressions.[2] CoffeeScript, however, does give a little help when you want to write those really long and complex regular expressions.

We've all had that regular expression that gets a bit unwieldy. We would love to split it up over several lines and comment each of the sections of the expression. Well, CoffeeScript is there to help us out.

To define a multiline regular expression, we wrap the expression with three forward slashes on either side of the expression, similar to heredocs and block comments.

Let's look at an actual usage of this from the CoffeeScript compiler source code:

Example: **(source: extended_regex.coffee)**

```
REGEX = /// ^
  (/ (?! [\s=] )   # disallow leading whitespace or equals signs
  [^ [ / \n \\ ]*  # every other thing
  (?:
    (?: \\[\s\S]   # anything escaped
      | \[         # character class
          [^ \] \n \\ ]*
          (?: \\[\s\S] [^ \] \n \\ ]* )*
        ]
    ) [^ [ / \n \\ ]*
  )*
  /) ([imgy]{0,4}) (?!\w)
///
```

Example: **(source: extended_regex.js)**

```
(function() {
  var REGEX;

  REGEX = /^(\/(?![\s=])[^[\/\n\\]*(?:(?:\\[\s\S]|\[[^\]\n\\]*(?:\\[\s\S]
➥[^\]\n\\]*)*])[^[\/\n\\]*)*\/)([imgy]{0,4})(?!\w)/;

}).call(this);
```

You can see how all the extra whitespace and the comments are removed from our JavaScript output.

Wrapping Up

Now that you understand the syntax of CoffeeScript, we can begin looking at more interesting and detailed parts of the language. If you don't understand anything we've covered so far, please take a few minutes to go back and reread this chapter again. It's important that you understand all that we have discussed here because it forms the basis for everything you will be learning throughout the rest of the book. When you're comfortable with everything, let's move on to the next chapter!

Notes

1. http://en.wikipedia.org/wiki/Heredoc
2. http://en.wikipedia.org/wiki/Regular_expressions

3

Control Structures

Almost all languages have the concept of operators[1] and conditionals;[2] JavaScript and CoffeeScript are no different. Operators and conditionals work hand in hand to form an important part of all programming languages. Operators let you do things such as add or subtract two numbers, compare two objects, shift bytes in an object, and so on. Conditionals, on the other hand, let us control the flow of our application based on certain predefined conditions. For example *if* a user is not logged in *then* send them to the login screen, *else* show them the secret page. That is a conditional statement.

In this chapter we take a look at both operators and conditionals and how they are defined in CoffeeScript.

Operators and Aliases

For the most part, JavaScript and CoffeeScript play nicely in terms of the operators behaving the same. However, in a few places CoffeeScript steps in to help make sure you don't step on some land mines that JavaScript has lurking about its innards. To make sure we understand fully what all the operators do, let's take a quick tour of the JavaScript operators, and I'll point out when they are different from their CoffeeScript counterparts. Before we continue, I want to say that I am assuming you know what all the JavaScript operators do. If you don't, now is a good time to brush up on them. If you need a reference, I recommend http://en.wikibooks.org/wiki/JavaScript/Operators. It offers a quick, but well written, overview of the operators available in JavaScript.

Arithmetic

Here is a list of each of the arithmetic operators in JavaScript:

- + Addition
- - Subtraction

- * Multiplication
- / Division (returns a floating-point value)
- % Modulus (returns the integer remainder)
- + Unary conversion of string to number
- - Unary negation (reverses the sign)
- ++ Increment (can be prefix or postfix)
- -- Decrement (can be prefix or postfix)

Now let's take a look at how those operators translate in the CoffeeScript world:

Example: **(source: arithmetic.coffee)**

```
console.log "+ Addition: #{1 + 1}"

console.log "- Subtraction: #{10 - 1}"

console.log "* Multiplication: #{5 * 5}"

console.log "/ Division: #{100 / 10}"

console.log "% Modulus: #{10 % 3}"

console.log "+ Unary conversion of string to number: #{+'100'}"

console.log "- Unary negation: #{-50}"

i = 1
x = ++i
console.log "++ Increment: #{x}"

i = 1
x = --i
console.log "-- Decrement: #{x}"
```

Example: **(source: arithmetic.js)**

```
(function() {
  var i, x;

  console.log("+ Addition: " + (1 + 1));

  console.log("- Subtraction: " + (10 - 1));
```

```
  console.log("* Multiplication: " + (5 * 5));

  console.log("/ Division: " + (100 / 10));

  console.log("% Modulus: " + (10 % 3));

  console.log("+ Unary conversion of string to number: " + (+'100'));

  console.log("- Unary negation: " + (-50));

  i = 1;

  x = ++i;

  console.log("++ Increment: " + x);

  i = 1;

  x = --i;

  console.log("-- Decrement: " + x);

}).call(this);
```

Output: **(source: arithmetic.coffee)**

```
+ Addition: 2
- Subtraction: 9
* Multiplication: 25
/ Division: 10
% Modulus: 1
+ Unary conversion of string to number: 100
- Unary negation: -50
++ Increment: 2
-- Decrement: 0
```

As we can see from the example, all our CoffeeScript arithmetic operators map directly to JavaScript, so we won't be losing any sleep at night trying to remember them.

Assignment

Now we'll move on to the assignment operators in JavaScript, which are presented in the following list:

- = Assign
- += Add and assign
- -= Subtract and assign
- *= Multiply and assign
- /= Divide and assign
- %= Modulus and assign
- ?= Exists or assign
- ||= Or or assign
- &&= Assign if both are true

How do they map to CoffeeScript?

Example: **(source: assignment.coffee)**

```
console.log "= Assign:"
x = 10
console.log x

console.log "+= Add and assign:"
x += 25
console.log x

console.log "-= Subtract and assign:"
x -= 25
console.log x

console.log "*= Multiply and assign:"
x *= 10
console.log x

console.log "/= Divide and assign:"
x /= 10
console.log x

console.log "%= Modulus and assign:"
x %= 3
console.log x

console.log "?= Exists or assign:"
y ?= 3
console.log y
y ?= 100
console.log y
```

```
console.log "||= Or or assign:"
z = null
z ||= 10
console.log z
z ||= 100
console.log z

console.log "&&= Assign if both are true:"
a = 1
b = 2
console.log a &&= b
console.log a
```

Example: **(source: assignment.js)**

```
(function() {
  var a, b, x, z;

  console.log("= Assign:");

  x = 10;

  console.log(x);

  console.log("+= Add and assign:");

  x += 25;

  console.log(x);

  console.log("-= Subtract and assign:");

  x -= 25;

  console.log(x);

  console.log("*= Multiply and assign:");

  x *= 10;

  console.log(x);

  console.log("/= Divide and assign:");

  x /= 10;
```

```
  console.log(x);

  console.log("%= Modulus and assign:");

  x %= 3;

  console.log(x);

  console.log("?= Exists or assign:");

  if (typeof y === "undefined" || y === null) y = 3;

  console.log(y);

  if (typeof y === "undefined" || y === null) y = 100;

  console.log(y);

  console.log("||= Or or assign:");

  z = null;

  z || (z = 10);

  console.log(z);

  z || (z = 100);

  console.log(z);

  console.log("&&= Assign if both are true:");

  a = 1;

  b = 2;

  console.log(a && (a = b));

  console.log(a);

}).call(this);
```

Output: **(source: assignment.coffee)**

```
= Assign:
10
+= Add and assign:
35
-= Subtract and assign:
10
*= Multiply and assign:
100
/= Divide and assign:
10
%= Modulus and assign:
1
?= Exists or assign:
3
3
||= Or or assign:
10
10
&&= Assign if both are true:
2
2
```

Again, all the operators map directly. Isn't life wonderful?

Comparison

Now let's take a look at the comparison operators and see how they map between CoffeeScript and JavaScript.

- == Equal
- != Not equal
- > Greater than
- >= Greater than or equal to
- < Less than
- <= Less than or equal to
- === Identical (equal and of the same type)
- !== Not identical

Okay, let's take a peek and see how these operators behave in CoffeeScript:

Example: **(source: comparison.coffee)**

```
console.log "== Equal: #{1 == 1}"

console.log "!= Not equal: #{1 != 2}"

console.log "> Greater than: #{2 > 1}"

console.log ">= Greater than or equal to: #{1 >= 1}"

console.log "< Less than: #{1 < 2}"

console.log "<= Less than or equal to: #{1 < 2}"

console.log "=== Identical: #{'a' === 'a'}"

console.log "!== Not identical: #{1 !== 2}"
```

Output: **(source: comparison.coffee)**

```
Error: In content/control_structures/comparison.coffee, Parse error on line 13:
➥Unexpected '='
    at Object.parseError
➥(/usr/local/lib/node_modules/coffee-script/lib/coffee-script/parser.js:470:11)
    at Object.parse
➥ (/usr/local/lib/node_modules/coffee-script/lib/coffee-script/parser.js:546:22)
    at /usr/local/lib/node_modules/coffee-script/lib/coffee-script/
➥ coffee-script.js:40:22
    at Object.run
➥ /usr/local/lib/node_modules/coffee-script/lib/coffee-script/coffee-script.js:68:34)
    at /usr/local/lib/node_modules/coffee-script/lib/coffee-script/command.js:135:29
    at /usr/local/lib/node_modules/coffee-script/lib/coffee-script/command.js:110:18
    at [object Object].<anonymous> (fs.js:114:5)
    at [object Object].emit (events.js:64:17)
    at afterRead (fs.js:1081:12)
    at Object.wrapper [as oncomplete] (fs.js:252:17)
```

Well, that doesn't look right, does it? Let's look at what happened there and why our example blew up. CoffeeScript does not allow the use of the === or !== operators. Hopefully, by the time this book goes to print a better error message will be presented that is both clearer and more informative. I can hear everyone crying out in horror because those are the comparison operators we should be using the most, but don't worry, CoffeeScript does have our backs here. Let me explain.

Let's rebuild our example code; this time we'll drop our === and !== examples:

Example: **(source: comparison2.coffee)**

```
console.log "== Equal: #{1 == 1}"

console.log "!= Not equal: #{1 != 2}"

console.log "> Greater than: #{2 > 1}"

console.log ">= Greater than or equal to: #{1 >= 1}"

console.log "< Less than: #{1 < 2}"

console.log "<= Less than or equal to: #{1 < 2}"
```

Example: **(source: comparison2.js)**

```
(function() {

  console.log("== Equal: " + (1 === 1));

  console.log("!= Not equal: " + (1 !== 2));

  console.log("> Greater than: " + (2 > 1));

  console.log(">= Greater than or equal to: " + (1 >= 1));

  console.log("< Less than: " + (1 < 2));

  console.log("<= Less than or equal to: " + (1 < 2));

}).call(this);
```

Output: **(source: comparison2.coffee)**

```
== Equal: true
!= Not equal: true
> Greater than: true
>= Greater than or equal to: true
< Less than: true
<= Less than or equal to: true
```

Great! Our examples didn't blow up this time, but you should've noticed something very interesting. Did you see how our `==` and `!=` examples converted when compiled in JavaScript? CoffeeScript compiled those examples into `===` and `!==` respectively. Why did CoffeeScript do that? Let's look at what happens in JavaScript when you use `==` and `!=`:

Example: **(source: javascript_comparison.js)**

```
x = 1;
y = '1';
console.log(x == y); // true
```

In the JavaScript example, `1` is equal to `"1"` despite the fact that they are different objects. The reason is that when using the `==` comparison operator in JavaScript it will automatically coerce the two objects to the same type of object and then do the comparison on it. The same holds true for the `!=` operator. This is the source of a great many JavaScript bugs. To get a true comparison of two objects you must use the `===` operator.

If we look at the same example again, only this time using the `===` operator, you see that we get `false` for our comparison instead of `true`:

Example: **(source: javascript_comparison2.js)**

```
x = 1;
y = '1';
console.log(x === y); // false
```

To make sure you don't run into these sorts of bugs, CoffeeScript automatically converts any `==` and `!=` operators into `===` and `!==` for you. Isn't that nice? CoffeeScript is helping you keep your bugs to a minimum. You should send it a thank you card. There is another way to use the `===` and `!==` operators, which we'll look at in a minute when we discuss aliases.

String

Finally, there are a few operators that work on strings.

- + Concatenation
- += Concatenate and assign

Here they are in CoffeeScript:

Example: **(source: string_operators.coffee)**

```
console.log "+ Concatenation: #{'a' + 'b'}"

x = 'Hello'
```

```
x += " World"
console.log "+= Concatenate and assign: #{x}"
```

Example: **(source: string_operators.js)**

```
(function() {
  var x;

  console.log("+ Concatenation: " + ('a' + 'b'));

  x = 'Hello';

  x += " World";

  console.log("+= Concatenate and assign: " + x);

}).call(this);
```

Output: **(source: string_operators.coffee)**

```
+ Concatenation: ab
+= Concatenate and assign: Hello World
```

Fortunately, these operators work just like they do in JavaScript.

The Existential Operator

When I first discovered CoffeeScript, I immediately fell in love with the existential operator. This operator lets you check, well, the existence of a variable or function, using a simple `?`.

Let's take a quick look:

Example: **(source: existential1.coffee)**

```
console.log x?
```

Example: **(source: existential1.js)**

```
(function() {

  console.log(typeof x !== "undefined" && x !== null);

}).call(this);
```

Output: **(source: existential1.coffee)**

```
false
```

As you can see in our example, CoffeeScript generates JavaScript that checks to see if the variable `x` is defined; if it is, then it checks to see if it is not null. This can make writing conditionals very powerful.

Example: **(source: existential_if.coffee)**

```
if html?
  console.log html
```

Example: **(source: existential_if.js)**

```
(function() {

  if (typeof html !== "undefined" && html !== null) console.log(html);

}).call(this);
```

The fun doesn't stop there with the existential operator. Using the existential operator, we can check the existence of something, and if it exists, call a function on it. My favorite example of this is with the `console` object. For those of you unfamiliar with the `console` object, it exists in most browsers as a way to write messages to the built-in JavaScript error console. Typically, this is used by developers as a way of logging messages at certain points in the code for either debugging or informational purposes. I've been using it in almost all the book examples as a way to demonstrate the output of our examples.

The problem with the `console` object is that it isn't always there (Internet Explorer, I'm looking at you!). If you attempt to call a function or call a property on a variable that doesn't exist, the browser will raise an exception and your program will not execute properly. The existential operator can help us get around the problem of calling functions on objects that are not defined, such as the `console` object in certain browsers.

First, let's look at an example where we don't use the existential operator:

Example: **(source: existential2.coffee)**

```
console.log "Hello, World"
console.log someObject.someFunction()
console.log "Goodbye, World"
```

Example: **(source: existential2.js)**

```
(function() {

  console.log("Hello, World");

  console.log(someObject.someFunction());

  console.log("Goodbye, World");

}).call(this);
```

Output: **(source: existential2.coffee)**

```
Hello, World
ReferenceError: someObject is not defined
    at Object.<anonymous> (.../control_structures/existential2.coffee:5:15)
    at Object.<anonymous> (.../control_structures/existential2.coffee:9:4)
    at Module._compile (module.js:432:26)
    at Object.run
➥(/usr/local/lib/node_modules/coffee-script/lib/coffee-script/coffee-script.js:68:25)
    at /usr/local/lib/node_modules/coffee-script/lib/coffee-script/command.js:135:29
    at /usr/local/lib/node_modules/coffee-script/lib/coffee-script/command.js:110:18
    at [object Object].<anonymous> (fs.js:114:5)
    at [object Object].emit (events.js:64:17)
    at afterRead (fs.js:1081:12)
    at Object.wrapper [as oncomplete] (fs.js:252:17)
```

Well, that's a nasty little error, isn't it? Our example is blowing up because it cannot find an object named `someObject` and we are attempting to call a function. Now, if we add the existential operator after `someObject`, let's see what happens.

Example: **(source: existential3.coffee)**

```
console.log "Hello, World"
console.log someObject?.someFunction()
console.log "Goodbye, World"
```

Example: **(source: existential3.js)**

```
(function() {

  console.log("Hello, World");
```

```
  console.log(typeof someObject !== "undefined" && someObject !== null ?
➥someObject.someFunction() : void 0);

  console.log("Goodbye, World");

}).call(this);
```

Output: **(source: existential3.coffee)**

```
Hello, World
undefined
Goodbye, World
```

That is definitely better. Although we got an `undefined` message when we tried to access our `someObject` variable, the program did fully execute. If this were a real-world example, we might want to log a message or possibly raise some sort of alert, but for now I think we've done our part to make our code a little safer.

Aliases

In an effort to make your code a little more user friendly, CoffeeScript has added a few aliases for some of the more common operators. Some of these aliases make wonderful additions to the language, but others are a little confusing. Table 3.1 shows the CoffeeScript aliases and their JavaScript counterparts.

Table 3.1 **CoffeeScript Aliases and Their JavaScript Counterparts**

CoffeeScript	JavaScript
`is`	`===`
`isnt`	`!==`
`not`	`!`
`and`	`&&`
`or`	`||`
`true, yes, on`	`true`
`false, no, off`	`false`
`@, this`	`this`
`of`	`in`
`in`	N/A

Let's take a look at all but the last two aliases. The last two aliases will be covered in Chapter 5, "Collections and Iterations."

The `is` and `isnt` Aliases

Here is an example of the `is`, `isnt` operator aliases in action:

Example: **(source: is_aliases.coffee)**

```
name = "mark"

console.log name is "mark"
console.log name isnt "bob"
```

Example: **(source: is_aliases.js)**

```
(function() {
  var name;

  name = "mark";

  console.log(name === "mark");

  console.log(name !== "bob");

}).call(this);
```

Output: **(source: is_aliases.coffee)**

```
true
true
```

As you can see, in our code the `is` alias mapped to the `===` and the `isnt` operator mapped to the `!==`. As you recall from our earlier discussions in this chapter, the `===` and `!==` operators are the comparison operators CoffeeScript not only wants you to use, but insists you use. CoffeeScript also would prefer you to use the `is` and `isnt` aliases. They are considered "the CoffeeScript way." Removing the `==` and `!=` as legal operators from CoffeeScript and forcing the use of the `is` and `isnt` operators only has been discussed. As of the time of this writing this has not happened, but it is something you should be aware of. This particular caveat holds true of all the aliases and their appropriate matching operator.

The `not` Alias

The not alias and I have a love/hate relationship. I love the way it makes my code look, but I hate the way it doesn't always behave the way I want it to. The idea of the not alias is the same as the ! operator in JavaScript; it will "flip" the Boolean state of a variable. That means it will make a true become false and vice versa.

Let's take a look at how the not alias behaves:

Example: **(source: not_alias.coffee)**

```
userExists = false

if not userExists
  console.log "the user doesn't exist!"
```

Example: **(source: not_alias.js)**

```
(function() {
  var userExists;

  userExists = false;

  if (!userExists) console.log("the user doesn't exist!");

}).call(this);
```

Output: **(source: not_alias.coffee)**

```
the user doesn't exist!
```

As you can see, we have to make sure to place a space between the not alias and the variable we are trying to "flip" Boolean states on.

So how does this get confusing? In CoffeeScript it is possible to write this code:

Example: **(source: not_alias_wrong.coffee)**

```
name = "mark"

console.log name isnt "bob"
console.log name is not "bob"
```

Example: **(source: not_alias_wrong.js)**

```
(function() {
  var name;

  name = "mark";

  console.log(name !== "bob");

  console.log(name === !"bob");

}).call(this);
```

Output: **(source: not_alias_wrong.coffee)**

```
true
false
```

Although grammatically those couple of lines look correct, they are actually very different lines of code. The line using the `isnt` alias is checking that the two objects are not equal. The line using the `is not` alias is checking the equality of the first variable to the "flipped" Boolean value of the second. This is an easy mistake to make, especially when you are first starting with CoffeeScript.

The `and` and `or` Aliases

I love these aliases. The `and` and `or` aliases not only read well in your code, but they do just what you would expect them to do! Here's an example:

Example: **(source: and_or.coffee)**

```
if true and true
  console.log "true and true really is true"

if false or true
  console.log "something was true"
```

Example: **(source: and_or.js)**

```
(function() {

  if (true && true) console.log("true and true really is true");

  if (false || true) console.log("something was true");

}).call(this);
```

Output: **(source: and_or.coffee)**

```
true and true really is true
something was true
```

Like I said, they do just what you would expect them to do.

The Boolean Aliases

CoffeeScript supports not just `true` and `false` for Booleans, but also took a page from the book of YAML[3] and added a few other aliases to make your code nicer to read.

Let's have a look:

Example: **(source: boolean_operators.coffee)**

```
myAnswer = true
console.log myAnswer is yes
console.log myAnswer is true

light = true
console.log light is on
console.log light is true

myAnswer = false
console.log myAnswer is no
console.log myAnswer is false

light = false
console.log light is off
console.log light is false
```

Example: **(source: boolean_operators.js)**

```
(function() {
  var light, myAnswer;

  myAnswer = true;

  console.log(myAnswer === true);

  console.log(myAnswer === true);

  light = true;

  console.log(light === true);
```

```
  console.log(light === true);

  myAnswer = false;

  console.log(myAnswer === false);

  console.log(myAnswer === false);

  light = false;

  console.log(light === false);

  console.log(light === false);

}).call(this);
```

Output: **(source: boolean_operators.coffee)**

```
true
true
true
true
true
true
true
true
```

As you can see the `yes`, `no`, `on`, and `off` aliases can make your code fun and easy to read.

The @ Alias

The last alias we look at before we move on is the `@` alias. We will revisit this alias from time to time throughout the book as we talk about different areas of CoffeeScript. For now let's talk about its most basic, and common, use: as an alias for the JavaScript keyword `this`.

Here is a very simple example of the `@` alias at work:

Example: **(source: at_alias.coffee)**

```
object = {
  name: 'mark'
  sayHi: ->
    console.log "Hello: #{@name}"
}
```

```
object.sayHi()

console.log @name
```

Example: **(source: at_alias.js)**

```
(function() {
  var object;

  object = {
    name: 'mark',
    sayHi: function() {
      return console.log("Hello: " + this.name);
    }
  };

  object.sayHi();

  console.log(this.name);

}).call(this);
```

Output: **(source: at_alias.coffee)**

```
Hello: mark
undefined
```

If you don't understand how `this` scoping in JavaScript works, or even what `this` is, I urge you to put this book down now and pick up a proper JavaScript book and read that first.

As you can see, if you compare our CoffeeScript example and its compiled JavaScript output, all references to `@` were replaced with `this.` when compiled. I find that my code is much easier to read when using the `@` symbol. I can easily distinguish between "local" variables, sometimes referred to as instance variables, within a function and variables and functions that are defined outside of the current function I'm working in.

If/Unless

In my travels as a developer, I have yet to meet a programming language that didn't have the concept of conditional statements. I'm sure somebody out there has written one, but I doubt that it is heavily used outside of that person's parent's basement.

Conditionals allow our programs to become intelligent. They let us program applications that can react to different situations. Is there a logged in user? If not, ask her to log in; otherwise, show her the secret account page. Has the current user paid his bill? If he has, give him access to his account; if not, tell him to pay. These are examples of conditional statements. The program takes a different path through its execution based on the answers to these questions.

CoffeeScript, like almost every other programming language, offers conditionals. These conditional statements will typically be used with the operators and aliases we've already seen in this chapter to help the program make more intelligent decisions.

The `if` Statement

Already in this book, you have seen examples of the `if` statement at work. The structure is pretty simple.

Example: **(source: if.coffee)**

```
if true
  console.log "the statement was true"
```

Example: **(source: if.js)**

```
(function() {

  if (true) console.log("the statement was true");

}).call(this);
```

Output: **(source: if.coffee)**

```
the statement was true
```

Our example, while incredibly contrived, illustrates the structure of an `if` statement. We follow the keyword `if` with whatever our conditional statement is. If that statement returns `true` we execute the block of code following it. If the conditional statement returns `false` we skip execution of the code block.

Here is a slightly less-contrived example:

Example: **(source: if2.coffee)**

```
today = "Sunday"
if today is "Sunday"
  console.log "Today is Sunday"
```

Example: **(source: if2.js)**

```
(function() {
  var today;

  today = "Sunday";

  if (today === "Sunday") console.log("Today is Sunday");

}).call(this);
```

Output: **(source: if2.coffee)**

```
Today is Sunday
```

The `if/else` Statement

There are times when we want to execute some code if the conditional statement is true, and there are times when we want to execute some other code if the statement is false. In these cases we can use the `if` statement we know and the `else` keyword to define a block of code to run, should the conditional statement be false.

For example:

Example: **(source: if_else.coffee)**

```
today = "Monday"
if today is "Sunday"
  console.log "Today is Sunday"
else
  console.log "Today is not Sunday"
```

Example: **(source: if_else.js)**

```
(function() {
  var today;

  today = "Monday";

  if (today === "Sunday") {
    console.log("Today is Sunday");
  } else {
    console.log("Today is not Sunday");
  }

}).call(this);
```

Output: **(source: if_else.coffee)**

```
Today is not Sunday
```

As you can see, in our example our conditional was false, so the block of code defined after the `else` keyword was executed.

CoffeeScript does allow you to write this in a single line of code, which would look something like this:

Example: **(source: if_else_1_line.coffee)**

```
today = "Monday"
console.log if today is "Sunday" then "Today is Sunday" else "Today is not Sunday"
```

Example: **(source: if_else_1_line.js)**

```
(function() {
  var today;

  today = "Monday";

  console.log(today === "Sunday" ? "Today is Sunday" : "Today is not Sunday");

}).call(this);
```

Output: **(source: if_else_1_line.coffee)**

```
Today is not Sunday
```

> **Tip**
>
> Personally, I think that the single line `if else then` statement is a bit wordy and hard to read, so I would very rarely, if ever, use it.

In JavaScript you can use what is called the ternary operator[4] to write that same example in one line of code, which is what CoffeeScript compiles it down to. However, CoffeeScript does not support the ternary operator, so any attempt to use it would result in some rather strange compiled JavaScript. Take a look for yourself:

Example: **(source: ternary.coffee)**

```
today = "Monday"
console.log today is "Sunday" ? "Today is Sunday" : "Today is not Sunday"
```

Example: **(source: ternary.js)**

```
(function() {
  var today, _ref;

  today = "Monday";

  console.log((_ref = today === "Sunday") != null ? _ref : {
    "Today is Sunday": "Today is not Sunday"
  });

}).call(this);
```

Output: **(source: ternary.coffee)**

```
false
```

I'm not going to explain what happened there. Make a note to yourself to revisit this example when you have finished this book to see if you can solve the riddle of why CoffeeScript generated that JavaScript.

The `if/else if` Statement

Let's pretend for a moment that we are writing a very basic todo application. When we look at the application we want it do one of three things. If today is Saturday, we want it to show us a list of todos for the day. If it's Sunday, we want it to tell us to relax and enjoy the day. Finally if it's neither Saturday nor Sunday, we want it tell us to get to work. How would we write that using the knowledge we have so far? It would look something like this:

Example: **(source: if_else_if_1.coffee)**

```
today = "Monday"
if today is "Saturday"
  console.log "Here are your todos for the day..."
if today is "Sunday"
  console.log "Go watch football and relax!"
if today isnt "Saturday" and today isnt "Sunday"
  console.log "Get to work you lazy bum!"
```

Example: **(source: if_else_if_1.js)**

```
(function() {
  var today;

  today = "Monday";

  if (today === "Saturday") console.log("Here are your todos for the day...");

  if (today === "Sunday") console.log("Go watch football and relax!");

  if (today !== "Saturday" && today !== "Sunday") {
    console.log("Get to work you lazy bum!");
  }

}).call(this);
```

Output: **(source: if_else_if_1.coffee)**

```
Get to work you lazy bum!
```

Although that code does work, it isn't the most efficient code. For a start we are checking each `if` statement, even if the first one was `true`, and we still check the other `if` statements in case they are also true, which we know will never be the case. Also, our last `if` statement is a bit repetitive because we are asking similar questions already. Finally, it is also error prone. If want to change from using full day names, like Sunday, to shortened ones, like Sun, we have to make sure we update every reference to Sunday we find.

Using the `else if` statement, we can easily clean up this example. Here's how:

Example: **(source: if_else_if_2.coffee)**

```
today = "Monday"
if today is "Saturday"
  console.log "Here are your todos for the day..."
else if today is "Sunday"
  console.log "Go watch football and relax!"
else
  console.log "Get to work you lazy bum!"
```

Example: **(source: if_else_if_2.js)**

```
(function() {
  var today;

  today = "Monday";
```

```
  if (today === "Saturday") {
    console.log("Here are your todos for the day...");
  } else if (today === "Sunday") {
    console.log("Go watch football and relax!");
  } else {
    console.log("Get to work you lazy bum!");
  }

}).call(this);
```

Output: **(source: if_else_if_2.coffee)**

```
Get to work you lazy bum!
```

Now doesn't that look a lot better? It is also a lot more efficient when executed. If today were Saturday, it would execute the first code block and then skip the rest of the `else if` and `else` statements, because they are unnecessary.

Later in this chapter we will rewrite this example using the `switch` statement, which will clean it up even further.

The `unless` Statement

The Ruby programming language has the concept of the `unless` statement, and the folks behind CoffeeScript thought it was such a great idea they stole it.

What does the `unless` statement do? In short, it enables you to put the `else` before the `if`. Now, I know you're scratching your head. It is confusing at first, but it really is straightforward.

When using the `unless` we are checking to see if our conditional statement is false. If the statement is false, we execute the code block defined below it. Here's an example:

Example: **(source: unless.\coffee)**

```
today = "Monday"
unless today is "Sunday"
  console.log "No football today!"
```

Example: **(source: unless.js)**

```
(function() {
  var today;

  today = "Monday";
```

```
  if (today !== "Sunday") console.log("No football today!");

}).call(this);
```

Output: **(source: unless.coffee)**

```
No football today!
```

The same example could be written in any of the following ways:

Example: **(source: unless_as_if.coffee)**

```
today = "Monday"
unless today is "Sunday"
  console.log "No football today!"

if not (today is "Sunday")
  console.log "No football today!"

if today isnt "Sunday"
  console.log "No football today!"
```

Example: **(source: unless_as_if.js)**

```
(function() {
  var today;

  today = "Monday";

  if (today !== "Sunday") console.log("No football today!");

  if (!(today === "Sunday")) console.log("No football today!");

  if (today !== "Sunday") console.log("No football today!");

}).call(this);
```

Output: **(source: unless_as_if.coffee)**

```
No football today!
No football today!
No football today!
```

Of the three examples, I prefer the last example using the `isnt` alias. I find it to be a bit cleaner and easier to read. The choice, however, is up to you. They are all valid ways of writing the same code.

Inline Conditionals

In addition to the `unless` keyword, the CoffeeScript team copped the idea of inline conditionals from Ruby. An inline conditional statement allows you to place both the conditional statement and the code block to execute on the same line.

This is easily demonstrated with an example:

Example: **(source: inline.coffee)**

```
today = "Sunday"
console.log "Today is Sunday" if today is "Sunday"
```

Example: **(source: inline.js)**

```
(function() {
  var today;

  today = "Sunday";

  if (today === "Sunday") console.log("Today is Sunday");

}).call(this);
```

Output: **(source: inline.coffee)**

```
Today is Sunday
```

When used with the existential operator, which we covered earlier in this chapter, the inline conditional can help to keep code clean.

Switch/Case Statements

Earlier when we talked about `else if` statements, I mentioned how we could clean up that code using a `switch` statement.[5] A `switch` statement lets us build a table of conditionals, which we can then match an object against. Should one of the conditionals match, appropriate code will be executed. We can also give our table an `else` clause to match, should none of the other conditionals match.

Let's take a look at our earlier `else if` example and rewrite it to use the `switch` statement in CoffeeScript.

Example: **(source: switch1.coffee)**

```
today = "Monday"
switch today
  when "Saturday"
    console.log "Here are your todos for the day..."
  when "Sunday"
    console.log "Go watch football and relax!"
  else
    console.log "Get to work you lazy bum!"
```

Example: **(source: switch1.js)**

```
(function() {
  var today;

  today = "Monday";

  switch (today) {
    case "Saturday":
      console.log("Here are your todos for the day...");
      break;
    case "Sunday":
      console.log("Go watch football and relax!");
      break;
    default:
      console.log("Get to work you lazy bum!");
  }

}).call(this);
```

Output: **(source: switch1.coffee)**

```
Get to work you lazy bum!
```

As you can see, our `today` variable is checked against the defined `case` statements. Because neither of the `case` statements matched the `today` variable we passed in, the program fell through to the `else` statement we defined at the end of the `switch` statement. It's worth pointing out that we don't need to define an `else` block at the end. If we didn't define the `else` in our example, nothing would have been printed out.

The more observant of you will have noticed the `break` keyword in the compiled JavaScript output at the end of each of the `case` statements. In JavaScript it is possible to let the `switch` statement keep falling through and keep matching more `case` statements. This is almost never wanted, and is often the source of many bugs. The most common bug is that it matches a case, executes the appropriate code, and ends up also executing the `default` code block at the bottom. The `break` keyword will tell the `switch` to stop executing and to stop trying to match other cases. This is another example of CoffeeScript trying to cover your back and help you write code with fewer bugs.

The `switch` statement also enables us to pass a comma-separated list of values to match against the `case` keyword. This makes it possible for us to execute the same code block for multiple matches. Suppose we wanted a program that would check to see if today was a weekend day. If it was indeed a weekend day, it would tell us to relax; otherwise, it would tell us to work. We could do that like this:

Example: **(source: switch2.coffee)**

```
today = "Sunday"
switch today
  when "Saturday", "Sunday"
    console.log "Enjoy your #{today}!"
  else
    console.log "Off to work you go. :("
```

Example: **(source: switch2.js)**

```
(function() {
  var today;

  today = "Sunday";

  switch (today) {
    case "Saturday":
    case "Sunday":
      console.log("Enjoy your " + today + "!");
      break;
    default:
      console.log("Off to work you go. :(");
  }

}).call(this);
```

Output: **(source: switch2.coffee)**

```
Enjoy your Sunday!
```

With that, our exploration of the wonderful `switch` statement comes to a close. There is a lot of debate among developers as to when, where, or if you should ever use `switch` statements. They are not something I use on a day-to-day basis, but they definitely have their place. I'll let you decide when they are of use to you and your application.

Wrapping Up

In this chapter we've covered a lot of ground. We've discussed the various operators in CoffeeScript and how, if at all, they map to JavaScript. We've seen a few of the places where CoffeeScript tries to help us write better JavaScript code. Aliases showed us how to write "prettier" code that reads more like English than "computer." You've seen how to build conditional statements to help make your programs more intelligent and to help execute the correct bit of code depending on certain conditions. Finally, we explored how the `switch` statement can help you clean up complex code.

In the original outline for this book, this chapter was originally part of Chapter 2, "The Basics," but I felt there was so much information here that it deserved its own chapter. This chapter could have been called "The Basics—Part 2." I'm telling you this because, armed with the knowledge contained within this chapter and Chapter 2, we have covered the basic building blocks of CoffeeScript. We can now start looking at the really fun stuff.

Notes

1. http://en.wikipedia.org/wiki/Operator_(programming)
2. http://en.wikipedia.org/wiki/Conditional_(programming)
3. http://www.yaml.org/spec/1.2/spec.html
4. http://en.wikipedia.org/wiki/Ternary_operation
5. http://en.wikipedia.org/wiki/Switch_statement

4

Functions and Arguments

In this chapter we are going to look at one of the most essential parts of any language, the function. Functions allow us to encapsulate reusable and discrete code blocks. Without functions our code would be one long, unreadable, and unmaintainable mess.

I wanted to give you an example of what JavaScript would look like if we were not able to use or write functions, but I was unable to. Even the simplest example of taking a string and making it lowercase requires the use of functions in JavaScript.

Because I can't show you an example devoid of functions, I'll show you an example of some CoffeeScript code that could use the help of a function or two, so you can see how important functions are to helping you keep your code manageable.

Example: **(source: no_functions_example.coffee)**

```
tax_rate = 0.0625

val = 100
console.log "What is the total of $#{val} worth of shopping?"
tax = val * tax_rate
total = val + tax
console.log "The total is #{total}"

val = 200
console.log "What is the total of $#{val} worth of shopping?"
tax = val * tax_rate
total = val + tax
console.log "The total is #{total}"
```

Example: **(source: no_functions_example.js)**

```
(function() {
  var tax, tax_rate, total, val;

  tax_rate = 0.0625;

  val = 100;

  console.log("What is the total of $" + val + " worth of shopping?");

  tax = val * tax_rate;

  total = val + tax;

  console.log("The total is " + total);

  val = 200;

  console.log("What is the total of $" + val + " worth of shopping?");

  tax = val * tax_rate;

  total = val + tax;

  console.log("The total is " + total);

}).call(this);
```

Output: **(source: no_functions_example.coffee)**

```
What is the total of $100 worth of shopping?
The total is 106.25
What is the total of $200 worth of shopping?
The total is 212.5
```

In our example, we are calculating the total value of goods purchased in-state with certain sales tax. Apart from the banality of the example, you can see that we are repeating our code to calculate the total value with tax several times.

Let's refactor our code a bit, add some functions, and try to clean it up.

Example: **(source: with_functions_example.coffee)**

```
default_tax_rate = 0.0625

calculateTotal = (sub_total, rate = default_tax_rate) ->
  tax = sub_total * rate
  sub_total + tax

val = 100
console.log "What is the total of $#{val} worth of shopping?"
console.log "The total is #{calculateTotal(val)}"

val = 200
console.log "What is the total of $#{val} worth of shopping?"
console.log "The total is #{calculateTotal(val)}"
```

Example: **(source: with_functions_example.js)**

```
(function() {
  var calculateTotal, default_tax_rate, val;

  default_tax_rate = 0.0625;

  calculateTotal = function(sub_total, rate) {
    var tax;
    if (rate == null) rate = default_tax_rate;
    tax = sub_total * rate;
    return sub_total + tax;
  };

  val = 100;

  console.log("What is the total of $" + val + " worth of shopping?");

  console.log("The total is " + (calculateTotal(val)));

  val = 200;

  console.log("What is the total of $" + val + " worth of shopping?");

  console.log("The total is " + (calculateTotal(val)));

}).call(this);
```

Output: **(source: with_functions_example.coffee)**

```
What is the total of $100 worth of shopping?
The total is 106.25
What is the total of $200 worth of shopping?
The total is 212.5
```

You probably don't understand everything we just did there, but don't worry, that's what this chapter is for. However, even without knowing the specifics of how functions are defined, and work, in CoffeeScript, you can see how much cleaner our code is between the two examples. In the refactored code, we are even able to pass in a different tax rate, should we need to. This also helps us keep our code DRY[1]: Don't Repeat Yourself. Not repeating your code makes for an easier-to-manage code base with, hopefully, fewer bugs.

Function Basics

We'll start with the very basics on how to define a function in CoffeeScript. The anatomy of a very simple function looks like this:

Example: **(source: simple_function.coffee)**

```
myFunction = ()->
  console.log "do some work here"

myFunction()
```

Example: **(source: simple_function.js)**

```
(function() {
  var myFunction;

  myFunction = function() {
    return console.log("do some work here");
  };

  myFunction();

}).call(this);
```

In that example we gave the function a name, `myFunction`, and a code block to go with it. The body of the function is the code that is indented below the ->, following the significant whitespace rules we learned about in Chapter 2, "The Basics."

The function does not accept any arguments. We know that by the empty parentheses prior to the ->. When calling a function in CoffeeScript that has no arguments, we are required to use parentheses, `myFunction()`.

Because our function has no arguments, we can drop the parentheses entirely when defining it, like so:

Example: **(source: simple_function_no_parens.coffee)**

```
myFunction = ->
  console.log "do some work here"

myFunction()
```

Example: **(source: simple_function_no_parens.js)**

```
(function() {
  var myFunction;

  myFunction = function() {
    return console.log("do some work here");
  };

  myFunction();

}).call(this);
```

There is one more way we can write this simple function. Because the body of our function is on only one line, we can collapse the whole function definition to one, like this:

Example: **(source: simple_function_one_line.coffee)**

```
myFunction = -> console.log "do some work here"

myFunction()
```

Example: **(source: simple_function_one_line.js)**

```
(function() {
  var myFunction;

  myFunction = function() {
    return console.log("do some work here");
  };

  myFunction();

}).call(this);
```

All three of the previous code examples produce the same JavaScript and are called in the same way.

> **Tip**
>
> Although you can write function definitions on one line, I prefer not to. Personally, I don't find it that much cleaner or easier to read. Also, by keeping the body of the function on a separate line, you make it easier to later augment your function with more code.
>
> You should also notice that the last line of each function contains a `return` keyword. CoffeeScript adds this automatically for you. Whatever the last line of your function is, that will be the function's return value. This is similar to languages such as Ruby. Because CoffeeScript will automatically add the `return` for you in the compiled JavaScript, the use of the `return` keyword in your CoffeeScript is optional.

> **Tip**
>
> I find that adding the `return` keyword can sometimes help make the meaning of your code a bit clearer. Use it where you find it will help make your code easier to read and understand.

> **Tip**
>
> If you want your functions to not return the last line of the function, you'll have to explicitly give it a new last line to return. Something like `return null` or `return undefined` will do the trick nicely.

Arguments

Just like in JavaScript, functions in CoffeeScript can also take arguments. Arguments let us pass objects into the function so that the function can then perform calculations, data manipulation, or whatever our little hearts desire.

In CoffeeScript, defining a function that takes arguments is not much different than in JavaScript. Inside our parentheses we define a comma-separated list of the names of the arguments we want the function to accept.

Example: **(source: function_with_args.coffee)**

```
calculateTotal = (sub_total, rate) ->
  tax = sub_total * rate
  sub_total + tax

console.log calculateTotal(100, 0.0625)
```

Example: **(source: function_with_args.js)**

```
(function() {
  var calculateTotal;

  calculateTotal = function(sub_total, rate) {
    var tax;
    tax = sub_total * rate;
    return sub_total + tax;
  };

  console.log(calculateTotal(100, 0.0625));

}).call(this);
```

Output: **(source: function_with_args.coffee)**

```
106.25
```

As you can see in our example, we defined our function to take in two arguments and to do some math with them to calculate a total value. When we called the function, we passed in the two values we wanted it to use.

In Chapter 2 we discussed briefly the rules around parentheses in CoffeeScript. I want to reiterate one of those rules. Because our function takes arguments, we are allowed to omit the parentheses when calling the function. This means we could also write our example like this:

Example: **(source: function_with_args_no_parens.coffee)**

```
calculateTotal = (sub_total, rate) ->
  tax = sub_total * rate
  sub_total + tax

console.log calculateTotal 100, 0.0625
```

Example: **(source: function_with_args_no_parens.js)**

```
(function() {
  var calculateTotal;

  calculateTotal = function(sub_total, rate) {
    var tax;
    tax = sub_total * rate;
    return sub_total + tax;
  };
```

```
  console.log(calculateTotal(100, 0.0625));

}).call(this);
```

Output: **(source: function_with_args_no_parens.coffee)**

```
106.25
```

As you can see, CoffeeScript correctly compiled the JavaScript for us, putting those parentheses back where they are needed.

> **Tip**
>
> The use of parentheses when calling functions is hotly contested in the CoffeeScript world. Personally, I tend to use them. I think it helps make my code a bit more readable, and it cuts down on potential bugs where parentheses were misplaced by the compiler. When in doubt, use parentheses. You won't regret it.

Default Arguments

In some languages, such as Ruby, it is possible to assign default values to arguments. This means that if you do not pass in some arguments, for whatever reason, then reasonable default values can be used in their place.

Let's revisit our calculator example again. We'll write it so that the tax rate is set to a default value should one not be passed in:

Example: **(source: default_args.coffee)**

```
calculateTotal = (sub_total, rate = 0.05) ->
  tax = sub_total * rate
  sub_total + tax

console.log calculateTotal 100, 0.0625
console.log calculateTotal 100
```

Example: **(source: default_args.js)**

```
(function() {
  var calculateTotal;

  calculateTotal = function(sub_total, rate) {
    var tax;
```

```
    if (rate == null) rate = 0.05;
    tax = sub_total * rate;
    return sub_total + tax;
  };

  console.log(calculateTotal(100, 0.0625));

  console.log(calculateTotal(100));

}).call(this);
```

Output: **(source: default_args.coffee)**

```
106.25
105
```

When defining our function, we told CoffeeScript to set the default value of the `tax_rate` argument equal to `0.05`. When we first call the `calculateTotal` function, we pass in a `tax_rate` argument of `0.0625`; the second time we omit the `tax_rate` argument altogether, and the code does the appropriate thing and uses `0.05` in its place.

We can take default arguments a step further and have them refer to other arguments. Consider this example:

Example: **(source: default_args_referring.coffee)**

```
href = (text, url = text) ->
  html = "<a href='#{url}'>#{text}</a>"
  return html

console.log href("Click Here", "http://www.example.com")
console.log href("http://www.example.com")
```

Example: **(source: default_args_referring.js)**

```
(function() {
  var href;

  href = function(text, url) {
    var html;
    if (url == null) url = text;
    html = "<a href='" + url + "'>" + text + "</a>";
    return html;
  };
```

```
  console.log(href("Click Here", "http://www.example.com"));

  console.log(href("http://www.example.com"));

}).call(this);
```

Output: **(source: default_args_referring.coffee)**

```
<a href='http://www.example.com'>Click Here</a>
<a href='http://www.example.com'>http://www.example.com</a>
```

Should no one pass in the `url` argument in our example, we will set it equal to the `text` argument that was passed in.

It is also possible to use functions as default values in the argument list. Because the default value will be called only if there is no argument passed in, there is no performance concern.

Example: **(source: default_args_with_function.coffee)**

```
defaultRate = -> 0.05

calculateTotal = (sub_total, rate = defaultRate()) ->
  tax = sub_total * rate
  sub_total + tax

console.log calculateTotal 100, 0.0625
console.log calculateTotal 100
```

Example: **(source: default_args_with_function.js)**

```
(function() {
  var calculateTotal, defaultRate;

  defaultRate = function() {
    return 0.05;
  };

  calculateTotal = function(sub_total, rate) {
    var tax;
    if (rate == null) rate = defaultRate();
    tax = sub_total * rate;
    return sub_total + tax;
  };
```

```
  console.log(calculateTotal(100, 0.0625));

  console.log(calculateTotal(100));

}).call(this);
```

Output: **(source: default_args_with_function.coffee)**

```
106.25
105
```

> **Tip**
>
> When using default arguments it is important to note that they must be at the *end* of the argument list. It is okay to have multiple arguments with defaults, but they all must be at the end.

Splats...

Sometimes when developing a function, we are not sure just how many arguments we are going to need. Sometimes we might get one argument; other times we might get a hundred. To help us easily solve this problem, CoffeeScript gives us the option of using splats when defining the argument list for a function. Splatted arguments are denoted by placing an ellipsis (`...`) after the method definition.

> **Tip**
>
> A great way to remember how to use splats is to treat the `...` suffix as if you were saying etc... Not only is that easy to remember, but if you use `etc...` in your code, you'll look cool.

When would you use splats? Splats can be used whenever your function will be taking in a variable number of arguments. Before we take a look at a detailed example, let's look quickly at a simple function that takes a splatted argument:

Example: **(source: splats.coffee)**

```
splatter = (etc...) ->
  console.log "Length: #{etc.length}, Values: #{etc.join(', ')}"

splatter()
splatter("a", "b", "c")
```

Example: **(source: splats.js)**

```
(function() {
  var splatter,
    __slice = Array.prototype.slice;

  splatter = function() {
    var etc;
    etc = 1 <= arguments.length ? __slice.call(arguments, 0) : [];
    return console.log("Length: " + etc.length + ", Values: " + (etc.join(', ')));
  };

  splatter();

  splatter("a", "b", "c");

}).call(this);
```

Output: **(source: splats.coffee)**

```
Length: 0, Values:
Length: 3, Values: a, b, c
```

As you can see, whatever arguments we pass into our function automatically get put into an array, and should we not send any arguments we get an empty array.

> **Tip**
>
> Splats are a great example of something that can be done in JavaScript but would require a lot of boilerplate code to implement. Look at the JavaScript output of a CoffeeScript splatted argument and you'll agree boilerplate code is no fun to write.

Unlike other languages that support a similar construct, CoffeeScript does not force you to only use splats as the last argument in the argument list. In fact, splatted arguments can appear anywhere in your argument list. A small caveat is that you can have only one splatted argument in the argument list.

To help illustrate how splats can be used in any part of the argument list, let's write a method that will take some arguments and spit out a string. When building this string, we make sure that the first and last arguments are uppercased; any other arguments will be lowercased. Then we'll concatenate the string using forward slashes.

Example: **(source: splats_arg_join.coffee)**

```
joinArgs = (first, middles..., last) ->
  parts = []

  if first?
    parts.push first.toUpperCase()

  for middle in middles
    parts.push middle.toLowerCase()

  if last?
    parts.push last.toUpperCase()

  parts.join('/')

console.log joinArgs("a")
console.log joinArgs("a", "b")
console.log joinArgs("a", "B", "C", "d")
```

Example: **(source: splats_arg_join.js)**

```
(function() {
  var joinArgs,
    __slice = Array.prototype.slice;

  joinArgs = function() {
    var first, last, middle, middles, parts, _i, _j, _len;
    first = arguments[0], middles = 3 <= arguments.length ? __slice.call(arguments, 1,
➥_i = arguments.length - 1) : (_i = 1, []), last = arguments[_i++];
    parts = [];
    if (first != null) parts.push(first.toUpperCase());
    for (_j = 0, _len = middles.length; _j < _len; _j++) {
      middle = middles[_j];
      parts.push(middle.toLowerCase());
    }
    if (last != null) parts.push(last.toUpperCase());
    return parts.join('/');
  };

  console.log(joinArgs("a"));

  console.log(joinArgs("a", "b"));

  console.log(joinArgs("a", "B", "C", "d"));

}).call(this);
```

Output: **(source: splats_arg_join.coffee)**

```
A
A/B
A/b/c/D
```

I admit that is a bit of a heavy example, but it illustrates how splats work. When we call the `joinArgs` function, the first argument we pass into the function call gets assigned to the `first` variable, the last argument we pass in gets assigned to the `last` variable, and if any other arguments are passed in between the first and the last arguments, those are put into an array and assigned to the `middles` variable.

> **Tip**
>
> We could have written our function to just take a splatted argument and extract the first and last elements from the `middles` array, but this function definition means we don't have to write all that code. Happy days.

Finally, when dealing with splats, you might have an array that you want passed in as individual arguments. That is possible.

Let's take a quick look at an example:

Example: **(source: splats_array.coffee)**

```
splatter = (etc...) ->
  console.log "Length: #{etc.length}, Values: #{etc.join(', ')}"

a = ["a", "b", "c"]
splatter(a)
splatter(a...)
```

Example: **(source: splats_array.js)**

```
(function() {
  var a, splatter,
    __slice = Array.prototype.slice;

  splatter = function() {
    var etc;
    etc = 1 <= arguments.length ? __slice.call(arguments, 0) : [];
    return console.log("Length: " + etc.length + ", Values: " + (etc.join(', ')));
  };

  a = ["a", "b", "c"];
```

```
  splatter(a);

  splatter.apply(null, a);

}).call(this);
```

Output: **(source: splats_array.coffee)**

```
Length: 1, Values: a,b,c
Length: 3, Values: a, b, c
```

Using our earlier `splatter` example, we can try first passing in an array, but as you can see, the `splatter` function sees the array as a single argument, because that is what it is. However, if we append `...` to the array as we pass it into our function call, the CoffeeScript will split up the array into separate arguments and pass them into the function.

Wrapping Up

There you have it—everything you've ever wanted to know about functions in CoffeeScript! First we looked at how to define a simple function; in fact, we saw several ways to define a function in CoffeeScript. We then took a look at how arguments to functions are defined and how to call a function, including a recap of when and where you do and do not have to use parentheses when calling a function. We also took a look at default arguments, one of my favorite features of CoffeeScript.

Finally, we explored splats and how they help us write functions that take variable arguments.

With our nickel tour of functions and arguments over with, we can move on to the next stop, Chapter 5, "Collections and Iterations." So go grab a cold one, and we'll meet there. Ready?

Notes

1. http://en.wikipedia.org/wiki/DRY

5

Collections and Iterations

Collections form an important part of almost any object-oriented programming language. They let us easily store multiple values either in a list, such as an array, or using a key/value pair, like objects in JavaScript. With objects we can represent an item, such as a book, and give it values such as a title, author, and publication date. Using an array we can then store a list of the book objects we create.

Along with collections come iterators. Iterators let us take our stored values, such as that list of books, and loop through them one at a time, allowing us to print each one to the screen, update some information on each book, or do whatever our application needs to do.

In the first half of this chapter we learn about arrays and objects in CoffeeScript. We'll see how they map to their JavaScript counterparts. Because this is CoffeeScript, we'll also look at some of the fun little hidden gems that are available to us with arrays and objects.

The second half of this chapter will focus on iterators. We'll take what we've learned about collections and learn how to loop through them and manipulate them.

Arrays

Without getting all geeky about how arrays are implemented in memory and such, let's agree that, for the premise of this book, arrays are simple data structures designed to store data in a sequential list. New items, unless otherwise stated, are added to the last slot in that list. In CoffeeScript, arrays don't look any different from JavaScript. Arrays in CoffeeScript use a zero index and are constructed in the same way as their JavaScript counterparts.

Example: **(source: array1.coffee)**

```
myArray = ["a", "b", "c"]

console.log myArray
```

Example: **(source: array1.js)**

```
(function() {
  var myArray;

  myArray = ["a", "b", "c"];

  console.log(myArray);

}).call(this);
```

Output: **(source: array1.coffee)**

```
[ 'a', 'b', 'c' ]
```

With the exception of a missing semicolon and `var` keyword, the CoffeeScript and JavaScript array implementations are almost identical. Just because they look identical, though, it doesn't mean that CoffeeScript doesn't have a few tricks up its sleeve when it comes to arrays.

In CoffeeScript we can declare the same array without the need for commas between each element in the array simply by placing each item on its own line:

Example: **(source: array2.coffee)**

```
myArray = [
            "a"
            "b"
            "c"
          ]

console.log myArray
```

Example: **(source: array2.js)**

```
(function() {
  var myArray;

  myArray = ["a", "b", "c"];
```

```
  console.log(myArray);

}).call(this);
```

Output: **(source: array2.coffee)**

```
[ 'a', 'b', 'c' ]
```

In this case, that is definitely a longer way to write the same array, but occasionally you'll find that splitting up your array definition to multiple lines can make your code easier to read. A combination of commas and new lines can also be used to make code more readable:

Example: **(source: array3.coffee)**

```
myArray = [
            "a", "b", "c"
            "d", "e", "f"
            "g", "h", "i"
          ]

console.log myArray
```

Example: **(source: array3.js)**

```
(function() {
  var myArray;

  myArray = ["a", "b", "c", "d", "e", "f", "g", "h", "i"];

  console.log(myArray);

}).call(this);
```

Output: **(source: array3.coffee)**

```
[ 'a', 'b', 'c', 'd', 'e', 'f', 'g', 'h', 'i' ]
```

Testing Inclusion

CoffeeScript arrays have the same functions available to them as JavaScript arrays do. There are a few things that are a bit difficult to do with JavaScript arrays that CoffeeScript tries to help you out with. We talk about a few of those things later in this chapter when we talk about ranges. Right now, however, I would like to talk about one area of working with arrays that CoffeeScript makes a whole lot easier—determining whether an array contains a particular value.

Example: **(source: in_array.coffee)**

```
myArray = ["a", "b", "c"]

if "b" in myArray
  console.log "I found 'b'."

unless "d" in myArray
  console.log "'d' was nowhere to be found."
```

Example: **(source: in_array.js)**

```
(function() {
  var myArray,
    __indexOf = Array.prototype.indexOf || function(item) { for (var i = 0, l =
➥this.length; i < l; i++) { if (i in this && this[i] === item) return i; }
➥return -1; };

  myArray = ["a", "b", "c"];

  if (__indexOf.call(myArray, "b") >= 0) console.log("I found 'b'.");

  if (__indexOf.call(myArray, "d") < 0) {
    console.log("'d' was nowhere to be found.");
  }

}).call(this);
```

Output: **(source: in_array.coffee)**

```
I found 'b'.
'd' was nowhere to be found.
```

As you can see, we can test an array to see if it contains a particular value using the `in` keyword. In the compiled JavaScript, a function is being created that will loop through the array and try to find the index of the value we're looking for. If it finds that value, it will return its index. Then the code checks to see if that returned index is greater than zero.

Swapping Assignment

At some point in your coding career, you will have two or more variables that need their values swapped. This can be more cumbersome in some languages than in others, but fortunately, CoffeeScript is not cumbersome.

Let's take a look at how this works by swapping the value of two variables:

Example: **(source: swap_assignment.coffee)**

```
x = "X"
y = "Y"

console.log "x is #{x}"
console.log "y is #{y}"

[x, y] = [y, x]

console.log "x is #{x}"
console.log "y is #{y}"
```

Example: **(source: swap_assignment.js)**

```
(function() {
  var x, y, _ref;

  x = "X";

  y = "Y";

  console.log("x is " + x);

  console.log("y is " + y);

  _ref = [y, x], x = _ref[0], y = _ref[1];

  console.log("x is " + x);

  console.log("y is " + y);

}).call(this);
```

Output: **(source: swap_assignment.coffee)**

```
x is X
y is Y
x is Y
y is X
```

In CoffeeScript we use the array syntax to create two arrays and assign those arrays to each other. In the first array, to the left of the =, we list the variables to which we would like to assign new values. In the second array, to the right of the =, we place the new values we would like our variables to have. CoffeeScript does the rest.

As we can see, when we print the values of our variables before and after the switch they have indeed switched values.

Multiple Assignment aka Destructing Assignment

Sometimes we will have a function that returns an array of values, and we want to quickly assign each element of that array to a variable for easier access later. Here is an example from the Ruby world. In Ruby there is a very popular library called Rack[1]. Rack's function is to provide a simple interface between web servers and application frameworks. The specification is pretty simple. Your framework must return an array. The first element of the array is an HTTP status code. The second element is a hash of HTTP headers. The third, and final, element is the body of the response. Now, that is a bit of an oversimplification of how Rack works, but it's good enough for our needs.

Now let's try to write a function that returns an array that meets the Rack specification. Then we'll assign the elements of that array to some useful variables.

Example: **(source: multiple_assignment.coffee)**

```
rack = ->
  [200, {"Content-Type": "text/html"}, "Hello Rack!"]

console.log rack()

[status, headers, body] = rack()

console.log "status is #{status}"
console.log "headers is #{JSON.stringify(headers)}"
console.log "body is #{body}"
```

Example: **(source: multiple_assignment.js)**

```
(function() {
  var body, headers, rack, status, _ref;
```

```
  rack = function() {
    return [
      200, {
        "Content-Type": "text/html"
      }, "Hello Rack!"
    ];
  };

  console.log(rack());

  _ref = rack(), status = _ref[0], headers = _ref[1], body = _ref[2];

  console.log("status is " + status);

  console.log("headers is " + (JSON.stringify(headers)));

  console.log("body is " + body);

}).call(this);
```

Output: **(source: multiple_assignment.coffee)**

```
[ 200, { 'Content-Type': 'text/html' }, 'Hello Rack!' ]
status is 200
headers is {"Content-Type":"text/html"}
body is Hello Rack!
```

Here we're using the same pattern as we did when we talked about swapping assignment. We have an array to the left of = containing the names of the variables that we want to assign values to. On the right side of the = we call the function that then returns an array of values we can use to assign to our variables.

Tip

Notice that with both swapping assignment and multiple assignment, we didn't need to first declare the names of the variables we wanted to use. CoffeeScript took care of that for us.

We can even use splats from Chapter 4, "Functions and Arguments," to capture multiple values:

Example: **(source: splat_assignment.coffee)**

```
myArray = ["A", "B", "C", "D"]

[start, middle..., end] = myArray

console.log "start is #{start}"
console.log "middle is #{middle}"
console.log "end is #{end}"
```

Example: **(source: splat_assignment.js)**

```
(function() {
  var end, middle, myArray, start, _i,
    __slice = Array.prototype.slice;

  myArray = ["A", "B", "C", "D"];

  start = myArray[0], middle = 3 <= myArray.length ? __slice.call(myArray, 1, _i =
➥myArray.length - 1) : (_i = 1, []), end = myArray[_i++];

  console.log("start is " + start);

  console.log("middle is " + middle);

  console.log("end is " + end);

}).call(this);
```

Output: **(source: splat_assignment.coffee)**

```
start is A
middle is B,C
end is D
```

So what happens if you want to assign values to more variables than there are values? Well, let's take a look:

Example: **(source: too_much_assignment.coffee)**

```
myArray = ["A", "B"]

[a, b, c] = myArray

console.log "a is #{a}"
console.log "b is #{b}"
console.log "c is #{c}"
```

Example: **(source: too_much_assignment.js)**

```
(function() {
  var a, b, c, myArray;

  myArray = ["A", "B"];

  a = myArray[0], b = myArray[1], c = myArray[2];

  console.log("a is " + a);

  console.log("b is " + b);

  console.log("c is " + c);

}).call(this);
```

Output: **(source: too_much_assignment.coffee)**

```
a is A
b is B
c is undefined
```

As you can see, our last variable was given the value of `undefined` because there was no value in the array to assign to it.

If we don't define enough variables for the amount of values in the array, such as in the following example, we simply don't assign the remaining values.

Example: **(source: too_little_assignment.coffee)**

```
myArray = ["A", "B", "C"]

[a, b] = myArray

console.log "a is #{a}"
console.log "b is #{b}"
```

Example: **(source: too_little_assignment.js)**

```
(function() {
  var a, b, myArray;

  myArray = ["A", "B", "C"];
```

```
  a = myArray[0], b = myArray[1];

  console.log("a is " + a);

  console.log("b is " + b);

}).call(this);
```

Output: **(source: too_little_assignment.coffee)**

```
a is A
b is B
```

Ranges

Ranges in CoffeeScript enable us to easily populate an array with numbers ranging from a start number to an end number. The syntax for building a range looks like so:

Example: **(source: range1.coffee)**

```
myRange = [1..10]
console.log myRange
```

Example: **(source: range1.js)**

```
(function() {
  var myRange;

  myRange = [1, 2, 3, 4, 5, 6, 7, 8, 9, 10];

  console.log(myRange);

}).call(this);
```

Output: **(source: range1.coffee)**

```
[ 1, 2, 3, 4, 5, 6, 7, 8, 9, 10 ]
```

By separating the start number and the end number with `..` we will get an array filled with numbers, starting with the first number and going up to and including the end number. If we want to exclude the end number, we would use `...` instead of `..`:

Example: **(source: range2.coffee)**

```
myRange = [1...10]
console.log myRange
```

Example: **(source: range2.js)**

```
(function() {
  var myRange;

  myRange = [1, 2, 3, 4, 5, 6, 7, 8, 9];

  console.log(myRange);

}).call(this);
```

Output: **(source: range2.coffee)**

```
[ 1, 2, 3, 4, 5, 6, 7, 8, 9 ]
```

As you can see, by using `...` instead of `..` we no longer have the number `10` in our array.

Using ranges, we can also build arrays of numbers in the reverse order:

Example: **(source: range3.coffee)**

```
myRange = [10..1]
console.log myRange
```

Example: **(source: range3.js)**

```
(function() {
  var myRange;

  myRange = [10, 9, 8, 7, 6, 5, 4, 3, 2, 1];

  console.log(myRange);

}).call(this);
```

Output: **(source: range3.coffee)**

```
[ 10, 9, 8, 7, 6, 5, 4, 3, 2, 1 ]
```

The same rules regarding `..` versus `...` apply when building reverse ranges.

As you can see, CoffeeScript has been creating JavaScript that builds out the full array by filling it with all the numbers we requested. The problem with this, although it is nice and simple, is that what if we want a hundred numbers in the array, or a thousand? Is CoffeeScript going to build a huge piece of JavaScript that is simply a list of a thousand numbers in between two brackets? Of course not. If CoffeeScript sees that array is going to go over a certain number of elements, it will switch to using a loop to build the elements of the range:

Example: **(source: range4.coffee)**

```
myRange = [1..50]
console.log myRange.join(", ")
```

Example: **(source: range4.js)**

```
(function() {
  var myRange, _i, _results;

  myRange = (function() {
    _results = [];
    for (_i = 1; _i <= 50; _i++){ _results.push(_i); }
    return _results;
  }).apply(this);

  console.log(myRange.join(", "));

}).call(this);
```

Output: **(source: range4.coffee)**

```
1, 2, 3, 4, 5, 6, 7, 8, 9, 10, 11, 12, 13, 14, 15, 16, 17, 18, 19, 20, 21, 22,
23, 24, 25, 26, 27, 28, 29, 30, 31, 32, 33, 34, 35, 36, 37, 38, 39, 40, 41, 42,
43, 44, 45, 46, 47, 48, 49, 50
```

> **Tip**
>
> For those of you wondering what number of elements in a range CoffeeScript thinks is too big to hard populate, that number is 22. I don't know why that number is 22, but it is. If you don't believe me, try it for yourself. I did.

Slicing Arrays

Using the power of ranges, we can easily slice up arrays in a number of ways.

Example: **(source: slice_array1.coffee)**

```
myArray = [1..10]

firstThree = myArray[0..2]
console.log firstThree
```

Example: **(source: slice_array1.js)**

```
(function() {
  var firstThree, myArray;

  myArray = [1, 2, 3, 4, 5, 6, 7, 8, 9, 10];

  firstThree = myArray.slice(0, 3);

  console.log(firstThree);

}).call(this);
```

Output: **(source: slice_array1.coffee)**

```
[ 1, 2, 3 ]
```

We could also write the same example using `0...3`, instead of `0..2`:

Example: **(source: slice_array2.coffee)**

```
myArray = [1..10]

firstThree = myArray[0...3]
console.log firstThree
```

Example: **(source: slice_array2.js)**

```
(function() {
  var firstThree, myArray;

  myArray = [1, 2, 3, 4, 5, 6, 7, 8, 9, 10];

  firstThree = myArray.slice(0, 3);

  console.log(firstThree);

}).call(this);
```

Output: **(source: slice_array2.coffee)**

```
[ 1, 2, 3 ]
```

We don't have to limit ourselves to getting only the first part of an array; we can get any part of the array that we like:

Example: **(source: slice_array3.coffee)**

```
myArray = [1..10]

middle = myArray[4..7]
console.log middle
```

Example: **(source: slice_array3.js)**

```
(function() {
  var middle, myArray;

  myArray = [1, 2, 3, 4, 5, 6, 7, 8, 9, 10];

  middle = myArray.slice(4, 8);

  console.log(middle);

}).call(this);
```

Output: **(source: slice_array3.coffee)**

```
[ 5, 6, 7, 8 ]
```

As you can see, we were able to grab the middle values from our array. Pretty cool stuff.

Replacing Array Values

We haven't quite finished yet with the power of ranges and its syntax. We can use the range syntax to replace the values of a section of an array.

Example: **(source: replace_array.coffee)**

```
myArray = [1..10]
console.log myArray

myArray[4..7] = ['a', 'b', 'c', 'd']
console.log myArray
```

Example: **(source: replace_array.js)**

```
(function() {
  var myArray, _ref;

  myArray = [1, 2, 3, 4, 5, 6, 7, 8, 9, 10];

  console.log(myArray);

  [].splice.apply(myArray, [4, 4].concat(_ref = ['a', 'b', 'c', 'd'])), _ref;

  console.log(myArray);

}).call(this);
```

Output: **(source: replace_array.coffee)**

```
[ 1, 2, 3, 4, 5, 6, 7, 8, 9, 10 ]
[ 1, 2, 3, 4, 'a', 'b', 'c', 'd', 9, 10 ]
```

I bet you didn't see that coming! That is definitely powerful.

Injecting Values

At times, you may want to inject the values of one array into the middle of another array at a particular position. To do this we employ a technique similar to what we did when we wanted to replace a range of values. The only difference is that instead of defining an end point in the range, we use `-1`.

Example: **(source: injecting_values.coffee)**

```
myArray = [1..10]
console.log myArray

myArray[4..-1] = ['a', 'b', 'c', 'd']
console.log myArray
```

Example: **(source: injecting_values.js)**

```
(function() {
  var myArray, _ref;

  myArray = [1, 2, 3, 4, 5, 6, 7, 8, 9, 10];

  console.log(myArray);
```

```
  [].splice.apply(myArray, [4, -1 - 4 + 1].concat(_ref = ['a', 'b', 'c', 'd'])), _ref;

  console.log(myArray);

}).call(this);
```

Output: **(source: injecting_values.coffee)**

```
[ 1, 2, 3, 4, 5, 6, 7, 8, 9, 10 ]
[ 1, 2, 3, 4, 'a', 'b', 'c', 'd', 5, 6, 7, 8, 9, 10 ]
```

As you can see, at the fifth slot of the first array, we injected the values from the second array. The original values of the first array were shifted further down the array to make room for the newly injected values.

Objects/Hashes

In JavaScript, objects are pretty simple. They are basically a holder of key/value pair information. The values of these objects can be other objects, functions, numbers, strings, and so on.

> **Tip**
>
> What JavaScript and CoffeeScript call objects are typically given names such as hash tables, hash maps, or, simply, hashes. Their title of 'object,' I think, is a bit of a misnomer because there are other types of objects in JavaScript. I tend to think of them purely as a key/value pair collection.

To create the most basic object possible in CoffeeScript, it would look like this:

Example: **(source: basic_object.coffee)**

```
obj = {}

console.log obj
```

Example: **(source: basic_object.js)**

```
(function() {
  var obj;

  obj = {};

  console.log(obj);

}).call(this);
```

Output: **(source: basic_object.coffee)**

```
{}
```

Admittedly, that is not very exciting. We can spice that object up a bit by adding a few key/value pairs to it:

Example: **(source: basic_object2.coffee)**

```
obj =
  firstName: "Mark"
  lastName: "Bates"

console.log obj
```

Example: **(source: basic_object2.js)**

```
(function() {
  var obj;

  obj = {
    firstName: "Mark",
    lastName: "Bates"
  };

  console.log(obj);

}).call(this);
```

Output: **(source: basic_object2.coffee)**

```
{ firstName: 'Mark', lastName: 'Bates' }
```

Notice that because we are listing our key/value pairs over several lines, we do not need to use commas to separate the key/value pairs. We were also able to drop the curly braces around the key/value pairs because we defined our object using the multiline syntax. We could also have written that same object on a single line, like this:

Example: **(source: basic_object2_single.coffee)**

```
obj = { firstName: "Mark", lastName: "Bates" }

console.log obj
```

Example: **(source: basic_object2_single.js)**

```
(function() {
  var obj;

  obj = {
    firstName: "Mark",
    lastName: "Bates"
  };

  console.log(obj);

}).call(this);
```

Output: **(source: basic_object2_single.coffee)**

```
{ firstName: 'Mark', lastName: 'Bates' }
```

Although that does save lines of code, we are forced to now use both curly braces and commas, and we do lose some readability along the way.

If we want to add a function to our object, we can do that very easily:

Example: **(source: basic_object3.coffee)**

```
obj =
  firstName: "Mark"
  lastName: "Bates"
  fullName: ->
    "#{@firstName} #{@lastName}"

console.log obj
```

Example: **(source: basic_object3.js)**

```
(function() {
  var obj;

  obj = {
    firstName: "Mark",
    lastName: "Bates",
    fullName: function() {
      return "" + this.firstName + " " + this.lastName;
    }
  };

  console.log(obj);

}).call(this);
```

Output: **(source: basic_object3.coffee)**

```
{ firstName: 'Mark', lastName: 'Bates', fullName: [Function] }
```

There is one more trick up CoffeeScript's sleeve when it comes to creating new objects. Occasionally we will have a few variables and we want to build an object using those variables, and we want the keys for those variables to have the same name as those variables, like this:

Example: **(source: object_keys1.coffee)**

```
foo = 'FOO'
bar = 'BAR'

obj =
  foo: foo
  bar: bar

console.log obj
```

Example: **(source: object_keys1.js)**

```
(function() {
  var bar, foo, obj;

  foo = 'FOO';

  bar = 'BAR';

  obj = {
    foo: foo,
    bar: bar
  };

  console.log(obj);

}).call(this);
```

Output: **(source: object_keys1.coffee)**

```
{ foo: 'FOO', bar: 'BAR' }
```

Doesn't that seem a bit redundant to you? Yeah, to me, too, and fortunately, CoffeeScript agrees. We can instead write the same object definition like this:

Example: **(source: object_keys2.coffee)**

```
foo = 'FOO'
bar = 'BAR'

obj = {
  foo
  bar
}

console.log obj
```

Example: **(source: object_keys2.js)**

```
(function() {
  var bar, foo, obj;

  foo = 'FOO';

  bar = 'BAR';

  obj = {
    foo: foo,
    bar: bar
  };

  console.log(obj);

}).call(this);
```

Output: **(source: object_keys2.coffee)**

```
{ foo: 'FOO', bar: 'BAR' }
```

The trade-off with that way to build objects is that you have to use curly braces; otherwise, CoffeeScript gets a bit confused as to what you are trying to do.

Finally, if we are defining an object as part of a call to a function, curly braces are optional, whether using multiline or single definitions:

Example: **(source: objects_into_functions.coffee)**

```
myFunc = (options) ->
  console.log options

myFunc(foo: 'Foo', bar: 'Bar')
```

Example: **(source: objects_into_functions.js)**

```
(function() {
  var myFunc;

  myFunc = function(options) {
    return console.log(options);
  };

  myFunc({
    foo: 'Foo',
    bar: 'Bar'
  });

}).call(this);
```

Output: **(source: objects_into_functions.coffee)**

```
{ foo: 'Foo', bar: 'Bar' }
```

And that, ladies and gentlemen, is all the different ways we can build objects in CoffeeScript.

Getting/Setting Attributes

When working with objects you will most likely, at some point in your code, want to be able to get access to some of the values that you stored in that object. Accessing those values in CoffeeScript is no different than in JavaScript. We can access the attribute using dot notation, or through the use of `[]`s.

Example: **(source: object_get_attributes.coffee)**

```
obj =
  firstName: "Mark"
  lastName: "Bates"
  fullName: ->
    "#{@firstName} #{@lastName}"

console.log obj.firstName
console.log obj['lastName']
console.log obj.fullName()
```

Example: **(source: object_get_attributes.js)**

```
(function() {
  var obj;

  obj = {
    firstName: "Mark",
    lastName: "Bates",
    fullName: function() {
      return "" + this.firstName + " " + this.lastName;
    }
  };

  console.log(obj.firstName);

  console.log(obj['lastName']);

  console.log(obj.fullName());

}).call(this);
```

Output: **(source: object_get_attributes.coffee)**

```
Mark
Bates
Mark Bates
```

The same goes for setting attributes:

Example: **(source: object_set_attributes.coffee)**

```
obj =
  firstName: "Mark"
  lastName: "Bates"
  fullName: ->
    "#{@firstName} #{@lastName}"

obj.firstName = 'MARK'
console.log obj.firstName
obj['lastName'] = 'BATES'
console.log obj['lastName']
```

Example: **(source: object_set_attributes.js)**

```
(function() {
  var obj;

  obj = {
    firstName: "Mark",
    lastName: "Bates",
    fullName: function() {
      return "" + this.firstName + " " + this.lastName;
    }
  };

  obj.firstName = 'MARK';

  console.log(obj.firstName);

  obj['lastName'] = 'BATES';

  console.log(obj['lastName']);

}).call(this);
```

Output: **(source: object_set_attributes.coffee)**

```
MARK
BATES
```

> **Tip**
>
> The popular JavaScript validation framework, JSLint[2], always recommends using dot notation for accessing attributes in an object. I tend to agree with them. I find the dot notation a bit nicer to read, and it's certainly less code to write, which is always good.

Destructuring Assignment

Earlier, when we talked about arrays, we talked about pulling certain elements out of the array and assigning them to variables. CoffeeScript lets us do the same thing with objects.

The syntax for extracting values from objects is not nearly as straightforward as it is for arrays. The syntax looks almost like the syntax for defining an object, except that instead of key/value pairs, you list the keys.

An example would probably clear that up a bit:

Example: **(source: object_destructuring.coffee)**

```
book =
  title: "Distributed Programming with Ruby"
  author: "Mark Bates"
  chapter_1:
    name: "Distributed Ruby (DRb)"
    pageCount: 33
  chapter_2:
    name: "Rinda"
    pageCount: 40

{author, chapter_1: {name, pageCount}} = book

console.log "Author: #{author}"
console.log "Chapter 1: #{name}"
console.log "Page Count: #{pageCount}"
```

Example: **(source: object_destructuring.js)**

```
(function() {
  var author, book, name, pageCount, _ref;

  book = {
    title: "Distributed Programming with Ruby",
    author: "Mark Bates",
    chapter_1: {
      name: "Distributed Ruby (DRb)",
      pageCount: 33
    },
    chapter_2: {
      name: "Rinda",
      pageCount: 40
    }
  };

  author = book.author, (_ref = book.chapter_1, name = _ref.name, pageCount =
➥_ref.pageCount);

  console.log("Author: " + author);

  console.log("Chapter 1: " + name);

  console.log("Page Count: " + pageCount);

}).call(this);
```

Output: **(source: object_destructuring.coffee)**

```
Author: Mark Bates
Chapter 1: Distributed Ruby (DRb)
Page Count: 33
```

Loops and Iteration

Being able to iterate over object keys and values and arrays in most applications is a must. Perhaps we have a list of books we want to print out to the screen, or maybe we want to mutate all the values in an object. Whatever it is, being able to iterate over these collections in CoffeeScript is incredibly easy. Let's see how it's done.

Iterating Arrays

One of my least favorite things to do in JavaScript is iterate over an array. It's messy and error prone. CoffeeScript has implemented a simple loop structure similar to that of the `for` loop in languages like Ruby.

Our `for` loop structure is very simple:

```
for <some name here> in <array here>
```

After we define our `for` loop, we use indentation to define the code we want to execute on each iteration, just like we did with `if` and `else` statements in Chapter 3, "Control Structures."

Let's loop over an array of letters and print out their uppercased values:

Example: **(source: iterating_arrays.coffee)**

```
myLetters = ["a", "b", "c", "d"]

for letter in myLetters
  console.log letter.toUpperCase()
```

Example: **(source: iterating_arrays.js)**

```
(function() {
  var letter, myLetters, _i, _len;

  myLetters = ["a", "b", "c", "d"];

  for (_i = 0, _len = myLetters.length; _i < _len; _i++) {
    letter = myLetters[_i];
    console.log(letter.toUpperCase());
  }

}).call(this);
```

Output: **(source: iterating_arrays.coffee)**

```
A
B
C
D
```

The `by` Keyword

Perhaps we have an array containing the letters of the alphabet, and we want to print out every other letter from the list. To do that we can use the `by` keyword when defining our `for` loop:

Example: **(source: iterating_arrays_by.coffee)**

```
letters = ["a", "b", "c", "d", "e", "f", "g", "h", "i", "j", "k", "l", "m", "n", "o",
➥"p", "q", "r", "s", "t", "u", "v", "w", "x", "y", "z"]
for letter in letters by 2
  console.log letter
```

Example: **(source: iterating_arrays_by.js)**

```
(function() {
  var letter, letters, _i, _len, _step;

  letters = ["a", "b", "c", "d", "e", "f", "g", "h", "i", "j", "k", "l", "m", "n",
➥"o", "p", "q", "r", "s", "t", "u", "v", "w", "x", "y", "z"];

  for (_i = 0, _len = letters.length, _step = 2; _i < _len; _i += _step) {
    letter = letters[_i];
    console.log(letter);
  }

}).call(this);
```

Output: **(source: iterating_arrays_by.coffee)**

```
a
c
e
g
i
k
m
o
q
```

```
s
u
w
y
```

We can use any number after the by keyword, and our for loop will step through the array accordingly.

The when Keyword

Using the when keyword, we can attach a simple condition to our for loop.

Suppose we have an array that has 10 numbers, but we want to print out only the numbers that are less than 5. We can write it like this:

Example: **(source: iterating_with_when1.coffee)**

```
a = [1..10]

for num in a
  if num < 5
    console.log num
```

Example: **(source: iterating_with_when1.js)**

```
(function() {
  var a, num, _i, _len;

  a = [1, 2, 3, 4, 5, 6, 7, 8, 9, 10];

  for (_i = 0, _len = a.length; _i < _len; _i++) {
    num = a[_i];
    if (num < 5) console.log(num);
  }

}).call(this);
```

Output: **(source: iterating_with_when1.coffee)**

```
1
2
3
4
```

We could also write the same example using the when keyword at the end of our for loop definition:

Example: **(source: iterating_with_when2.coffee)**

```
a = [1..10]

for num in a when num < 5
  console.log num
```

Example: **(source: iterating_with_when2.js)**

```
(function() {
  var a, num, _i, _len;

  a = [1, 2, 3, 4, 5, 6, 7, 8, 9, 10];

  for (_i = 0, _len = a.length; _i < _len; _i++) {
    num = a[_i];
    if (num < 5) console.log(num);
  }

}).call(this);
```

Output: **(source: iterating_with_when2.coffee)**

```
1
2
3
4
```

Iterating Objects

Iterating over objects in CoffeeScript is almost as straightforward as iterating over arrays.

The for loop syntax for iterating over objects looks like this:

```
for <key name here>, <value name here> of <object here>
```

Let's look at an example:

Example: **(source: iterating_objects.coffee)**

```
person =
  firstName: "Mark"
  lastName: "Bates"

for key, value of person
  console.log "#{key} is #{value}"
```

Example: **(source: iterating_objects.js)**

```
(function() {
  var key, person, value;

  person = {
    firstName: "Mark",
    lastName: "Bates"
  };

  for (key in person) {
    value = person[key];
    console.log("" + key + " is " + value);
  }

}).call(this);
```

Output: **(source: iterating_objects.coffee)**

```
firstName is Mark
lastName is Bates
```

There are two big differences between the `for` loop syntax with objects and arrays: First, we need to define the names of two variables in the `for` loop for an object, one for the key and the other for the value of the key/value pairs in the object. The other difference is instead of using the keyword `in`, like we do for arrays, we use the keyword `of`.

The `by` Keyword

Unfortunately, the `by` keyword is not useable when looping through the key/value pairs of objects, because there is no way to step over the key/value pairs in the object like you can with elements of an array.

The `when` Keyword

Unlike the `by` keyword, we can use the `when` keyword when defining `for` loops for objects.

Here we want to print out key/value pairs only where the length of the value is less than five:

Example: **(source: iterating_objects_with_when.coffee)**

```
person =
  firstName: "Mark"
  lastName: "Bates"
```

```
for key, value of person when value.length < 5
  console.log "#{key} is #{value}"
```

Example: **(source: iterating_objects_with_when.js)**

```
(function() {
  var key, person, value;

  person = {
    firstName: "Mark",
    lastName: "Bates"
  };

  for (key in person) {
    value = person[key];
    if (value.length < 5) console.log("" + key + " is " + value);
  }

}).call(this);
```

Output: **(source: iterating_objects_with_when.coffee)**

```
firstName is Mark
```

The `own` Keyword

In JavaScript it is possible to add functions or values on to all objects of the system using the `prototype`[3] function. This is how libraries such as jQuery are able to add special functions onto arrays, strings, and so on.

Following is an example of this in action:

Example: **(source: iterating_objects_without_own.coffee)**

```
myObject =
  name: "Mark"

for key, value of myObject
  console.log "#{key}: #{value}"

Object.prototype.dob = new Date(1976, 7, 24)

for key, value of myObject
  console.log "#{key}: #{value}"
```

```
anotherObject =
  name: "Bob"

for key, value of anotherObject
  console.log "#{key}: #{value}"
```

Example: **(source: iterating_objects_without_own.js)**

```
(function() {
  var anotherObject, key, myObject, value;

  myObject = {
    name: "Mark"
  };

  for (key in myObject) {
    value = myObject[key];
    console.log("" + key + ": " + value);
  }

  Object.prototype.dob = new Date(1976, 7, 24);

  for (key in myObject) {
    value = myObject[key];
    console.log("" + key + ": " + value);
  }

  anotherObject = {
    name: "Bob"
  };

  for (key in anotherObject) {
    value = anotherObject[key];
    console.log("" + key + ": " + value);
  }

}).call(this);
```

Output: **(source: iterating_objects_without_own.coffee)**

```
name: Mark
name: Mark
dob: Tue Aug 24 1976 00:00:00 GMT-0400 (EDT)
name: Bob
dob: Tue Aug 24 1976 00:00:00 GMT-0400 (EDT)
```

When we first loop through the key/value pairs of `myObject`, we see only the `name` value that we defined. However, after we add `dob` to the `prototype` of `Object` we now see `dob` print out when we loop through the key/value pairs of `myObject`.

So what do we do if we want to see only the key/value pairs that explicitly belong to our object? In JavaScript we would use the `hasOwnProperty` function to test to see if the key was defined by that object or the global `Object` prototype. In CoffeeScript, however, we can change our `for` loop to be a `for own` loop:

Example: **(source: iterating_objects_with_own.coffee)**

```
myObject =
  name: "Mark"

for own key, value of myObject
  console.log "#{key}: #{value}"

Object.prototype.dob = new Date(1976, 7, 24)

for own key, value of myObject
  console.log "#{key}: #{value}"

anotherObject =
  name: "Bob"

for own key, value of anotherObject
  console.log "#{key}: #{value}"
```

Example: **(source: iterating_objects_with_own.js)**

```
(function() {
  var anotherObject, key, myObject, value,
    __hasProp = Object.prototype.hasOwnProperty;

  myObject = {
    name: "Mark"
  };

  for (key in myObject) {
    if (!__hasProp.call(myObject, key)) continue;
    value = myObject[key];
    console.log("" + key + ": " + value);
  }

  Object.prototype.dob = new Date(1976, 7, 24);
```

```
  for (key in myObject) {
    if (!__hasProp.call(myObject, key)) continue;
    value = myObject[key];
    console.log("" + key + ": " + value);
  }

  anotherObject = {
    name: "Bob"
  };

  for (key in anotherObject) {
    if (!__hasProp.call(anotherObject, key)) continue;
    value = anotherObject[key];
    console.log("" + key + ": " + value);
  }

}).call(this);
```

Output: **(source: iterating_objects_with_own.coffee)**

```
name: Mark
name: Mark
name: Bob
```

Perfect! Now we are only getting the key/value pairs that are defined for `myObject`.

`while` Loops

Occasionally we have the need as developers to have a section of code repeat while a particular condition is true. Maybe we want to print something out `n` number of times, or maybe we want to display some "Please wait" text while we load a file. Whatever it is you are trying to do, you can do it using a `while` loop in CoffeeScript.

Let's write a function that will execute a block of code `n` times:

Example: **(source: while_loop.coffee)**

```
times = (number_of_times, callback)->
  index = 0
  while index++ < number_of_times
    callback(index)
  return null

times 5, (index)->
  console.log index
```

Example: **(source: while_loop.js)**

```
(function() {
  var times;

  times = function(number_of_times, callback) {
    var index;
    index = 0;
    while (index++ < number_of_times) {
      callback(index);
    }
    return null;
  };

  times(5, function(index) {
    return console.log(index);
  });

}).call(this);
```

Output: **(source: while_loop.coffee)**

```
1
2
3
4
5
```

In our `times` function, we have a `while` loop that will keep executing our callback function as long as the `index` is less than the `number_of_times` argument.

> **Tip**
>
> In the `while` loop example, we see the code `index++`. For those of you who might be unfamiliar with what the ++ operator does, it increments the variable by 1 and returns the newly incremented number. It is the equivalent of `index = index + 1`.

`until` Loops

As you might expect by its name, an `until` loop is the opposite of a `while` loop. A `while` loop will keep executing its code block as long as the condition is true. An `until` loop will keep executing its code block as long as the condition is false.

We can rewrite our `while` loop example like this, using an `until` loop:

Example: **(source: until_loop.coffee)**

```
times = (number_of_times, callback)->
  index = 0
  until index++ >= number_of_times
    callback(index)
  return null

times 5, (index)->
  console.log index
```

Example: **(source: until_loop.js)**

```
(function() {
  var times;

  times = function(number_of_times, callback) {
    var index;
    index = 0;
    while (!(index++ >= number_of_times)) {
      callback(index);
    }
    return null;
  };

  times(5, function(index) {
    return console.log(index);
  });

}).call(this);
```

Output: **(source: until_loop.coffee)**

```
1
2
3
4
5
```

Tip

To help you remember which loop is which, think of it like this: A `while` loop runs while the condition is true. An `until` loop runs until the condition is true. It may sound silly to some of you, but a lot of people have trouble remembering which is which.

Comprehensions

In a lot of our iterating examples, we've had very simple code blocks we wanted to execute, like this one:

Example: **(source: iterating_arrays.coffee)**

```
myLetters = ["a", "b", "c", "d"]

for letter in myLetters
  console.log letter.toUpperCase()
```

Because we are using a single line code block with our `for` loop, we are able to take advantage of what CoffeeScript calls *comprehensions*. Comprehensions are, essentially, loops and their code blocks on the same line.

Here's what that same example would look like using comprehensions:

Example: **(source: iterating_arrays_comprehension.coffee)**

```
myLetters = ["a", "b", "c", "d"]

console.log letter.toUpperCase() for letter in myLetters
```

Example: **(source: iterating_arrays_comprehension.js)**

```
(function() {
  var letter, myLetters, _i, _len;

  myLetters = ["a", "b", "c", "d"];

  for (_i = 0, _len = myLetters.length; _i < _len; _i++) {
    letter = myLetters[_i];
    console.log(letter.toUpperCase());
  }

}).call(this);
```

Output: **(source: iterating_arrays_comprehension.coffee)**

```
A
B
C
D
```

As you can see, we took the code block off of its own line and placed it before the `for` loop on the same line.

We also can use comprehensions to help us capture the results of a `for` loop. Using our same example let's capture the results of the uppercased letters into a new array:

Example: **(source: iterating_arrays_comprehension_capture.coffee)**

```
myLetters = ["a", "b", "c", "d"]

upLetters = (letter.toUpperCase() for letter in myLetters)

console.log upLetters
```

Example: **(source: iterating_arrays_comprehension_capture.js)**

```
(function() {
  var letter, myLetters, upLetters;

  myLetters = ["a", "b", "c", "d"];

  upLetters = (function() {
    var _i, _len, _results;
    _results = [];
    for (_i = 0, _len = myLetters.length; _i < _len; _i++) {
      letter = myLetters[_i];
      _results.push(letter.toUpperCase());
    }
    return _results;
  })();

  console.log(upLetters);

}).call(this);
```

Output: **(source: iterating_arrays_comprehension_capture.coffee)**

```
[ 'A', 'B', 'C', 'D' ]
```

By wrapping our comprehension statement in parentheses, we can capture the results of the iteration into another variable. It should be noted that we can also capture the results of a `for` loop even if you are using the multiline version:

Example: **(source: iterating_arrays_capture.coffee)**

```
myLetters = ["a", "b", "c", "d"]

upLetters = for letter in myLetters
  letter.toUpperCase()

console.log upLetters
```

Example: **(source: iterating_arrays_capture.js)**

```
(function() {
  var letter, myLetters, upLetters;

  myLetters = ["a", "b", "c", "d"];

  upLetters = (function() {
    var _i, _len, _results;
    _results = [];
    for (_i = 0, _len = myLetters.length; _i < _len; _i++) {
      letter = myLetters[_i];
      _results.push(letter.toUpperCase());
    }
    return _results;
  })();

  console.log(upLetters);

}).call(this);
```

Output: **(source: iterating_arrays_capture.coffee)**

```
[ 'A', 'B', 'C', 'D' ]
```

> **Tip**
>
> I'm not necessarily advocating everything I just showed you in this section. CoffeeScript touts the "power" of comprehensions a lot. I agree they can be powerful, but I think they can also be very hard to read and even harder to maintain. Use them where you see fit and the need is warranted.

The `do` Keyword

Scope, as we discussed in Chapter 2, "The Basics," in JavaScript can be a real pain to deal with sometimes—no more so than in loops. Because of the asynchronous nature of JavaScript, it is possible that we have lost the scope of a variable while we're doing something as simple as looping through a few numbers.

Let's look at an example. In this example we want to loop through a few numbers and print them out. However, before we print them out we want to wait one second.

Example: **(source: do.coffee)**

```
for x in [1..5]
  setTimeout ->
    console.log x
  , 1
```

Example: **(source: do.js)**

```
(function() {
  var x;

  for (x = 1; x <= 5; x++) {
    setTimeout(function() {
      return console.log(x);
    }, 1);
  }

}).call(this);
```

Output: **(source: do.coffee)**

```
6
6
6
6
6
```

Wow! That wasn't at all what we wanted! We were hoping to print out the numbers 1 through 5. Instead we got the number 6 printed out 5 times. What happened? The answer is that we lost track of the scope of the variable `x`.

While we waited the second to print out the number, the variable was being incremented in the loop. The reason we saw the number 6 is because the last time through the loop it incremented it up to 6, which is greater than 5, so the loop didn't execute.

So how do we prevent this from happening and keep track of the variable's value that we actually want? We can do this using the do keyword:

Example: **(source: do2.coffee)**

```
for x in [1..5]
  do (x) ->
    setTimeout ->
      console.log x
    , 1
```

Example: **(source: do2.js)**

```
(function() {
  var x, _fn;

  _fn = function(x) {
    return setTimeout(function() {
      return console.log(x);
    }, 1);
  };
  for (x = 1; x <= 5; x++) {
    _fn(x);
  }

}).call(this);
```

Output: **(source: do2.coffee)**

```
1
2
3
4
5
```

The do keyword will create a wrapper function around the code we want to execute, and it will take in, and hold onto, the variable at the time we called it. Very useful, indeed!

Wrapping Up

Well, there we have it—everything you've always wanted to know about collections and iterating in CoffeeScript.

We first looked at arrays and what makes them tick in CoffeeScript. We looked at a few fun tricks CoffeeScript makes possible when dealing with arrays: testing to see if a value is in an array, swapping assignment of variables, and, finally, capturing the elements of an array easily into variables.

Next we looked at ranges. We saw how to construct arrays of numbers using the range syntax. We also looked at how ranges can be used to manipulate existing arrays by grabbing sections of the array and even replacing sections of an array with other values.

After ranges, we moved on to objects in CoffeeScript. We looked at the different rules around constructing objects. We looked at how to set and get attributes on the objects we create. Using a modified object syntax, we saw how we could pull out deeply nested attributes in an object and assign them to variables.

Next came iterations. We looked at how to iterate over the elements of an array and how to iterate over the key/value pairs of an object. We looked at the `by` and `when` keywords to help us write cleaner loops. Then we examined how `while` and `until` loops worked and how they differ from each other.

We looked at the comprehensions syntax for helping us write single line loops and code blocks.

Finally, we looked at how the `do` keyword can help us keep track of the scope of our variables while doing things such as looping through a collection.

With collections now behind us, we can next look at a different type of collection, the class.

Notes

1. http://rack.rubyforge.org/
2. http://www.jslint.com/
3. http://en.wikipedia.org/wiki/JavaScript#Prototype-based

6

Classes

Classes[1] are essentially a blueprint for creating new instances of an object with predefined functions and variables. These instances can then store state related to that individual instance. Over the years, JavaScript has constantly come under attack for its lack of any real support for classes.

In Chapter 5, "Collections and Iterations," we looked at objects in JavaScript. In each example we hand rolled a brand new object and gave that new object a set of functions and values. This works great for the occasional simple object, but what if we wanted to have a more complex data model? More importantly, what if we wanted to have more than one of those complex data models? That is typically where classes come in.

Fortunately, CoffeeScript steps up to the plate with full class support. So if JavaScript does not have any real support for classes, how does CoffeeScript solve the problem? The short answer is through the use of some clever scoping and the use of functions and objects. The long answer is, read the rest of this chapter.

Defining Classes

Defining classes in CoffeeScript can be as simple and as straightforward as one line:

Example: **(source: simple_class1.coffee)**

```
class Employee
```

Example: **(source: simple_class1.js)**

```
(function() {
  var Employee;

  Employee = (function() {
```

```
    function Employee() {}

    return Employee;

  })();

}).call(this);
```

With that, we have defined a simple new class called `Employee`. We can instantiate new instances of that object like so:

Example: **(source: simple_class2.coffee)**

```
class Employee

emp1 = new Employee()
emp2 = new Employee()
```

Example: **(source: simple_class2.js)**

```
(function() {
  var Employee, emp1, emp2;

  Employee = (function() {

    function Employee() {}

    return Employee;

  })();

  emp1 = new Employee();

  emp2 = new Employee();

}).call(this);
```

We call the `new` keyword before the name of our class, and we get a brand-new instance of that object to do with as we like.

> **Tip**
>
> When creating new instances of objects with the `new` keyword, it isn't required to put the parentheses at the end, as we do in our examples, but I find it looks nice and makes the code a bit easier to read. Do whatever feels right to you.

Defining Functions

When defining functions on our classes we follow the same rules, and syntax, that we would if we were defining a function on a simple object—because that is exactly what we are doing.

Example: **(source: simple_class_with_function.coffee)**

```
class Employee

  dob: (year = 1976, month = 7, day = 24)->
    new Date(year, month, day)

emp1 = new Employee()
console.log emp1.dob()
emp2 = new Employee()
console.log emp2.dob(1979, 3, 28)
```

Example: **(source: simple_class_with_function.js)**

```
(function() {
  var Employee, emp1, emp2;

  Employee = (function() {

    function Employee() {}

    Employee.prototype.dob = function(year, month, day) {
      if (year == null) year = 1976;
      if (month == null) month = 7;
      if (day == null) day = 24;
      return new Date(year, month, day);
    };

    return Employee;

  })();

  emp1 = new Employee();

  console.log(emp1.dob());

  emp2 = new Employee();

  console.log(emp2.dob(1979, 3, 28));

}).call(this);
```

Output: **(source: simple_class_with_function.coffee)**

```
Tue, 24 Aug 1976 04:00:00 GMT
Sat, 28 Apr 1979 05:00:00 GMT
```

The `constructor` Function

CoffeeScript lets us define a function called `constructor` that will be called when we create a new instance of an object. The `constructor` is like every other function we've talked about. The only thing special about the `constructor` function is that it will be called automatically when we instantiate a new instance of an object without us having to call it explicitly.

> **Tip**
>
> I told a little white lie earlier when I said that the `constructor` function gets called automatically when we create a new instance of an object. In reality, when we create a new instance of an object like this, `new Employee()`, we are calling that `constructor` function directly. It's just renamed.

Example: **(source: simple_class3.coffee)**

```
class Employee

  constructor: ->
    console.log "Instantiated a new Employee object"

  dob: (year = 1976, month = 7, day = 24)->
    new Date(year, month, day)

emp1 = new Employee()
console.log emp1.dob()

emp2 = new Employee()
console.log emp2.dob(1979, 3, 28)
```

Example: **(source: simple_class3.js)**

```
(function() {
  var Employee, emp1, emp2;

  Employee = (function() {

    function Employee() {
      console.log("Instantiated a new Employee object");
```

```
    }

    Employee.prototype.dob = function(year, month, day) {
      if (year == null) year = 1976;
      if (month == null) month = 7;
      if (day == null) day = 24;
      return new Date(year, month, day);
    };

    return Employee;

  })();

  emp1 = new Employee();

  console.log(emp1.dob());

  emp2 = new Employee();

  console.log(emp2.dob(1979, 3, 28));

}).call(this);
```

Output: **(source: simple_class3.coffee)**

```
Instantiated a new Employee object
Tue, 24 Aug 1976 04:00:00 GMT
Instantiated a new Employee object
Sat, 28 Apr 1979 05:00:00 GMT
```

As you can see in our example, every time we create a new `Employee` object, it will print a message out to the console to let us know that it's been created.

As we'll see in this chapter, the `constructor` function can provide an easy way to quickly set up your new object with any custom data for that object.

Scope in Classes

At their heart, classes in CoffeeScript are just glorified objects that produce a lot of boilerplate JavaScript code to let them do the things they do. Because classes are just plain objects—granted, objects with a lot of window dressing—scope of variables, attributes, and functions behave the same as they do in regular objects.

Let's investigate by taking our `Employee` class again. Employees in real life have names, so let's make sure our `Employee` class can reflect it. When we create a new instance of the `Employee` class, we want to have the name passed in and assigned to an attribute that is scoped to the instance of the new `Employee` object.

Example: **(source: class_scope.coffee)**

```
class Employee

  constructor: (name)->
    @name = name

  dob: (year = 1976, month = 7, day = 24)->
    new Date(year, month, day)

emp1 = new Employee("Mark")
console.log emp1.name
console.log emp1.dob()

emp2 = new Employee("Rachel")
console.log emp2.name
console.log emp2.dob(1979, 3, 28)
```

Example: **(source: class_scope.js)**

```
(function() {
  var Employee, emp1, emp2;

  Employee = (function() {

    function Employee(name) {
      this.name = name;
    }

    Employee.prototype.dob = function(year, month, day) {
      if (year == null) year = 1976;
      if (month == null) month = 7;
      if (day == null) day = 24;
      return new Date(year, month, day);
    };

    return Employee;

  })();

  emp1 = new Employee("Mark");

  console.log(emp1.name);
```

```
  console.log(emp1.dob());

  emp2 = new Employee("Rachel");

  console.log(emp2.name);

  console.log(emp2.dob(1979, 3, 28));

}).call(this);
```

Output: **(source: class_scope.coffee)**

```
Mark
Tue, 24 Aug 1976 04:00:00 GMT
Rachel
Sat, 28 Apr 1979 05:00:00 GMT
```

As we discussed earlier, the `constructor` function is no different from any other function, so the same scope and definition rules apply. Knowing that we are now passing in an argument called `name`, we set the `name` argument onto an attribute on the object instance using `@name = name`. Remember from Chapter 3, "Control Structures," that the `@` alias is equal to `this`.

With the attribute set on the object instance, we can then call it like any other attribute on the object.

There is an even easier and cleaner way to achieve the same goal, and it's quite possibly one of my favorite features of CoffeeScript (and one I wish other languages would implement). We can trim our `constructor` down by doing the following:

Example: **(source: class_scope1.coffee)**

```
class Employee

  constructor: (@name)->

  dob: (year = 1976, month = 7, day = 24)->
    new Date(year, month, day)

emp1 = new Employee("Mark")
console.log emp1.name
console.log emp1.dob()

emp2 = new Employee("Rachel")
console.log emp2.name
console.log emp2.dob(1979, 3, 28)
```

Example: **(source: class_scope1.js)**

```
(function() {
  var Employee, emp1, emp2;

  Employee = (function() {

    function Employee(name) {
      this.name = name;
    }

    Employee.prototype.dob = function(year, month, day) {
      if (year == null) year = 1976;
      if (month == null) month = 7;
      if (day == null) day = 24;
      return new Date(year, month, day);
    };

    return Employee;

  })();

  emp1 = new Employee("Mark");

  console.log(emp1.name);

  console.log(emp1.dob());

  emp2 = new Employee("Rachel");
  console.log(emp2.name);
  console.log(emp2.dob(1979, 3, 28));

}).call(this);
```

Output: **(source: class_scope1.coffee)**

```
Mark
Tue, 24 Aug 1976 04:00:00 GMT
Rachel
Sat, 28 Apr 1979 05:00:00 GMT
```

By adding the `@` operator in front of the definition of the `name` argument, we tell CoffeeScript that we want it to generate JavaScript that will assign that argument to an attribute with the same name, in this case called `name`.

We can also easily access that attribute in the other functions of the class. Let's update the example again, this time to add a method that prints out the employee's name and birth date:

Example: **(source: class_scope2.coffee)**

```
class Employee

  constructor: (@name)->

  dob: (year = 1976, month = 7, day = 24)->
    new Date(year, month, day)

  printInfo: (year = 1976, month = 7, day = 24)->
    console.log "Name: #{@name}"
    console.log "DOB: #{@dob(year, month, day)}"


emp1 = new Employee("Mark")
emp1.printInfo(1976, 7, 24)

emp2 = new Employee("Rachel")
emp2.printInfo(1979, 3, 28)
```

Example: **(source: class_scope2.js)**

```
(function() {
  var Employee, emp1, emp2;

  Employee = (function() {

    function Employee(name) {
      this.name = name;
    }

    Employee.prototype.dob = function(year, month, day) {
      if (year == null) year = 1976;
      if (month == null) month = 7;
      if (day == null) day = 24;
      return new Date(year, month, day);
    };

    Employee.prototype.printInfo = function(year, month, day) {
      if (year == null) year = 1976;
      if (month == null) month = 7;
      if (day == null) day = 24;
      console.log("Name: " + this.name);
      return console.log("DOB: " + (this.dob(year, month, day)));
    };

    return Employee;
```

```
  })();

  emp1 = new Employee("Mark");

  emp1.printInfo(1976, 7, 24);

  emp2 = new Employee("Rachel");

  emp2.printInfo(1979, 3, 28);

}).call(this);
```

Output: **(source: class_scope2.coffee)**

```
Name: Mark
DOB: Tue Aug 24 1976 00:00:00 GMT-0400 (EDT)
Name: Rachel
DOB: Sat Apr 28 1979 00:00:00 GMT-0500 (EST)
```

I would be remiss if we left this section with the code looking like that. I don't want to have to keep passing in the year, month, and day every time I want to print out the employee's information. I want to pass a birth date into the `constructor` function and then access it whenever I want. So let's do that:

Example: **(source: class_scope_refactor_1.coffee)**

```
class Employee

  constructor: (@name, @dob)->

  printInfo: ->
    console.log "Name: #{@name}"
    console.log "DOB: #{@dob}"


emp1 = new Employee("Mark", new Date(1976, 7, 24))
emp1.printInfo()

emp2 = new Employee("Rachel", new Date(1979, 3, 28))
emp2.printInfo()
```

Example: **(source: class_scope_refactor_1.js)**

```
(function() {
  var Employee, emp1, emp2;

  Employee = (function() {
```

```
    function Employee(name, dob) {
      this.name = name;
      this.dob = dob;
    }

    Employee.prototype.printInfo = function() {
      console.log("Name: " + this.name);
      return console.log("DOB: " + this.dob);
    };

    return Employee;

  })();

  emp1 = new Employee("Mark", new Date(1976, 7, 24));

  emp1.printInfo();

  emp2 = new Employee("Rachel", new Date(1979, 3, 28));

  emp2.printInfo();

}).call(this);
```

Output: **(source: class_scope_refactor_1.coffee)**

```
Name: Mark
DOB: Tue Aug 24 1976 00:00:00 GMT-0400 (EDT)
Name: Rachel
DOB: Sat Apr 28 1979 00:00:00 GMT-0500 (EST)
```

That is certainly cleaner and a little more DRY.[2] Therefore, when I see two arguments for a function I start asking the question, will there be more arguments? If the answer is yes, I reconsider how I'm defining my function; in this case I'm concerned about the `constructor` function. What happens when we need to pass in other information, such as salary, department, manager, and so on? Let's do a bit more refactoring:

Example: **(source: class_scope_refactor_2.coffee)**

```
class Employee

  constructor: (@attributes)->

  printInfo: ->
    console.log "Name: #{@attributes.name}"
    console.log "DOB: #{@attributes.dob}"
```

```
    if @attributes.salary
      console.log "Salary: #{@attributes.salary}"
    else
      console.log "Salary: Unknown"

emp1 = new Employee
  name: "Mark"
  dob: new Date(1976, 7, 24)
  salary: "$1.00"

emp1.printInfo()

emp2 = new Employee
  name: "Rachel"
  dob: new Date(1979, 3, 28)

emp2.printInfo()
```

Example: **(source: class_scope_refactor_2.js)**

```
(function() {
  var Employee, emp1, emp2;

  Employee = (function() {

    function Employee(attributes) {
      this.attributes = attributes;
    }

    Employee.prototype.printInfo = function() {
      console.log("Name: " + this.attributes.name);
      console.log("DOB: " + this.attributes.dob);
      if (this.attributes.salary) {
        return console.log("Salary: " + this.attributes.salary);
      } else {
        return console.log("Salary: Unknown");
      }
    };

    return Employee;

  })();

  emp1 = new Employee({
    name: "Mark",
    dob: new Date(1976, 7, 24),
```

```
    salary: "$1.00"
  });

  emp1.printInfo();
  emp2 = new Employee({
    name: "Rachel",
    dob: new Date(1979, 3, 28)
  });

  emp2.printInfo();

}).call(this);
```

Output: **(source: class_scope_refactor_2.coffee)**

```
Name: Mark
DOB: Tue Aug 24 1976 00:00:00 GMT-0400 (EDT)
Salary: $1.00
Name: Rachel
DOB: Sat Apr 28 1979 00:00:00 GMT-0500 (EST)
Salary: Unknown
```

Now we can pass any arguments we want into the `Employee` class, and they'll be available to us through the `attributes` attribute on the object. That is definitely a lot nicer, and it certainly is more extensible down the line.

As you can see with the first employee, we passed in a third attribute, `salary`, that we didn't pass in for the second employee. We could pass in a hundred different attributes to our `Employee` class now and our code doesn't have to change.

One last thing before we leave this section. Some of you might have come up with what you think of as a great idea. What if you use the knowledge you gained in Chapter 5, "Collections and Iterations," about looping through the `attributes` argument and assigning each key/value pair directly to the object so you don't have to keep calling `@attributes` everywhere in the code?

Well, let's see how you would do that, and we can also see why that could be a *very* bad idea:

Example: **(source: class_scope_refactor_3.coffee)**

```
class Employee

  constructor: (@attributes)->
    for key, value of @attributes
      @[key] = value
```

```
  printInfo: ->
    console.log "Name: #{@name}"
    console.log "DOB: #{@dob}"
    if @salary
      console.log "Salary: #{@salary}"
    else
      console.log "Salary: Unknown"

emp1 = new Employee
  name: "Mark"
  dob: new Date(1976, 7, 24)
  salary: "$1.00"

emp1.printInfo()

emp2 = new Employee
  name: "Rachel",
  dob: new Date(1979, 3, 28)
  printInfo: ->
    console.log "I've hacked your code!"

emp2.printInfo()
```

Example: **(source: class_scope_refactor_3.js)**

```
(function() {
  var Employee, emp1, emp2;

  Employee = (function() {

    function Employee(attributes) {
      var key, value, _ref;
      this.attributes = attributes;
      _ref = this.attributes;
      for (key in _ref) {
        value = _ref[key];
        this[key] = value;
      }
    }

    Employee.prototype.printInfo = function() {
      console.log("Name: " + this.name);
      console.log("DOB: " + this.dob);
      if (this.salary) {
        return console.log("Salary: " + this.salary);
      } else {
        return console.log("Salary: Unknown");
      }
```

```
    };

    return Employee;

  })();

  emp1 = new Employee({
    name: "Mark",
    dob: new Date(1976, 7, 24),
    salary: "$1.00"
  });

  emp1.printInfo();

  emp2 = new Employee({
    name: "Rachel",
    dob: new Date(1979, 3, 28),
    printInfo: function() {
      return console.log("I've hacked your code!");
    }
  });

  emp2.printInfo();

}).call(this);
```

Output: **(source: class_scope_refactor_3.coffee)**

```
Name: Mark
DOB: Tue Aug 24 1976 00:00:00 GMT-0400 (EDT)
Salary: $1.00
I've hacked your code!
```

Uh-oh! We were easily able to override the `printInfo` function when we passed in the list of attributes for our second employee. The code is definitely easier to read, but it's also easier to hack, and who wants that? JavaScript is easy enough to modify on its own, so why should we make it even easier? With that said, let's move on, pretending we didn't just do that last refactor.

Extending Classes

When writing object-oriented programs, developers often come across the need for inheritance.[3] Inheritance lets us take a class, such as our `Employee` class, and create a variant on that class.

In a business, everyone is an employee, but not everybody is a manager. So let's define a `Manager` class that inherits, or extends, from our `Employee` class:

Example: **(source: manager1.coffee)**

```
class Employee

  constructor: (@attributes)->

  printInfo: ->
    console.log "Name: #{@attributes.name}"
    console.log "DOB: #{@attributes.dob}"
    console.log "Salary: #{@attributes.salary}"

class Manager extends Employee

employee = new Employee
  name: "Mark"
  dob: new Date(1976, 7, 24)
  salary: 50000

employee.printInfo()

manager = new Manager
  name: "Rachel"
  dob: new Date(1979, 3, 28)
  salary: 100000

manager.printInfo()
```

Example: **(source: manager1.js)**

```
(function() {
  var Employee, Manager, employee, manager,
    __hasProp = Object.prototype.hasOwnProperty,
    __extends = function(child, parent) { for (var key in parent) { if
(__hasProp.call(parent, key)) child[key] = parent[key]; } function ctor() {
this.constructor = child; } ctor.prototype = parent.prototype; child.prototype =
new ctor; child.__super__ = parent.prototype; return child; };

  Employee = (function() {
    function Employee(attributes) {
      this.attributes = attributes;
    }

    Employee.prototype.printInfo = function() {
      console.log("Name: " + this.attributes.name);
```

```
      console.log("DOB: " + this.attributes.dob);
      return console.log("Salary: " + this.attributes.salary);
    };

    return Employee;

  })();

  Manager = (function(_super) {

    __extends(Manager, _super);

    function Manager() {
      Manager.__super__.constructor.apply(this, arguments);
    }

    return Manager;

  })(Employee);

  employee = new Employee({
    name: "Mark",
    dob: new Date(1976, 7, 24),
    salary: 50000
  });

  employee.printInfo();

  manager = new Manager({
    name: "Rachel",
    dob: new Date(1979, 3, 28),
    salary: 100000
  });

  manager.printInfo();

}).call(this);
```

Output: **(source: manager1.coffee)**

```
Name: Mark
DOB: Tue Aug 24 1976 00:00:00 GMT-0400 (EDT)
Salary: 50000
Name: Rachel
DOB: Sat Apr 28 1979 00:00:00 GMT-0500 (EST)
Salary: 100000
```

> **Tip**
>
> In the real world we would probably use roles to define different types of employees, but for the sake of discussion let's pretend that this is the best way to solve our problem of different types of employees.

The basic definition of our `Manager` class was simple, `class Manager`, but by using the keyword `extends` and giving it the name of the class we wanted to extend, `Employee`, we were able to gain all the functionality from the `Employee` class in our `Manager` class.

Let's take it a step further and learn about how to override methods in subclasses. Let's add a function, `bonus`, to our `Employee` class that returns `0`. Regular employees apparently don't get bonuses. Managers, however, get a 10% bonus, so we want to make sure when we call the `bonus` function on managers we get the right value.

Example: **(source: manager2.coffee)**

```
class Employee

  constructor: (@attributes)->

  printInfo: ->
    console.log "Name: #{@attributes.name}"
    console.log "DOB: #{@attributes.dob}"
    console.log "Salary: #{@attributes.salary}"
    console.log "Bonus: #{@bonus()}"

  bonus: ->
    0

class Manager extends Employee

  bonus: ->
    @attributes.salary * .10

employee = new Employee
  name: "Mark"
  dob: new Date(1976, 7, 24)
  salary: 50000

employee.printInfo()

manager = new Manager
  name: "Rachel"
  dob: new Date(1979, 3, 28)
  salary: 100000

manager.printInfo()
```

Example: **(source: manager2.js)**

```
(function() {
  var Employee, Manager, employee, manager,
    __hasProp = Object.prototype.hasOwnProperty,
    __extends = function(child, parent) { for (var key in parent) { if
(__hasProp.call(parent, key)) child[key] = parent[key]; } function ctor() {
this.constructor = child; } ctor.prototype = parent.prototype; child.prototype =
new ctor; child.__super__ = parent.prototype; return child; };

  Employee = (function() {

    function Employee(attributes) {
      this.attributes = attributes;
    }

    Employee.prototype.printInfo = function() {
      console.log("Name: " + this.attributes.name);
      console.log("DOB: " + this.attributes.dob);
      console.log("Salary: " + this.attributes.salary);
      return console.log("Bonus: " + (this.bonus()));
    };

    Employee.prototype.bonus = function() {
      return 0;
    };

    return Employee;

  })();

  Manager = (function(_super) {
    __extends(Manager, _super);

    function Manager() {
      Manager.__super__.constructor.apply(this, arguments);
    }

    Manager.prototype.bonus = function() {
      return this.attributes.salary * .10;
    };

    return Manager;

  })(Employee);
```

```
  employee = new Employee({
    name: "Mark",
    dob: new Date(1976, 7, 24),
    salary: 50000
  });

  employee.printInfo();

  manager = new Manager({
    name: "Rachel",
    dob: new Date(1979, 3, 28),
    salary: 100000
  });

  manager.printInfo();

}).call(this);
```

Output: **(source: manager2.coffee)**

```
Name: Mark
DOB: Tue Aug 24 1976 00:00:00 GMT-0400 (EDT)
Salary: 50000
Bonus: 0
Name: Rachel
DOB: Sat Apr 28 1979 00:00:00 GMT-0500 (EST)
Salary: 100000
Bonus: 10000
```

Overriding functions on the subclass is as simple as redefining the function again with new functionality. But what about if we want to call the original function and maybe add a little bit to it. Here's an example.

Employees get really upset when they see their bonus amount as 0 in the `printInfo`, so we're going to take it out entirely, but we still want managers to see that information when we call `printInfo`. We can do this using the `super` keyword:

Example: **(source: manager3.coffee)**

```
class Employee

  constructor: (@attributes)->

  printInfo: ->
    console.log "Name: #{@attributes.name}"
    console.log "DOB: #{@attributes.dob}"
    console.log "Salary: #{@attributes.salary}"
```

```
  bonus: ->
    0

class Manager extends Employee

  bonus: ->
    @attributes.salary * .10

  printInfo: ->
    super
    console.log "Bonus: #{@bonus()}"

employee = new Employee
  name: "Mark"
  dob: new Date(1976, 7, 24)
  salary: 50000

employee.printInfo()

manager = new Manager
  name: "Rachel"
  dob: new Date(1979, 3, 28)
  salary: 100000

manager.printInfo()
```

Example: **(source: manager3.js)**

```
(function() {
  var Employee, Manager, employee, manager,
    __hasProp = Object.prototype.hasOwnProperty,
    __extends = function(child, parent) { for (var key in parent) { if
(__hasProp.call(parent, key)) child[key] = parent[key]; } function ctor() {
this.constructor = child; } ctor.prototype = parent.prototype; child.prototype =
new ctor; child.__super__ = parent.prototype; return child; };

  Employee = (function() {

    function Employee(attributes) {
      this.attributes = attributes;
    }

    Employee.prototype.printInfo = function() {
      console.log("Name: " + this.attributes.name);
      console.log("DOB: " + this.attributes.dob);
      return console.log("Salary: " + this.attributes.salary);
    };
```

```
    Employee.prototype.bonus = function() {
      return 0;
    };

    return Employee;

  })();

  Manager = (function(_super) {

    __extends(Manager, _super);

    function Manager() {
      Manager.__super__.constructor.apply(this, arguments);
    }

    Manager.prototype.bonus = function() {
      return this.attributes.salary * .10;
    };

    Manager.prototype.printInfo = function() {
      Manager.__super__.printInfo.apply(this, arguments);
      return console.log("Bonus: " + (this.bonus()));
    };

    return Manager;

  })(Employee);

  employee = new Employee({
    name: "Mark",
    dob: new Date(1976, 7, 24),
    salary: 50000
  });

  employee.printInfo();

  manager = new Manager({
    name: "Rachel",
    dob: new Date(1979, 3, 28),
    salary: 100000
  });

  manager.printInfo();

}).call(this);
```

Output: **(source: manager3.coffee)**

```
Name: Mark
DOB: Tue Aug 24 1976 00:00:00 GMT-0400 (EDT)
Salary: 50000
Name: Rachel
DOB: Sat Apr 28 1979 00:00:00 GMT-0500 (EST)
Salary: 100000
Bonus: 10000
```

In the `printInfo` function we defined in the `Manager` class, we first called `super`. When we call `super`, that will call the original `printInfo` function from the `Employee` class with any arguments that might have come into the function. After we call `super` we then print out the bonus information for the manager.

> **Tip**
>
> The call to `super` can be called at any point in the function that is overriding it; it doesn't have to be first (as in some languages). Subsequently, you don't have to call the `super` method at all.

> **Tip**
>
> When calling `super` we do not need to explicitly pass in arguments. By default, any arguments that come into the function that is overriding `super` will be passed to `super` when called. You can, however, explicitly pass any arguments you want when calling `super`. This can be useful if you want to augment or mutate the arguments before they go to the `super` method.

Class-Level Functions

Class-level functions are functions that don't require an instance of the class in order to be called. These functions can be incredibly useful. One of the best uses is to provide a sort of namespacing for your functions. An example of this in JavaScript is `Math.random()`. You don't need to instantiate a new `Math` object to get a random number. But by hanging the `random` function off of the `Math` class, you avoid the risk that there is another function called `random` that might override your function.

> **Tip**
>
> In reality, `Math` isn't a class; it's just a plain object that is used for namespacing. Occasionally I twist the truth a little bit to help get my point across.

You can also use class-level functions to do things that might affect multiple instances of a class, like search for them in a database.

We could write a couple of class-level functions on the `Employee` class. Since we don't have a full database at our disposal, we'll just keep track of how many employee instances we create and report that number. To keep track of which employees we hire, we create a class-level function called `hire` that will take the newly hired employees and add them to an array that will act as our impromptu database. We'll also add a `total` class-level function that will return the total number of employees we have in our faux database.

Example: **(source: class_level.coffee)**

```
class Employee

  constructor: ->
    Employee.hire(@)

  @hire: (employee) ->
    @allEmployees ||= []
    @allEmployees.push employee

  @total: ->
    console.log "There are #{@allEmployees.length} employees."
    @allEmployees.length

new Employee()
new Employee()
new Employee()

Employee.total()
```

Example: **(source: class_level.js)**

```
(function() {
  var Employee;

  Employee = (function() {

    function Employee() {
      Employee.hire(this);
    }

    Employee.hire = function(employee) {
      this.allEmployees || (this.allEmployees = []);
      return this.allEmployees.push(employee);
    };

    Employee.total = function() {
      console.log("There are " + this.allEmployees.length + " employees.");
```

```
      return this.allEmployees.length;
    };

    return Employee;

  })();

  new Employee();

  new Employee();

  new Employee();

  Employee.total();

}).call(this);
```

Output: **(source: class_level.coffee)**

```
There are 3 employees.
```

So how did we create those class-level functions? By prepending the function name with `@` we are telling CoffeeScript that we want that function to be at the class level. In the JavaScript world this works because when we replace `@` with `this.` the `this` context is that of the `Employee` class, not an instance of that class.

The inside class-level functions scope is limited to other class-level functions and attributes.

> **Tip**
>
> I routinely create class definitions that are nothing but a bunch of class-level methods. This is great for building utility packages and to make sure that I have nicely scoped functions. And, if I ever want to, or need to, I can inherit from these classes and override certain functions for a particular need.

The use of `super` is limited, however, when dealing with class-level functions and attributes. You can use `super` when you want to call the original function that you have overridden in the subclass. However, and this is big, if the function you are calling using `super` tries to make reference to any class-level attributes, you'll get a big fat error.

Let's take a look at what happens when we override the `total` class-level function in the `Manager` class and then try to call `super`:

Example: **(source: class_level_super.coffee)**

```
class Employee

  constructor: ->
    Employee.hire(@)

  @hire: (employee) ->
    @allEmployees ||= []
    @allEmployees.push employee

  @total: ->
    console.log "There are #{@allEmployees.length} employees."
    @allEmployees.length

class Manager extends Employee

  @total: ->
    console.log "There are 0 managers."
    super

new Employee()
new Employee()
new Employee()

Manager.total()
```

Example: **(source: class_level_super.js)**

```
(function() {
  var Employee, Manager,
    __hasProp = Object.prototype.hasOwnProperty,
    __extends = function(child, parent) { for (var key in parent) { if
(__hasProp.call(parent, key)) child[key] = parent[key]; } function ctor() {
this.constructor = child; } ctor.prototype = parent.prototype; child.prototype =
new ctor; child.__super__ = parent.prototype; return child; };

  Employee = (function() {

    function Employee() {
      Employee.hire(this);
    }

    Employee.hire = function(employee) {
      this.allEmployees || (this.allEmployees = []);
      return this.allEmployees.push(employee);
    };
```

```
    Employee.total = function() {
      console.log("There are " + this.allEmployees.length + " employees.");
      return this.allEmployees.length;
    };

    return Employee;

  })();

  Manager = (function(_super) {

    __extends(Manager, _super);

    function Manager() {
      Manager.__super__.constructor.apply(this, arguments);
    }

    Manager.total = function() {
      console.log("There are 0 managers.");
      return Manager.__super__.constructor.total.apply(this, arguments);
    };

    return Manager;

  })(Employee);

  new Employee();

  new Employee();

  new Employee();

  Manager.total();

}).call(this);
```

Output: **(source: class_level_super.coffee)**

```
There are 0 managers.
TypeError: Cannot read property 'length' of undefined
    at Function.<anonymous> (.../classes/class_level_super.coffee:18:51)
    at Function.total (.../classes/class_level_super.coffee:36:50)
    at Object.<anonymous> (.../classes/class_level_super.coffee:49:11)
    at Object.<anonymous> (.../classes/class_level_super.coffee:51:4)
    at Module._compile (module.js:432:26)
    at Object.run (/usr/local/lib/node_modules/coffee-script/lib/coffee-script/
➥coffee-script.js:68:25)
```

```
    at /usr/local/lib/node_modules/coffee-script/lib/coffee-script/command.js:135:29
    at /usr/local/lib/node_modules/coffee-script/lib/coffee-script/command.js:110:18
    at [object Object].<anonymous> (fs.js:114:5)
    at [object Object].emit (events.js:64:17)
```

As you can see, when we tried to call `length` on the `@allEmployees` attribute we got the following error:

```
TypeError: Cannot read property 'length' of undefined
```

The reason for this is straightforward, but it might take a minute for it to sink in. Because JavaScript doesn't have true inheritance, CoffeeScript has to cheat and do some magic, as we talked about earlier, to give the illusion of classes and inheritance. Because of this, the subclass `Manager` is a different object from the `Employee` class, and because the attributes are being set on the `Employee` class and not the `Manager` class, the `Manager` class doesn't have access to them. I told you it was a bit to wrap your head around.

> **Tip**
>
> I find it best to try to avoid using `super` at the class level. I also try to keep all my class-level functions self-contained so I don't run into these sorts of issues.

Prototype Functions

In JavaScript, you can add functions and attributes to all instances of an object by adding those functions and attributes to the object's prototype using the aptly named `prototype` attribute.

In CoffeeScript we can do this using the `::` operator. Let's add a `size` function to all instances of array. We want the `size` function to return the length of the array.

Example: **(source: prototypes.coffee)**

```
myArray = [1..10]

try
  console.log myArray.size()
catch error
  console.log error

Array::size = -> @length
console.log myArray.size()

myArray.push(11)
console.log myArray.size()
```

Example: **(source: prototypes.js)**

```
(function() {
  var myArray;

  myArray = [1, 2, 3, 4, 5, 6, 7, 8, 9, 10];

  try {
    console.log(myArray.size());
  } catch (error) {
    console.log(error);
  }

  Array.prototype.size = function() {
    return this.length;
  };

  console.log(myArray.size());

  myArray.push(11);

  console.log(myArray.size());

}).call(this);
```

Output: **(source: prototypes.coffee)**

```
[TypeError: Object 1,2,3,4,5,6,7,8,9,10 has no method 'size']
10
11
```

The first time we try to call the `size` function on our array we get an error because the function doesn't exist. However, after we add the `size` function to the `Array` class's prototype, it behaves just as we hoped it would the next couple of times we call it.

> **Tip**
>
> The `::` operator is there for convenience. You can still access the `prototype` attribute directly, but I find that typing all those extra characters isn't worth it.

Binding (-> Versus =>)

JavaScript is an asynchronous[4] or "evented" programming language. In non-asynchronous programming, each time a function is called execution of the rest of the program would be halted until the aforementioned function has returned. In JavaScript, this is not necessarily the case. It is quite common for the program to continue executing after calling a function, even though the function has yet to return. If it helps, think of this style of programming as "fire and forget;" the program fires off a call to a function and then forgets all about it. Let's look at a quick example of how an asynchronous program runs.

Example: **(source: fire_and_forget.coffee)**

```
fire = (msg, wait)->
  setTimeout ->
    console.log msg
  , wait

fire("Hello", 3000)
fire("World", 1000)
```

Example: **(source: fire_and_forget.js)**

```
(function() {
  var fire;

  fire = function(msg, wait) {
    return setTimeout(function() {
      return console.log(msg);
    }, wait);
  };

  fire("Hello", 3000);

  fire("World", 1000);

}).call(this);
```

Output: **(source: fire_and_forget.coffee)**

```
World
Hello
```

As you can see, our program first said "World" and then "Hello." In non-asynchronous programming we would have first seen the word "Hello" followed a few seconds later by the word "World." Asynchronous programming can be incredibly powerful but can also be a bit cumbersome and confusing. Let's look at how things can start to get a bit muddled up.

Let's write a `log` method. This method will log to the console that we are about to execute a callback function; then it will execute the callback; and finally, it will log to the console that we have executed the function.

Example: **(source: unbound.coffee)**

```
class User

  constructor: (@name) ->

  sayHi: ->
    console.log "Hello #{@name}"

bob = new User('bob')
mary = new User('mary')

log = (callback)->

  console.log "about to execute callback..."
  callback()
  console.log "...executed callback"

log(bob.sayHi)
log(mary.sayHi)
```

Example: **(source: unbound.js)**

```
(function() {
  var User, bob, log, mary;

  User = (function() {

    function User(name) {
      this.name = name;
    }

    User.prototype.sayHi = function() {
      return console.log("Hello " + this.name);
    };

    return User;

  })();

  bob = new User('bob');

  mary = new User('mary');

  log = function(callback) {
    console.log("about to execute callback...");
    callback();
    return console.log("...executed callback");
```

```
  };

  log(bob.sayHi);

  log(mary.sayHi);

}).call(this);
```

Output: **(source: unbound.coffee)**

```
about to execute callback...
Hello undefined
...executed callback
about to execute callback...
Hello undefined
...executed callback
```

Well, I'm pretty sure that code was not supposed to say hello to `undefined`. So what happened there? When the `log` function called the callback function we passed in, that callback had lost the original context from which it came. The callback no longer had reference to the `name` variable we set in our class. This type of problem is quite common in JavaScript, particularly when using libraries like jQuery when making AJAX requests or binding to events.

So how do we fix this? How do we give our callback back its context? The answer is to use =>, also known as the fat arrow, instead of -> when defining our `sayHi` function in the `User` class. Here is the same example, only this time I changed `sayHi: ->` to `sayHi: =>`. Let's see what happens:

Example: **(source: bound.coffee)**

```
class User

  constructor: (@name) ->

  sayHi: =>
    console.log "Hello #{@name}"

bob = new User('bob')
mary = new User('mary')

log = (callback)->
  console.log "about to execute callback..."
  callback()
  console.log "...executed callback"

log(bob.sayHi)
log(mary.sayHi)
```

Example: **(source: bound.js)**

```
(function() {
  var User, bob, log, mary,
    __bind = function(fn, me){ return function(){ return fn.apply(me, arguments); }; };

  User = (function() {

    function User(name) {
      this.name = name;
      this.sayHi = __bind(this.sayHi, this);
    }

    User.prototype.sayHi = function() {
      return console.log("Hello " + this.name);
    };

    return User;

  })();

  bob = new User('bob');

  mary = new User('mary');

  log = function(callback) {
    console.log("about to execute callback...");
    callback();
    return console.log("...executed callback");
  };

  log(bob.sayHi);

  log(mary.sayHi);

}).call(this);
```

Output: **(source: bound.coffee)**

```
about to execute callback...
Hello bob
...executed callback
about to execute callback...
Hello mary
...executed callback
```

Amazing! One simple character did so much there. Let's compare the JavaScript output of our unbound and bound examples to better understand what that one character did to our code:

Example: **(source: unbound.js)**

```
(function() {
  var User, bob, log, mary;

  User = (function() {

    function User(name) {
      this.name = name;
    }

    User.prototype.sayHi = function() {
      return console.log("Hello " + this.name);
    };

    return User;

  })();

  bob = new User('bob');

  mary = new User('mary');

  log = function(callback) {
    console.log("about to execute callback...");
    callback();
    return console.log("...executed callback");
  };

  log(bob.sayHi);

  log(mary.sayHi);
}).call(this);
```

Example: **(source: bound.js)**

```
(function() {
  var User, bob, log, mary,
    __bind = function(fn, me){ return function(){ return fn.apply(me, arguments); }; };

  User = (function() {

    function User(name) {
```

```
      this.name = name;
      this.sayHi = __bind(this.sayHi, this);
    }

    User.prototype.sayHi = function() {
      return console.log("Hello " + this.name);
    };

    return User;

  })();

  bob = new User('bob');

  mary = new User('mary');

  log = function(callback) {
    console.log("about to execute callback...");
    callback();
    return console.log("...executed callback");
  };

  log(bob.sayHi);

  log(mary.sayHi);

}).call(this);
```

I will explain some of what is going on here, but if you don't understand what the `apply` function does, I suggest reading up on it in a JavaScript book. There are two differences between the two JavaScript files. The first is the existence of the `__bind` function found in our => example. This function accepts two parameters, the first being the function that you would like to bind, and the second being the context to which you would like to bind the function. The `__bind` will return a new function that will call the original function using `apply` and passing in the context you provided.

The next difference is in the constructor for the `User` class. We are redefining the `sayHi` function by calling `__bind` and passing in the original definition of `sayHi` and the context of the class instance we are in.

If all that just confused you, don't worry—you are not alone. Context and binding are very confusing subjects in JavaScript. If you don't understand it, I recommend two things: First, get a good JavaScript book, and second, read "Understanding JavaScript Function Invocation and 'this.'"[5] Yehuda does a great job explaining it all in a couple-page blog post.

If you do understand the JavaScript that is going on here, you are probably smiling right now, knowing that you don't have to deal with troublesome binding anymore. You can use => and your life will instantly be better. You'll see this in action in Chapter 11, "Example: Todo List Part 2 (Client-side w/ jQuery)."

Wrapping Up

Well, wasn't that fun? Classes in CoffeeScript are, for me at least, one of the biggest selling points of the language. I hope this chapter helped to sell you on them.

We covered a lot in this chapter. We looked at what a class is in CoffeeScript and how to define the most basic class possible.

Next, we looked at the "special" `constructor` function and talked a lot about scope in our classes.

We talked about how to extend classes in CoffeeScript using the `extends` keyword. We also learned how `super` can help us extend the original functionality of a `super` class's function in a subclass.

After that, we talked in depth about class-level functions and prototype functions. We also learned about the trouble `super` can cause at the class level if we're not careful.

We ended the chapter by looking at the rather complex, but insanely powerful, concept of bound functions using =>, also known as the fat arrow.

At this point you have learned pretty much all there is to learn about CoffeeScript. Congratulations! You are ready to leave the temple. This ends Part I of this book, "Core CoffeeScript." Part II, "CoffeeScript in Practice," will take all that we've learned from Part I and put it into practice using a few popular JavaScript libraries.

Notes

1. http://en.wikipedia.org/wiki/Class_(computer_programming)
2. http://en.wikipedia.org/wiki/DRY
3. http://en.wikipedia.org/wiki/Inheritance_(computer_science)
4. http://en.wikipedia.org/wiki/Asynchronous_I/O
5. http://yehudakatz.com/2011/08/11/understanding-javascript-function-invocation-and-this/

Part II

CoffeeScript in Practice

In this half of the book, we're going to take all that great CoffeeScript knowledge you've learned and put it into practical use. This will help reinforce what you've learned, and hopefully you'll pick up a few tips and tricks along the way. We'll do this using some of the more popular tools that are commonly used with CoffeeScript.

We'll build Cakefiles so we can run common tasks in our applications. We'll see how easy it is to test our CoffeeScript using CoffeeScript with the Jasmine test framework. Then we'll take a quick tour of Node.js and build a small application server to compile CoffeeScript as it's requested.

Finally, we're going to build a full application, the canonical "todo" application. We'll build the todo application over three chapters. First, we'll build the backend application needed to serve up our todos and persist them. Second, we'll build the front end of the application using the popular library jQuery. Third, we'll replace our handcrafted jQuery[1] code with the Backbone.js[2] framework. We're going to use some fun libraries with this application: jQuery, Backbone.js, Mongoose[3], Express[4], and, of course, CoffeeScript.

As we look at these different technologies and build our application and examples, we're not going to do a deep dive into these libraries. Instead, we'll touch on the highlights and those parts that are necessary to the job at hand. So, with all that said, this is the fun part of the book! Let's go!

Notes

1. http://jquery.com
2. http://documentcloud.github.com/backbone/
3. http://mongoosejs.com/
4. http://expressjs.com/

7

Cake and Cakefiles

CoffeeScript offers a simple build tool, called Cake, that is very similar in nature to Ruby's Rake[1] tool. Cake enables you to define simple tasks to help with your CoffeeScript projects. Perhaps you need a task to run your tests or a task to build your files. Cake lets you define those tasks easily in a file called a Cakefile.

In this chapter you'll learn how to define and execute Cake tasks, and of course, we'll be doing it all using CoffeeScript.

> **Tip**
>
> "Wait a minute, how do we install Cake?" You don't have to! When you installed CoffeeScript, the installer also installed Cake and its command-line tool, aptly named `cake`. You don't have to do anything extra to get access to this tool.

Getting Started

Before we write our first Cake task, it's important that we understand a few things about how Cake works. The first thing we need to know about Cake is that all tasks must live in a file named Cakefile and that this file must live in the directory in which you want to run your Cake tasks. Typically, this is the root directory of your project.

The only other thing you need to know about Cake and Cakefiles is that the Cakefile must be written in CoffeeScript. Cakefiles also have a few special functions already available to help you write your tasks. We'll see those in action as we build some Cake tasks.

Creating Cake Tasks

Let's build our first Cake task—a simple "hello world" task:

Example: **(source: example1/Cakefile)**

```
task "greet", "Say hi to the nice people", ->
  console.log "Hello, World!"
```

Example: **(source: example1/Cakefile.js)**

```
(function() {

  task("greet", "Say hi to the nice people", function() {
    return console.log("Hello, World!");
  });

}).call(this);
```

> **Tip**
>
> Although you will never see the JavaScript that is generated under the covers for Cakefiles, I decided to still include its output in this chapter to better help you further grasp what your CoffeeScript is doing.

To define our Cake task, we have to call the `task` function that gets automatically added to every Cakefile. The first argument is the name of the task; this is what we will use on the command line to execute the task. The second argument, which is optional, is a description of the task. If supplied, the description will appear when we print out a list of tasks that are available to us. The last argument we pass into the `task` function is a function that will be executed when we execute the task. This function is where the heavy lifting of our task is done.

To print out which tasks are available, we can use the `cake` command-line tool:

```
> cake
```

If we were to run that against our Cakefile, we would get the following output:

Output: **(source: example1/Cakefile)**

```
Cakefile defines the following tasks:

cake greet                # Say hi to the nice people
```

As you can see in the output, we see the name of the task we defined, preceded with the `cake` command, as well as the description we gave to the task.

> **Tip**
>
> Being able to get a list of available tasks is incredibly useful if you start requiring libraries that may have their own built-in Cake tasks.

Running Cake Tasks

Now that we've created our first task, how do we run it? Easy. When I ran the `cake` command against our example, it told us to run our task. Simply type in `cake` followed by the name of the task you would like to run, like this:

```
> cake greet
```

That will run our `greet` Cake task.

Output:

```
Hello, World!
```

Using Options

We have our first task written, and we know how to execute it, but what if we want to pass some arguments into it? For example, what if we want our `greet` task to accept an option so we can customize who we greet? Let's look at how Cake lets us do that.

The first step in being able to pass options to our tasks is to define the option. We do this using the special `option` function that Cake gives us. This function takes three arguments. The first argument is the "short" form of the option, the second argument is the "long" form of the option, and the final argument is a simple description of what the option does. Let's take a look at our `greet` task again, and this time let's define an option so we can customize the greeting.

> **Tip**
>
> When I talk about the "long" or "short" form of an option, I really am talking about how much typing the user has to do. For example, `-n` is a short option and `--name` is a long option.

Example: **(source: example2/Cakefile)**

```
option '-n', '--name [NAME]', 'name you want to greet'
task "greet", "Say hi to someone", (options)->
  message = "Hello, "
  if options.name?
    message += options.name
```

```
  else
    message += "World"
  console.log message
```

Example: **(source: example2/Cakefile.js)**

```
(function() {

  option('-n', '--name [NAME]', 'name you want to greet');

  task("greet", "Say hi to someone", function(options) {
    var message;
    message = "Hello, ";
    if (options.name != null) {
      message += options.name;
    } else {
      message += "World";
    }
    return console.log(message);
  });

}).call(this);
```

As you can see, before our task definition we called the `option` function and passed it the three arguments it expects. The first argument is `-n`, the short form of the option. The second is `--name`, the long form of the option. Notice that in the example, as part of the long form option, I have also put `[NAME]`, which tells Cake that you are expecting a value there. If you do not put something like `[NAME]`, Cake will raise an error if you try to pass in a value with the option, the last argument being the description.

> **Tip**
>
> Although all three arguments are required for the `option` function, only the last two arguments are truly necessary. You have to provide both the long form option as well as the description, but the short form of the option is not required. If you don't want to have a short form for the option, either pass in an empty string or `null` as the first parameter.

Now when we run the `cake` command to see the list of available tasks, we should see this:

Output: **(source: example2/Cakefile)**

```
Cakefile defines the following tasks:

cake greet                # Say hi to someone

  -n, --name         name you want to greet
```

At the bottom of the output we can see the list of available options for the tasks.

> **Tip**
>
> I want to point out what I feel to be a shortcoming of Cake options. Options are not defined for a specific task; instead, they are available for all tasks. If, in addition to our `greet` task, we were to have a second task, both tasks would accept the `name` option we defined. Although this isn't the end of the world, it does mean that some care does need to be taken when naming the options and providing their descriptions.

If we look at our `greet` task again, we can see that we are passing an object, `options`, into the function that will be executed when the task is executed:

Example: **(source: example2/Cakefile)**

```
option '-n', '--name [NAME]', 'name you want to greet'
task "greet", "Say hi to someone", (options)->
  message = "Hello, "
  if options.name?
    message += options.name
  else
    message += "World"
  console.log message
```

Example: **(source: example2/Cakefile.js)**

```
(function() {

  option('-n', '--name [NAME]', 'name you want to greet');

  task("greet", "Say hi to someone", function(options) {
    var message;
    message = "Hello, ";
    if (options.name != null) {
      message += options.name;
    } else {
      message += "World";
    }
    return console.log(message);
  });

}).call(this);
```

With the `options` object, we can determine if someone has called the task with the `name` option. If the task is run with the `name` option, we will greet that name; if not, we will use a generic greeting.

We can run our greet task with the name option like this:

```
> cake -n Mark greet
```

Output: **(source: example2a/Cakefile)**

```
Hello, Mark
```

If you want an option to be required, you would have to do that manually in the task definition itself by checking the existence of the option and throwing an error if it doesn't exist:

Example: **(source: example2a/Cakefile)**

```
option '-n', '--name [NAME]', 'name you want to greet'
task "greet", "Say hi to someone", (options)->
  throw new Error("[NAME] is required") unless options.name?
  console.log "Hello, #{options.name}"
```

Example: **(source: example2a/Cakefile.js)**

```
(function() {

  option('-n', '--name [NAME]', 'name you want to greet');

  task("greet", "Say hi to someone", function(options) {
    if (options.name == null) throw new Error("[NAME] is required");
    return console.log("Hello, " + options.name);
  });

}).call(this);
```

Output: **(source: example2a/Cakefile)**

```
node.js:201
        throw e; // process.nextTick error, or 'error' event on first tick
              ^

Error: [NAME] is required
    at Object.action (.../cake/example2a/Cakefile:6:37)
    at /usr/local/lib/node_modules/coffee-script/lib/coffee-script/cake.js:39:26
    at Object.run (/usr/local/lib/node_modules/coffee-script/lib/coffee-script/
➥cake.js:62:21)
    at Object.<anonymous> (/usr/local/lib/node_modules/coffee-script/bin/cake:7:38)
    at Module._compile (module.js:432:26)
    at Object..js (module.js:450:10)
    at Module.load (module.js:351:31)
    at Function._load (module.js:310:12)
    at Array.0 (module.js:470:10)
    at EventEmitter._tickCallback (node.js:192:40)
```

> **Tip**
>
> When running a Cake task with options, it is important to note that all options must be placed *before* the name of the task. If the options are placed after the task, you will be greeted with a rather unfriendly error. To me this seems backward. I would prefer `cake greet -n Mark`, but, unfortunately, at the time of writing that's not possible.

Invoking Other Tasks

There will come a time when you want to execute other tasks from inside another task. Here's an example: Two common tasks you might have in a project would be a task to clean up your build directories and another task to compile and build your project. Let's write these two tasks:

Example: **(source: example3/Cakefile)**

```
task "clean", "Clean up build directories", ->
  console.log "cleaning up..."

task "build", "Build the project files", ->
  console.log "building..."
```

Example: **(source: example3/Cakefile.js)**

```
(function() {

  task("clean", "Clean up build directories", function() {
    return console.log("cleaning up...");
  });

  task("build", "Build the project files", function() {
    return console.log("building...");
  });

}).call(this);
```

Output: **(source: example3/Cakefile)**

```
Cakefile defines the following tasks:

cake clean                # Clean up build directories
cake build                # Build the project files
```

After using these tasks for a while, you realize that you are always running the `clean` task and then the `build` task. You can run both tasks with one command, like this:

```
> cake clean build
```

That will run both tasks for you. But what if want to have a third task, `package`, that will package up your project for you? Before you can neatly package up your project, you want to first make sure you build it—and before you build it, you want to make sure that the build directories are clean. You could do it like this:

```
> cake clean build package
```

The problem is that this approach is error prone. What if you forget to call the `build` or `clean` tasks first? What happens? Fortunately, Cake lets us invoke other tasks from inside a task. To do that, we can call the `invoke` function that Cake provides for us and give it the name of the task we want to call:

Example: **(source: example4/Cakefile)**

```
task "clean", "Clean up build directories", ->
  console.log "cleaning up..."

task "build", "Build the project files", ->
  console.log "building..."

task "package", "Clean, build, and package the project", ->
  invoke "clean"
  invoke "build"
  console.log "packaging..."
```

Example: **(source: example4/Cakefile.js)**

```
(function() {

  task("clean", "Clean up build directories", function() {
    return console.log("cleaning up...");
  });

  task("build", "Build the project files", function() {
    return console.log("building...");
  });

  task("package", "Clean, build, and package the project", function() {
    invoke("clean");
    invoke("build");
    return console.log("packaging...");
  });

}).call(this);
```

Output: **(source: example4/Cakefile)**

```
Cakefile defines the following tasks:

cake clean                # Clean up build directories
cake build                # Build the project files
cake package              # Clean, build, and package the project
```

Now we can call the `package` task and see that both the `clean` and `build` tasks are also being executed:

```
> cake package
```

Output: **(source: example4/Cakefile)**

```
cleaning up...
building...
packaging...
```

> **Tip**
>
> It's important to note that when invoking other tasks, they will be run asynchronously. So in our example, there is no guarantee that the `clean` task will be finished before the `build` task is run. This could potentially cause issues, so be careful. The same is true of executing them by chaining them to a single `cake` command on the command line. Caveat emptor.

Wrapping Up

In this chapter we dug through the build tool that ships with CoffeeScript, called Cake. You learned how to define new tasks and see which tasks are available. You saw how to execute tasks, give them options, and run multiple tasks at once. You might feel as though you didn't really learn much about writing useful Cake tasks. The reason is that this is all that Cake offers. It is up to you to fill those tasks with what you need. The Node.js[2] project, which I talk about in Chapter 9, "Intro to Node.js," is a great place to start when looking for useful modules you can use to read and write files and directories, compile CoffeeScript files, make HTTP requests, and more. Other chapters will include Cakefiles to do things such as run tests, so be on the lookout for those examples.

Although Cake is a good tool, and it's nice to have it automatically installed with CoffeeScript, I do find it a bit too weak with too many awkward idiosyncrasies for it to be useful for most tasks I want to write. When combined with modules from Node[3] and other available modules, it can be quite powerful, but I still find myself falling back to my Ruby roots and using Rake because it's much more polished than Cake.

However, I highly encourage you to give it a shot. It might be exactly the right tool for you, especially if you're limited in what languages you can use and have installed; then it's a no-brainer.

Notes

1. https://github.com/jimweirich/rake
2. http://nodejs.org/
3. http://nodejs.org/

8

Testing with Jasmine

To me there is no greater sin than writing code that doesn't have tests. It is my belief that testing is not an option.[1] Testing is required. I feel so strongly in that statement that I practice what is known as TDD.[2] TDD, or test-driven development, is a philosophy of writing code that states you should always write your tests first and your code last. By practicing TDD you can sleep well at night, knowing that your code is well tested and that should anything crop up, you can quickly and easily fix it with the comfort and knowledge that you haven't broken anything else.

The art of TDD can be daunting; a lot of people don't know where to begin. If you need some guidance on how to become a test-driven developer, might I recommend a little blog post written by yours truly, titled "How to Become a Test-driven Developer."[3]

In this chapter I want to take a quick look at what I consider to be one of the best testing tools out there for testing JavaScript applications—Jasmine.[4]

> **Tip**
>
> Jasmine isn't the only testing tool for JavaScript; in fact, there are quite a few. I think Jasmine is one of the nicest ones around because it emulates my favorite Ruby testing framework, RSpec.[5] Other JavaScript testing frameworks to check out include QUnit,[6] JsTestDriver,[7] and YUI Test.[8]

I won't be covering Jasmine in great detail here. You can find a number of great articles and videos on the Internet covering Jasmine in more detail. Instead, I want to show you how to use Jasmine with CoffeeScript and to give you a feel for what it can do.

Installing Jasmine

Typically, as you may remember from the beginning of this book, I don't like to cover installation of tools in a book. The reason is pretty obvious—the instructions tend to be out of date by the time I finish typing, let alone by the time the book goes to print. The same is true here.

With that out of the way, I will point out what I consider to be the best way to install and set up Jasmine with CoffeeScript support. That would be to use the jasmine-headless-webkit[9] Ruby gem. Because this is a Ruby gem it requires Ruby to be installed. It also features a few other dependencies. The link in the footnote has detailed instructions on how to get it set up.

There are ways of setting up Jasmine that aren't as tricky. However, they don't have native CoffeeScript support and require all sorts of precompilation of both your source files and your tests, and let's be honest, who wants to deal with all of that?

If you don't want to use jasmine-headless-webkit and instead use another version of Jasmine, that's fine. For this chapter we will be using jasmine-headless-webkit, so I would recommend using that if you plan to follow along.

Setting Up Jasmine

I'm going to assume that you have installed Jasmine and are ready to go. So let's get started.

In this chapter we are going to build a simple calculator project. It will do the basic stuff that calculators do: add, subtract, multiply, and divide. Create a new folder for the project. Inside the project folder run the following command to set up Jasmine:

```
> jasmine init
```

When you do that, Jasmine should create a bunch of new files and folders in the project directory that look something like this:

```
public/
  javascripts/
    Player.js
    Song.js
Rakefile
spec/
  javascripts/
    helpers/
      SpecHelper.js
    PlayerSpec.js
  support/
    jasmine.yml
    jasmine_config.rb
    jasmine_runner.rb
```

Jasmine throws a few example files in there to give us a feeling for how Jasmine works and to help us make sure that it has been set up and configured correctly. Let's test that now:

```
> jasmine-headless-webkit -c
```

With any luck you should see output similar to the following:

```
Running Jasmine specs...
.....
PASS: 5 tests, 0 failures, 0.009 secs.
```

Great! We now have Jasmine up and running. Things look good. Well, everything except that awful command we have to execute on the command line whenever we want to run our tests. Let's use what we learned in Chapter 7, "Cake and Cakefiles," and write up a quick Cake task to help keep things simple.

First, I'll show you the Cakefile and then I'll explain it.

Example: **(source: calc.1/Cakefile)**

```
exec = require('child_process').exec

task "test", (options) =>
  exec "jasmine-headless-webkit -c", (error, stdout, stderr)->
    console.log stdout
```

Example: **(source: calc.1/Cakefile.js)**

```
(function() {
  var exec,
    _this = this;

  exec = require('child_process').exec;

  task("test", function(options) {
    return exec("jasmine-headless-webkit -c", function(error, stdout, stderr) {
      return console.log(stdout);
    });
  });

}).call(this);
```

Output: **(source: calc.1/Cakefile)**

```
Cakefile defines the following tasks:

cake test
```

This is definitely not the most complex Cakefile or Cake task you'll ever see, but it does deserve a bit of explaining. The real magic of this Cake task is happening in the first line. In this line we import the `child_process` module from the Node.js[10] toolset. Don't worry if you don't understand what it's doing or how it works; we'll cover importing modules a bit more in Chapter 9, "Intro to Node.js."

What we get with the `child_process` module, in particular, is the `exec` function. The `exec` function lets us send commands to the console and then capture the output of that command when it finishes, which is exactly what we're doing with our Cake task.

We've created a Cake task called `test` that sends our command, `jasmine-headless-webkit -c`, to the command line, where the tests are run. When the tests have finished, our callback function is executed, and the results of the tests print out to the console.

Now if you type the following in the console:

```
> cake test
```

you should see the results of the tests, just like we did earlier.

With the command line cleaned up a bit, let's do some final configuration of our project before we dive into writing some tests.

First, we'll clean up the project a bit and get rid of all those example files that were generated for us that we don't want. You should delete files and directories until your project directory looks like this:

```
src/
Rakefile
spec/
  javascripts/
    helpers/
  support/
    jasmine.yml
    jasmine_config.rb
    jasmine_runner.rb
```

Okay, we are almost there. The last thing we need to do is configure the `spec/javascripts/support/jasmine.yml` file to give it the specifics of our project:

Example: **(source: calc.2/spec/javascripts/support/jasmine.yml)**

```
src_files:
  - "**/*.coffee"

helpers:
    - "helpers/**/*.coffee"

spec_files:
  - /**/*_spec.coffee
```

```
src_dir: "src"

spec_dir: spec/javascripts
```

Now we are finally ready to start looking at Jasmine code!

Introduction to Jasmine

So what does a Jasmine test look like? Let's build a simple one and you'll see.

In our `spec` directory, let's create a new file called `calculator_spec.coffee`. This file is where we will build all the tests, or specs as they're sometimes known, for our calculator. Let's first see what our simple test will look at, and then we'll dissect it to understand better what it's doing.

Example: **(source: calc.3/spec/javascripts/calculator_spec.coffee)**

```
describe "Calculator", ->

  it "does something", ->
    expect(1 + 1).toEqual 2
    expect(1 + 1).not.toEqual 3
```

Example: **(source: calc.3/spec/javascripts/calculator_spec.js)**

```
(function() {

  describe("Calculator", function() {
    return it("does something", function() {
      expect(1 + 1).toEqual(2);
      return expect(1 + 1).not.toEqual(3);
    });
  });

}).call(this);
```

First, we need to create what is called a "describe" block. This is where we tell Jasmine what the "noun" is that we are going to be testing. We usually describe classes or functions. In this case we want to describe the `Calculator` class we're going to build. The first argument to the `describe` function is a string that represents the noun "Calculator." The second argument is going to be a function that will contain all the tests associated with that noun.

Inside the callback function we give to the `describe` function we can define "it" blocks. An "it" block, which is just a function, is similar to the "describe" function, or block, in that it takes two arguments. The first argument is a string that represents what we plan on testing now. In this short example we want to test that the "Calculator" "does something." The second argument is a function that contains the assertions to prove what it is we are testing.

In our "does something" test, we are asserting that `1 + 1` equals `2`. We are also rather triumphantly asserting that `1 + 1` does not equal `3`. We did these tests using what are called `matchers`; in this case we used the `toEqual` matcher. Matchers have one simple rule: if the matcher returns `true` the test passes; otherwise, the test fails.

So what does the `expect` function do and why do we need it? The `expect` function takes as its argument the statement you want to test, so for us it would be `1 + 1`, and returns a special object that has the matcher functions on it. In a nutshell, it's there to make Jasmine's life a little easier. It also helps the readability of your tests a bit.

> **Tip**
>
> Jasmine ships with a handful of matchers that you can use to test almost anything. You can find a list of these matchers on the documentation[11] site for Jasmine.

Unit Testing

Now that we have a basic understanding of how to write a Jasmine test, let's flesh out what the tests are going to look like for our `Calculator` class. We'll start by removing our example test and adding four `describe` blocks to test addition, subtraction, multiplication, and division:

Example: **(source: calc.4/spec/javascripts/calculator_spec.coffee)**

```
describe "Calculator", ->

  describe "#add", ->

    it "adds two numbers", ->

  describe "#subtract", ->

    it "subtracts two numbers", ->

  describe "#multiply", ->

    it "multiplies two numbers", ->

  describe "#divide", ->

    it "divides two numbers", ->
```

Example: **(source: calc.4/spec/javascripts/calculator_spec.js)**

```
(function() {

  describe("Calculator", function() {
    describe("#add", function() {
      return it("adds two numbers", function() {});
    });
    describe("#subtract", function() {
      return it("subtracts two numbers", function() {});
    });
    describe("#multiply", function() {
      return it("multiplies two numbers", function() {});
    });
    return describe("#divide", function() {
      return it("divides two numbers", function() {});
    });
  });

}).call(this);
```

After looking at that code, you are probably wondering why there are multiple "describe" blocks under our initial "describe." We do that because we are going to be writing tests for each of the four functions we're going to have on our `Calculator` class. Each of these functions is a noun that we are going to be testing. Below each of those nouns are the "it" blocks that state what we will be testing.

We can run our tests with this:

```
> cake test
```

The output of our tests should look like this:

```
Running Jasmine specs...
....
PASS: 4 tests, 0 failures, 0.02 secs.
```

> **Tip**
>
> There is a # before each of the function names in our test because that is a common testing style that indicates that function is an instance-level function. If we were to describe class-level functions, we would preface the function name with `.` instead of #.

Our tests all pass because there is nothing inside of the "it" blocks. Let's flesh them all out a bit:

Example: **(source: calc.5/spec/javascripts/calculator_spec.coffee)**

```
describe "Calculator", ->

  describe "#add", ->

    it "adds two numbers", ->
      calculator = new Calculator()
      expect(calculator.add(1, 1)).toEqual 2

  describe "#subtract", ->

    it "subtracts two numbers", ->
      calculator = new Calculator()
      expect(calculator.subtract(10, 1)).toEqual 9

  describe "#multiply", ->

    it "multiplies two numbers", ->
      calculator = new Calculator()
      expect(calculator.multiply(5, 4)).toEqual 20

  describe "#divide", ->

    it "divides two numbers", ->
      calculator = new Calculator()
      expect(calculator.divide(20, 5)).toEqual 4
```

Example: **(source: calc.5/spec/javascripts/calculator_spec.js)**

```
(function() {

  describe("Calculator", function() {
    describe("#add", function() {
      return it("adds two numbers", function() {
        var calculator;
        calculator = new Calculator();
        return expect(calculator.add(1, 1)).toEqual(2);
      });
    });
    describe("#subtract", function() {
      return it("subtracts two numbers", function() {
        var calculator;
        calculator = new Calculator();
        return expect(calculator.subtract(10, 1)).toEqual(9);
      });
    });
```

```
    describe("#multiply", function() {
      return it("multiplies two numbers", function() {
        var calculator;
        calculator = new Calculator();
        return expect(calculator.multiply(5, 4)).toEqual(20);
      });
    });
    return describe("#divide", function() {
      return it("divides two numbers", function() {
        var calculator;
        calculator = new Calculator();
        return expect(calculator.divide(20, 5)).toEqual(4);
      });
    });
  });

}).call(this);
```

Now we're starting to get somewhere. We have nice looking tests that describe and test the four functions we're going to have on our `Calculator` class, so what happens if we run the tests?

```
Running Jasmine specs...
FFFF

Calculator #add adds two numbers.
➥(../jasmine/calc.5/spec/javascripts/calculator_spec.coffee:5)
  ReferenceError: Can't find variable: Calculator in ../jasmine/calc.5/spec/
➥ javascripts/calculator_spec.coffee (line ~6)


Calculator #subtract subtracts two numbers.
➥ (../jasmine/calc.5/spec/javascripts/calculator_spec.coffee:11)
  ReferenceError: Can't find variable: Calculator in ../jasmine/calc.5/spec/
➥ javascripts/calculator_spec.coffee (line ~13)


Calculator #multiply multiplies two numbers.
➥ (../jasmine/calc.5/spec/javascripts/calculator_spec.coffee:17)
  ReferenceError: Can't find variable: Calculator in ../jasmine/calc.5/spec/
➥ javascripts/calculator_spec.coffee (line ~20)


Calculator #divide divides two numbers.
➥ (../jasmine/calc.5/spec/javascripts/calculator_spec.coffee:23)
  ReferenceError: Can't find variable: Calculator in ../jasmine/calc.5/spec/
➥ javascripts/calculator_spec.coffee (line ~27)

FAIL: 4 tests, 4 failures, 0.017 secs.
```

All tests are now failing, and they're failing for a very good reason—we haven't written our `Calculator` class yet! So let's do that; it's a pretty simple class:

Example: **(source: calc.6/src/calculator.coffee)**

```
class @Calculator

  add: (a, b) ->
    a + b

  subtract: (a, b) ->
    a - b

  multiply: (a, b) ->
    a * b

  divide: (a, b) ->
    a / b
```

Example: **(source: calc.6/src/calculator.js)**

```
(function() {

  this.Calculator = (function() {

    function Calculator() {}

    Calculator.prototype.add = function(a, b) {
      return a + b;
    };

    Calculator.prototype.subtract = function(a, b) {
      return a - b;
    };

    Calculator.prototype.multiply = function(a, b) {
      return a * b;
    };

    Calculator.prototype.divide = function(a, b) {
      return a / b;
    };

    return Calculator;

  })();

}).call(this);
```

Now when we run our tests again we should see them all passing:

```
Running Jasmine specs...
....
PASS: 4 tests, 0 failures, 0.021 secs.
```

Before and After

Our tests look pretty good now, but a lot of duplication occurs in each test. In each test we are creating a new instance of our `Calculator` class. Jasmine will help us clean that up a bit using the `beforeEach` function.

> **Tip**
>
> As you might guess, there is also an `afterEach` function. The `afterEach` is great for resetting databases, files, or other fixture data back to where it was before the test was run.

Let's move the creation of an instance of the `Calculator` class to a `beforeEach` call. We do that by passing a function to the `beforeEach` function that will be called before each "it" block in the current "describe" block, as well as any subsequent "describe" blocks.

Example: **(source: calc.7/spec/javascripts/calculator_spec.coffee)**

```
describe "Calculator", ->

  beforeEach ->
    @calculator = new Calculator()

  describe "#add", ->

    it "adds two numbers", ->
      expect(@calculator.add(1, 1)).toEqual 2

  describe "#subtract", ->

    it "subtracts two numbers", ->
      expect(@calculator.subtract(10, 1)).toEqual 9

  describe "#multiply", ->

    it "multiplies two numbers", ->
      expect(@calculator.multiply(5, 4)).toEqual 20

  describe "#divide", ->

    it "divides two numbers", ->
      expect(@calculator.divide(20, 5)).toEqual 4
```

Example: **(source: calc.7/spec/javascripts/calculator_spec.js)**

```
(function() {

  describe("Calculator", function() {
    beforeEach(function() {
      return this.calculator = new Calculator();
    });
    describe("#add", function() {
      return it("adds two numbers", function() {
        return expect(this.calculator.add(1, 1)).toEqual(2);
      });
    });
    describe("#subtract", function() {
      return it("subtracts two numbers", function() {
        return expect(this.calculator.subtract(10, 1)).toEqual(9);
      });
    });
    describe("#multiply", function() {
      return it("multiplies two numbers", function() {
        return expect(this.calculator.multiply(5, 4)).toEqual(20);
      });
    });
    return describe("#divide", function() {
      return it("divides two numbers", function() {
        return expect(this.calculator.divide(20, 5)).toEqual(4);
      });
    });
  });

}).call(this);
```

> **Tip**
>
> The scope of `beforeEach` and `afterEach` calls can be a bit confusing. It helps to try to think of it a bit like a waterfall. The calls trickle down from the current "describe" block scope to all "describe" blocks that are nested below. It does this for as many levels of "describe" blocks there are.

When writing `beforeEach` functions, it's important to know that you can have as many as you want, and they can be at any level of your tests as you need. Let's see this in action with our `Calculator` class.

Let's add a flag to our `Calculator` that tells the calculator whether it should operate in scientific mode.

Example: **(source: calc.8/src/calculator.coffee)**

```
class @Calculator

  constructor: (@scientific = false)->

  add: (a, b) ->
    a + b

  subtract: (a, b) ->
    a - b

  multiply: (a, b) ->
    a * b

  divide: (a, b) ->
    a / b
```

Example: **(source: calc.8/src/calculator.js)**

```
(function() {

  this.Calculator = (function() {

    function Calculator(scientific) {
      this.scientific = scientific != null ? scientific : false;
    }

    Calculator.prototype.add = function(a, b) {
      return a + b;
    };

    Calculator.prototype.subtract = function(a, b) {
      return a - b;
    };

    Calculator.prototype.multiply = function(a, b) {
      return a * b;
    };

    Calculator.prototype.divide = function(a, b) {
      return a / b;
    };

    return Calculator;

  })();

}).call(this);
```

Next, let's add a test that asserts that its default state is not scientific mode:

Example: **(source: calc.8/spec/javascripts/calculator_spec.coffee)**

```
describe "Calculator", ->

  beforeEach ->
    @calculator = new Calculator()

  it "is not in scientific mode by default", ->
    expect(@calculator.scientific).toBeFalse()

  describe "#add", ->

    it "adds two numbers", ->
      expect(@calculator.add(1, 1)).toEqual 2

  describe "#subtract", ->

    it "subtracts two numbers", ->
      expect(@calculator.subtract(10, 1)).toEqual 9

  describe "#multiply", ->

    it "multiplies two numbers", ->
      expect(@calculator.multiply(5, 4)).toEqual 20

  describe "#divide", ->

    it "divides two numbers", ->
      expect(@calculator.divide(20, 5)).toEqual 4
```

Example: **(source: calc.8/spec/javascripts/calculator_spec.js)**

```
(function() {

  describe("Calculator", function() {
    beforeEach(function() {
      return this.calculator = new Calculator();
    });
    it("is not in scientific mode by default", function() {
      return expect(this.calculator.scientific).toBeFalse();
    });
    describe("#add", function() {
      return it("adds two numbers", function() {
        return expect(this.calculator.add(1, 1)).toEqual(2);
```

```
      });
    });
    describe("#subtract", function() {
      return it("subtracts two numbers", function() {
        return expect(this.calculator.subtract(10, 1)).toEqual(9);
      });
    });
    describe("#multiply", function() {
      return it("multiplies two numbers", function() {
        return expect(this.calculator.multiply(5, 4)).toEqual(20);
      });
    });
    return describe("#divide", function() {
      return it("divides two numbers", function() {
        return expect(this.calculator.divide(20, 5)).toEqual(4);
      });
    });
  });

}).call(this);

Running Jasmine specs...
....
PASS: 5 tests, 0 failures, 0.021 secs.
```

Now we'll write another "describe" block to describe our `Calculator` class when it's in scientific mode and we'll add a `beforeEach` call in that describe block to create a new `Calculator` that is in scientific mode. Let's also write a test to assert that when we tell it to be in scientific mode, it actually is:

Example: **(source: calc.9/spec/javascripts/calculator_spec.coffee)**

```
describe "Calculator", ->

  beforeEach ->
    @calculator = new Calculator()

  it "is not in scientific mode by default", ->
    expect(@calculator.scientific).toBeFalse()

  describe "scientific mode", ->

    beforeEach ->
      @calculator = new Calculator(true)
```

```
    it "is in scientific mode when set", ->
      expect(@calculator.scientific).toBeTruth()

  describe "#add", ->

    it "adds two numbers", ->
      expect(@calculator.add(1, 1)).toEqual 2

  describe "#subtract", ->

    it "subtracts two numbers", ->
      expect(@calculator.subtract(10, 1)).toEqual 9

  describe "#multiply", ->

    it "multiplies two numbers", ->
      expect(@calculator.multiply(5, 4)).toEqual 20

  describe "#divide", ->

    it "divides two numbers", ->
      expect(@calculator.divide(20, 5)).toEqual 4
```

Example: **(source: calc.9/spec/javascripts/calculator_spec.js)**

```
(function() {

  describe("Calculator", function() {
    beforeEach(function() {
      return this.calculator = new Calculator();
    });
    it("is not in scientific mode by default", function() {
      return expect(this.calculator.scientific).toBeFalse();
    });
    describe("scientific mode", function() {
      beforeEach(function() {
        return this.calculator = new Calculator(true);
      });
      return it("is in scientific mode when set", function() {
        return expect(this.calculator.scientific).toBeTruth();
      });
    });
    describe("#add", function() {
      return it("adds two numbers", function() {
        return expect(this.calculator.add(1, 1)).toEqual(2);
      });
    });
```

```
    describe("#subtract", function() {
      return it("subtracts two numbers", function() {
        return expect(this.calculator.subtract(10, 1)).toEqual(9);
      });
    });
    describe("#multiply", function() {
      return it("multiplies two numbers", function() {
        return expect(this.calculator.multiply(5, 4)).toEqual(20);
      });
    });
    return describe("#divide", function() {
      return it("divides two numbers", function() {
        return expect(this.calculator.divide(20, 5)).toEqual(4);
      });
    });
  });

}).call(this);

Running Jasmine specs...
......
PASS: 6 tests, 0 failures, 0.017 secs.
```

Custom Matchers

Before we wrap up the development of our `Calculator` class, we can clean up our tests a bit more by using a custom matcher to test whether the calculator in question is in scientific mode. Jasmine provides a nice, simple way of letting us define our own matchers.

In our `spec/javascripts/helpers` directory, let's create a file called `to_be_scientific.coffee`.

> **Tip**
>
> The names of the files in the `spec/javascripts/helpers` directory don't really matter, but I like to make sure they're fairly descriptive. Using the name of the matcher we're going to write in that file is a great way to easily find it later when you need to make changes to it.

Let's add the following to that file:

Example: **(source: calc.10/spec/javascripts/helpers/to_be_scientific.coffee)**

```
beforeEach ->
  @addMatchers
    toBeScientific: ->
      @actual.scientific is true
```

Example: **(source: calc.10/spec/javascripts/helpers/to_be_scientific.js)**

```
(function() {

  beforeEach(function() {
    return this.addMatchers({
      toBeScientific: function() {
        return this.actual.scientific === true;
      }
    });
  });

}).call(this);
```

> **Tip**
>
> Custom matchers don't need to be placed into their own files. You could define them all in one helper file. I like to write one per file. I find it makes my code base a littler cleaner and saner. You can also write one-off matchers in a "describe" block for a particular test should the whim strike you.

To write our custom matcher, the first thing we need to do is add a `beforeEach` call that will get called before every test in our entire test suite. Inside of that `beforeEach` call we want to call the built-in Jasmine function, `addMatchers`, that does just what its name says. It takes an object that contains the names of the matchers you want to add and the function that represents each of those custom matchers. It is important that the custom matcher returns either true or false as the result. Remember earlier in the chapter when I said that in Jasmine if an assertion returns `true` the test passes; otherwise, the test fails? This is where you define that behavior.

In our matcher, `toBeScientific`, we are going to assert whether the `Calculator` instance we are testing has the `scientific` flag set on it and return `true` or `false` based on that flag.

With our custom matcher in place, we can update our tests to use it like so:

Example: **(source: calc.10/spec/javascripts/calculator_spec.coffee)**

```
describe "Calculator", ->

  beforeEach ->
    @calculator = new Calculator()

  it "is not in scientific mode by default", ->
    expect(@calculator).not.toBeScientific()

  describe "scientific mode", ->
```

```
    beforeEach ->
      @calculator = new Calculator(true)

    it "is in scientific mode when set", ->
      expect(@calculator).toBeScientific()

  describe "#add", ->

    it "adds two numbers", ->
      expect(@calculator.add(1, 1)).toEqual 2

  describe "#subtract", ->

    it "subtracts two numbers", ->
      expect(@calculator.subtract(10, 1)).toEqual 9

  describe "#multiply", ->

    it "multiplies two numbers", ->
      expect(@calculator.multiply(5, 4)).toEqual 20

  describe "#divide", ->

    it "divides two numbers", ->
      expect(@calculator.divide(20, 5)).toEqual 4
```

Example: **(source: calc.10/spec/javascripts/calculator_spec.js)**

```
(function() {

  describe("Calculator", function() {
    beforeEach(function() {
      return this.calculator = new Calculator();
    });
    it("is not in scientific mode by default", function() {
      return expect(this.calculator).not.toBeScientific();
    });
    describe("scientific mode", function() {
      beforeEach(function() {
        return this.calculator = new Calculator(true);
      });
      return it("is in scientific mode when set", function() {
        return expect(this.calculator).toBeScientific();
      });
    });
    describe("#add", function() {
```

```
      return it("adds two numbers", function() {
        return expect(this.calculator.add(1, 1)).toEqual(2);
      });
    });
    describe("#subtract", function() {
      return it("subtracts two numbers", function() {
        return expect(this.calculator.subtract(10, 1)).toEqual(9);
      });
    });
    describe("#multiply", function() {
      return it("multiplies two numbers", function() {
        return expect(this.calculator.multiply(5, 4)).toEqual(20);
      });
    });
    return describe("#divide", function() {
      return it("divides two numbers", function() {
        return expect(this.calculator.divide(20, 5)).toEqual(4);
      });
    });
  });

}).call(this);
```

See how much cleaner that looks? Our custom matcher is pretty simple, but we could easily put a lot more logic in there to clean up several lines of code. For example, if our `Calculator` class had a GUI, we could test in our `toBeScientific` matcher that the `scientific` flag was set and the GUI keyboard had switched to a scientific keyboard instead of the standard one.

Wrapping Up

There you have it—a very quick and dirty whirlwind tour of the Jasmine test framework. In this chapter we talked a bit about why testing is important and how test-driven development can make your life a little bit nicer. I hope that I was able to show you that TDD is easy to do and can be worthwhile.

We talked briefly about a few of the ways to install Jasmine, as well as how to configure it for the way we want to work, in particular using Jasmine with CoffeeScript. After we had Jasmine set up and running, we looked at what makes up a Jasmine test.

Next we defined our tests for our `Calculator` class and saw them all fail because we had yet to write our implementation of the class itself. After we wrote the implementation, we saw our tests all pass.

Finally we did several iterations of our specs and learned how to use `beforeEach` hooks and how to write custom matchers that are more expressive for our code base.

I hope you enjoyed this quick tour of Jasmine. There are plenty of third-party libraries that can help you to write better tests, including ones that help you test your UI elements effectively. A quick search of GitHub[12] will help you find some great little libraries that inspire your tests.

One last thing before I end this chapter: I want you to promise me right here and now that you will write tests for *all* of your code, whether that code is written in CoffeeScript, JavaScript, Java, ColdFusion, or Cobalt. Hold up your hand and say the following oath:

"
```
I solemnly swear to test all of my code.
I will not test just part of my code, but rather all of it.
I understand that failure to test my code
will result in Mark finding me and beating me with my own shoes.
I do this, not just for me,
but for all developers who have to work with my code base.
I also pledge to make other developers take this pledge.
Should they refuse to take this pledge I will tell Mark
and he will beat them with their own shoes.
Viva La Tests!
```
"

Congratulations. Now go forth and test!

Notes

1. http://www.metabates.com/2010/07/01/testing-is-not-an-option/
2. http://en.wikipedia.org/wiki/Test-driven_development
3. http://www.metabates.com/2010/10/12/how-to-become-a-test-driven-developer/
4. http://pivotal.github.com/jasmine/
5. https://github.com/rspec/rspec
6. http://docs.jquery.com/QUnit
7. http://code.google.com/p/js-test-driver/
8. http://yuilibrary.com/yui/docs/test/
9. http://johnbintz.github.com/jasmine-headless-webkit/
10. http://nodejs.org
11. https://github.com/pivotal/jasmine/wiki/Matchers
12. http://github.com

9

Intro to Node.js

Over the past year or so, a platform written by Joyent[1] has been taking the web development world by storm. This platform is called Node.js,[2] commonly referred to as Node (and will be from here on).

> **Tip**
>
> If you don't believe that Node is taking the web development world by storm, just ask companies like LinkedIn,[3] who announced in 2011 that it had rewritten its API from Ruby on Rails[4] to Node. That's a pretty big endorsement.

So what is Node exactly, and why are we talking about it in a CoffeeScript book? In this chapter, you'll find out.

What Is Node.js?

Node is an implementation of server-side JavaScript that sits atop Google's V8[5] JavaScript engine. Node is part framework, runtime, and language. Because of that, people are sometimes confused about what exactly Node is and when and why they should use it.

Node's main goal in life is to help developers write evented, asynchronous applications. In Node every request is handled asynchronously, and almost all I/O is nonblocking. Because of this, a Node application is very efficient in terms of memory and can handle very large numbers of "concurrent" connections.

There are three reasons why we are covering Node.js in a book about CoffeeScript. First, because Node applications are written using JavaScript, we can write those same applications using CoffeeScript instead and enjoy all that CoffeeScript has to offer. Second, the `coffee` command we've been using throughout this book uses Node under the covers for some of its magic, so CoffeeScript and Node already enjoy a kinship. Third, Node ships with a package management system, NPM.[6] NPM lets developers package up and distribute bundles of code that can later be imported into other Node applications. These NPM modules are incredibly helpful even when not building a Node application; for example, by importing them into a Cakefile to help us perform certain tasks.

In this chapter we build a simple web server that will serve static files out of a directory. It will also compile any CoffeeScript assets in real-time and return the compiled JavaScript to the browser. Of course, we are going to write this server using CoffeeScript.

Installing Node

I think by now you probably know that I have a penchant for pushing you off to a vendor's site for installation instructions. So, to learn how to install Node on your platform of choice, I recommend that you check out Node's installation page, http://nodejs.org/#download. I will let you in on a little secret, if you've been following along with the code in this book and trying it out for yourself; there's a good chance you already have Node installed. Even if you do, this is a great chance to upgrade to the latest and greatest version.

With Node installed, let's give it a little spin. We can fire up a Node REPL like so:

```
> node
```

Then, inside the Node REPL, we can execute any JavaScript we'd like:

```
node> 1 + 1
```

In addition to the Node REPL we can also execute JavaScript files, much the same way we did CoffeeScript files. Take this JavaScript file for example:

Example: **(source: example.js)**

```
(function() {
  var sayHi;

  sayHi = function(name) {
    if (name == null) name = 'World';
    return console.log("Hello, " + name);
  };

  sayHi('Mark');

}).call(this);
```

We would run that file like this:

```
> node example.js
```

And we should get this output:

Output: **(source: example.js)**

```
Hello, Mark
```

Getting Started

Now that we have Node installed and we know how to run JavaScript using it, let's write a little "Hello, World" server using Node. I'll show you the code for the server and then we'll go over it in more detail.

Example: **(source: server.1/server.coffee)**

```
http = require('http')

port = 3000
ip = "127.0.0.1"

server = http.createServer (req, res) ->
  data = "Hello World!"
  res.writeHead 200,
    "Content-Type": "text/plain"
    "Content-Length": Buffer.byteLength(data, "utf-8")
  res.write(data, "utf-8")
  res.end()

server.listen(port, ip)

console.log "Server running at http://#{ip}:#{port}/"
```

Example: **(source: server.1/server.js)**

```
(function() {
  var http, ip, port, server;

  http = require('http');

  port = 3000;

  ip = "127.0.0.1";

  server = http.createServer(function(req, res) {
    var data;
    data = "Hello World!";
```

```
    res.writeHead(200, {
      "Content-Type": "text/plain",
      "Content-Length": Buffer.byteLength(data, "utf-8")
    });
    res.write(data, "utf-8");
    return res.end();
  });

  server.listen(port, ip);

  console.log("Server running at http://" + ip + ":" + port + "/");

}).call(this);
```

Before I explain our little server, let's first fire up the server to see what happens:

```
> coffee server.1/server.coffee
```

Now, if you navigate to `http://127.0.0.1:3000` you should be properly greeted.

So, let's start with the obvious question: Why did we run our file with the `coffee` command and not the `node` command we just learned about? The reason is that the `node` command does not know how to compile or execute CoffeeScript. If we were to try to run our CoffeeScript file using the `node` command, it would blow up in a most extraordinary fashion. Fortunately, the `coffee` command sits on top of Node, so we can achieve the desired results that way.

> **Tip**
>
> If we really wanted to, we could precompile our CoffeeScript file in JavaScript and then execute that using the `node` command, but why go through that extra step when we can use the `coffee` command?

Let's dissect our server and find out what exactly is making it tick.

The first thing we need to do is to import the `http` Node module. That will give us everything we need to both receive and handle HTTP requests. To do that we can use the `require` function that Node provides. Next, we create some variables to represent the port and the IP address we want to bind our server to.

Then we define the actual bulk of our server using the aptly named `createServer` function in the `http` module. We pass the `createServer` function a callback function that will be executed each time a new request comes in. The nice part of this is that the callback function we pass in *only* gets called when a request comes in; the rest of the time the server sits idle and uses very little resources. Let's skip over the callback function for just a minute and finish looking at the rest of the file. All that is left to do is to tell the server which port and IP address to listen on for requests.

Inside our callback function, we are expecting two arguments. The first argument represents the request and the last argument is the response we are going to send back. The request object, our `req` argument, is filled with a tremendous amount of useful data—the page requested, the browser type, the query string, and so on.

> **Tip**
>
> I recommend that you put a `console.log` statement in the callback function to print the request out to the screen and see exactly what data is in there. It's a quick and easy way to know what you have access to for each request.

When a request comes in to our server, our callback will be called with the corresponding request and an object we can use to handle the response. The first thing we want to do is define a variable named `data` to hold our response. In this case our response will be a simple "Hello World!"

Now that we know what we want to say, we can start writing that response back to the client. To do so we must first write our headers and our response code; for that we will use the `writeHead` function on the response. The first argument that `writeHead` takes is an HTTP status code. In this case `200` is appropriate because everything went well. The second argument is an object representing any HTTP headers we want to send back. In our case we want to send back two headers. The first header is `Content-Type`, which for this example is `text/plain` because we're not sending any binary data or HTML. The second header we need to send back is `Content-Length`. This header tells the client just how big, in bytes, our response will be. Node provides a nice little utility to do this: `Buffer.byteLength`. Simply pass in the data we want to know the byte length of, and it will take care of the rest.

With our status code and headers written out to the client, we can actually write our data back to the client using the `write` function.

With our data written to the client, we can finally call the `end` function, which does exactly what its name implies—it ends the response. With that we have built our first very simple Node server. Congratulations.

Streaming Responses

When writing a Node application, it's important to note that you are not limited to calling the `write` function only once in your response. You can call it as many times as you want before you call the `end` function. This is a great way to write streaming APIs for your application. Let's take a quick look at what this would look like.

We'll write a simple server that prints out the classic line from *The Shining*,[7] "All work and no play makes Jack a dull boy." Let's print that line out to the browser for 30 seconds and then stop.

Example: **(source: streaming/server.coffee)**

```
http = require('http')

port = 3000
ip = "127.0.0.1"

server = http.createServer (req, res) ->
  res.writeHead 200,
    "Content-Type": "text/plain"
  setInterval ->
    res.write("All work and no play makes Jack a dull boy. ")
  , 10
  setTimeout ->
    res.end()
  , 30000

server.listen(port, ip)

console.log "Server running at http://#{ip}:#{port}/"
```

Example: **(source: streaming/server.js)**

```
(function() {
  var http, ip, port, server;

  http = require('http');

  port = 3000;

  ip = "127.0.0.1";

  server = http.createServer(function(req, res) {
    res.writeHead(200, {
      "Content-Type": "text/plain"
    });
    setInterval(function() {
      return res.write("All work and no play makes Jack a dull boy. ");
    }, 10);
    return setTimeout(function() {
      return res.end();
    }, 30000);
  });

  server.listen(port, ip);

  console.log("Server running at http://" + ip + ":" + port + "/");
```

```
}).call(this);

> coffee streaming/server.coffee
```

If you navigate your browser to `http://127.0.0.1:3000`, you should see our creepy message being printed to the screen and then stopping after 30 seconds. If this was a nonstreaming application, we would be looking at a blank screen for 30 seconds wondering whether our application was working before we got hit with a huge response all of a sudden.

In our callback function we set up a `setInterval` loop to write our message out to the response every 10 milliseconds. Then we wrote a `setTimeout` block to end our response after 30 seconds.

All in all, it is pretty easy to set a streaming server using Node. If you want to see something really cool, open up multiple browser windows and navigate to our server. You'll see that Node easily serves up the streaming request to each of the browsers with no extra-special code handling.

Building a CoffeeScript Server

Let's build something that might be useful to us—an app server. Our spec for our server is going to be pretty simple. It's going to look at the requests that come in and then do one of three things. If the file requested is a JavaScript file, it is going to look in the `src` directory for the corresponding CoffeeScript file, compile that file into JavaScript, and return that. If the requested file or path is not JavaScript, the server will find the corresponding file in the `public` directory and serve up that file. Finally, if there is no matching CoffeeScript in the `src` directory or no matching file in the `public` directory, the server should respond with a simple `404` page.

We know what we want to build, but before we build it, you should know that the code we will build in this section is going to get a bit big, and we're going to be iterating over it. Because of this, I am not going to show you the compiled JavaScript until we have finished writing our server. Trust me, you will thank me for it. Now, let's get building.

Thinking ahead, I know that this is going to be too much code to go in a simple callback function. So let's put it all into a class and go from there. We'll write our callback function for our server as if we've coded the class that's going to do all the work, so we can get a feel for what we want that class to look like.

Example: **(source: server.2/server.coffee)**

```
http = require('http')

port = 3000
ip = "127.0.0.1"
```

```
server = http.createServer (req, res) ->
  app = new Application(req, res)
  app.process()

server.listen(port, ip)

console.log "Server running at http://#{ip}:#{port}/"
```

> **Tip**
>
> By not putting all our code in the callback function, we are also getting another great benefit from it: easier testing. If we create a couple of classes to process our requests, we can easily use what we learned in Chapter 8, "Testing with Jasmine," to test each of the files to make sure they're doing just what we want them to, and we don't need to run a server in the background to test them.

If we tried to run that code, it wouldn't run because we don't actually have an `Application` class, so let's stub out the class based off of what we just wrote:

Example: **(source: server.3/server.coffee)**

```
http = require('http')

class Application

  constructor: (@req, @res) ->

  process: ->


port = 3000
ip = "127.0.0.1"

server = http.createServer (req, res) ->
  app = new Application(req, res)
  app.process()

server.listen(port, ip)

console.log "Server running at http://#{ip}:#{port}/"
```

That is a nice stub of an `Application` class. Now let's put a little more flesh on its bones.

Example: **(source: server.4/server.coffee)**

```
http = require('http')
url = require('url')

class Application

  constructor: (@req, @res) ->
    @pathInfo = url.parse(@req.url, true)

  process: ->
    if /^\/javascripts\//.test @pathInfo.pathname
      new JavaScriptProcessor(@req, @res, @pathInfo).process()
    else
      new PublicProcessor(@req, @res, @pathInfo).process()

port = 3000
ip = "127.0.0.1"

server = http.createServer (req, res) ->
  app = new Application(req, res)
  app.process()

server.listen(port, ip)

console.log "Server running at http://#{ip}:#{port}/"
```

First we need to import the `url` Node module. This module provides a few helper functions, which we can use to split up the requested path into its various components. In the constructor of the `Application` class we are doing just that.

In our `process` function, things really start to get interesting. We first need to detect what kind of a request it is and then handle it accordingly. We know from our spec that we are going to handle two types of requests: JavaScript files and everything else. So let's write two classes, one that will handle all our JavaScript files and another to handle the files from the `public` directory. A very simple regular expression test on the path will tell us which kind of request we are dealing with. We can then call the correct class to handle that request type.

> **Tip**
>
> It's worth noting that if this was a real application, I would highly recommend splitting these class definitions into their own separate files, but for right now, let's just make life easier.

Next, let's stub out the functions we are going to need on our different processors. We can probably guess that both our `JavascriptProcessor` and our `PublicProcessor` class are going to have some common functionality, and because of that we should probably create a parent class for them both to extend to get that common functionality. So with that in mind let's stub out the parent class, `Processor`, as well as `JavascriptProcessor` and `PublicProcessor`:

Example: **(source: server.5/server.coffee)**

```
http = require('http')
url = require('url')

class Application

  constructor: (@req, @res) ->
    @pathInfo = url.parse(@req.url, true)

  process: ->
    if /^\/javascripts\//.test @pathInfo.pathname
      new JavaScriptProcessor(@req, @res, @pathInfo).process()
    else
      new PublicProcessor(@req, @res, @pathInfo).process()

class Processor

  constructor: (@req, @res, @pathInfo) ->

  contentType: ->
    throw new Error("must be implemented!")

  process: ->
    throw new Error("must be implemented!")

  pathname: ->

  write: (data, status = 200, headers = {}) ->

class JavaScriptProcessor extends Processor

  contentType: ->

  process: ->

class PublicProcessor extends Processor

  contentType: ->
  process: ->

port = 3000
ip = "127.0.0.1"

server = http.createServer (req, res) ->
```

```
  app = new Application(req, res)
  app.process()

server.listen(port, ip)

console.log "Server running at http://#{ip}:#{port}/"
```

Looking at our `Processor` class first, it looks like there are five functions that we'll need. The first is the `constructor` function. The `constructor` will take the request, response, and the object that represents the requested path details.

The next two functions, `contentType` and `process`, need to be implemented by the subclasses. The `contentType` function will return the appropriate content type of the file for the headers when we go to write the response back to the client. The `process` function will do the heavy lifting of either reading the file from the `public` directory or compiling the CoffeeScript file that was requested.

The next method, `pathname`, will be used to calculate the name of the file on disk that we'll be looking for. This will be optional for the subclasses to implement because we can put in a simple default value that maps to the requested path, as we'll see in a few minutes.

The final method, `write`, will do all the heavy lifting of writing out the response status, headers, and body for the processors. As you can see, we've set a default `status` value of `200` and are setting an empty object as the default for our response headers. When we fill out this method in a few minutes, we'll set some pretty good default values on that `headers` object.

Before we move on to the `JavascriptProcessor` and `PublicProcessor` classes, let's finish implementing our parent class, `Processor`.

Example: **(source: server.6/server.coffee)**

```
http = require('http')
url = require('url')

class Application

  constructor: (@req, @res) ->
    @pathInfo = url.parse(@req.url, true)

  process: ->
    if /^\/javascripts\//.test @pathInfo.pathname
      new JavaScriptProcessor(@req, @res, @pathInfo).process()
    else
      new PublicProcessor(@req, @res, @pathInfo).process()

class Processor

  constructor: (@req, @res, @pathInfo) ->
```

```
  contentType: ->
    throw new Error("must be implemented!")

  process: ->
    throw new Error("must be implemented!")

  pathname: ->
    @pathInfo.pathname

  write: (data, status = 200, headers = {}) ->
    headers["Content-Type"] ||= @contentType()
    headers["Content-Length"] ||= Buffer.byteLength(data, "utf-8")
    @res.writeHead(status, headers)
    @res.write(data, "utf-8")
    @res.end()

class JavaScriptProcessor extends Processor

  contentType: ->

  process: ->

class PublicProcessor extends Processor

  contentType: ->

  process: ->

port = 3000
ip = "127.0.0.1"

server = http.createServer (req, res) ->
  app = new Application(req, res)
  app.process()
server.listen(port, ip)

console.log "Server running at http://#{ip}:#{port}/"
```

All we needed to do here was to set the default return value of the `pathname` function to match that of the path that was requested by the client. The implementation of the `write` function was also pretty straightforward and not too dissimilar to what we've already talked about earlier in this chapter.

Let's implement the more interesting of the two processors, the `JavascriptProcessor` class. To implement this class, we are going to need to override three functions from our super class and include two more Node modules. Let's take a look:

Example: **(source: server.7/server.coffee)**

```
http = require('http')
url = require('url')
fs = require('fs')
CoffeeScript = require('coffee-script')

class Application

  constructor: (@req, @res) ->
    @pathInfo = url.parse(@req.url, true)

  process: ->
    if /^\/javascripts\//.test @pathInfo.pathname
      new JavaScriptProcessor(@req, @res, @pathInfo).process()
    else
      new PublicProcessor(@req, @res, @pathInfo).process()

class Processor

  constructor: (@req, @res, @pathInfo) ->

  contentType: ->
    throw new Error("must be implemented!")

  process: ->
    throw new Error("must be implemented!")

  pathname: ->
    @pathInfo.pathname

  write: (data, status = 200, headers = {}) ->
    headers["Content-Type"] ||= @contentType()
    headers["Content-Length"] ||= Buffer.byteLength(data, "utf-8")
    @res.writeHead(status, headers)
    @res.write(data, "utf-8")
    @res.end()

class JavaScriptProcessor extends Processor

  contentType: ->
    "application/x-javascript"
```

```
  pathname: ->
    file = (/\/javascripts\/(.+)\.js/.exec(@pathInfo.pathname))[1]
    return "#{file}.coffee"

  process: ->
    fs.readFile "src/#{@pathname()}", "utf-8", (err, data) =>
      if err?
        @write("", 404)
      else
        @write(CoffeeScript.compile(data))

class PublicProcessor extends Processor

  contentType: ->

  process: ->

port = 3000
ip = "127.0.0.1"

server = http.createServer (req, res) ->
  app = new Application(req, res)
  app.process()

server.listen(port, ip)

console.log "Server running at http://#{ip}:#{port}/"
```

We first need to require the `fs` Node module. This rather vaguely named module gives us functions that let us access the file system. We are going to need to access the file system so we can read our CoffeeScript files from the disk before we compile them. We are also going to need to read the files in our `public` directory later when we implement the `PublicProcessor` class.

The next module we have to include is the `coffee-script` module. I know, we're getting a bit meta here, aren't we? We need this module so we can compile our CoffeeScript source files into JavaScript when they're requested.

> **Tip**
>
> The `coffee-script` module gives us more than just a `compile` function, but that's all we need here. I highly recommend you dig into it a bit and see what else it can do.

With our required modules in place, we can start to implement the necessary functions for the `JavascriptProcessor` class. Implementing the `contentType` function is straightforward as we know that the content type for JavaScript is `application/x-javascript`.

> **Tip**
>
> If you are having some troubles with the content type, chances are you are using certain versions of Internet Explorer. Try changing the content type to `text/javascript`; that should do the trick for you.

Implementing the `pathname` function wasn't as straightforward as the `contentType` function, but it isn't overly complex either. We can use a regular expression to strip off the `javascripts/` and `.js` parts of the requested path, leaving us with what's in the middle. For example, if the path requested was `javascripts/foo.js`, our regular expression would leave us with just `foo`. With that, all we need to do is return the captured part of path along with `.coffee` and we are good to go.

Finally, we needed to implement the `process` function. In some ways I think this is more self-explanatory and straightforward than the `pathname` function we just implemented. Using the `readFile` function from the `fs` module, we attempt to read in the CoffeeScript file from the `src` directory. The `readFile` function will then execute our callback function we pass in.

The callback function we passed into `readFile` has two arguments. The first is an object that represents any errors that may have occurred while trying to read the file, such as the file not existing. The second argument is the actual data from the file that was read.

In the callback function, if there is an error, we check for this using the `?` existential operator we learned about in Chapter 3, "Control Structures," and then we call the `write` function from our super class, passing it an empty body and a status code of `404`. If there aren't any errors, we call the `compile` function from the `coffee-script` module, passing it the contents of our CoffeeScript file we just read off disk. This function will return the compiled JavaScript code. We can then pass that compiled JavaScript code into our `write` function to be written back to the client. Pretty nifty, eh?

All that is left now is to implement the same three functions on the `PublicProcessor` class, and we'll have our completed server.

Example: **(source: final/server.coffee)**

```
http = require('http')
url = require('url')
fs = require('fs')
CoffeeScript = require('coffee-script')

class Application

  constructor: (@req, @res) ->
    @pathInfo = url.parse(@req.url, true)

  process: ->
    if /^\/javascripts\//.test @pathInfo.pathname
      new JavaScriptProcessor(@req, @res, @pathInfo).process()
```

```
    else
      new PublicProcessor(@req, @res, @pathInfo).process()

class Processor

  constructor: (@req, @res, @pathInfo) ->

  contentType: ->
    throw new Error("must be implemented!")

  process: ->
    throw new Error("must be implemented!")

  pathname: ->
    @pathInfo.pathname

  write: (data, status = 200, headers = {}) ->
    headers["Content-Type"] ||= @contentType()
    headers["Content-Length"] ||= Buffer.byteLength(data, "utf-8")
    @res.writeHead(status, headers)
    @res.write(data, "utf-8")
    @res.end()

class JavaScriptProcessor extends Processor

  contentType: ->
    "application/x-javascript"

  pathname: ->
    file = (/\/javascripts\/(.+)\.js/.exec(@pathInfo.pathname))[1]
    return "#{file}.coffee"
  process: ->
    fs.readFile "src/#{@pathname()}", "utf-8", (err, data) =>
      if err?
        @write("", 404)
      else
        @write(CoffeeScript.compile(data))

class PublicProcessor extends Processor

  contentType: ->
    ext = (/\.(.+)$/.exec(@pathname()))[1].toLowerCase()
    switch ext
      when "png", "jpg", "jpeg", "gif"
        "image/#{ext}"
      when "css"
        "text/css"
```

```
      else
        "text/html"

  process: ->
    fs.readFile "public/#{@pathname()}", "utf-8", (err, data) =>
      if err?
        @write("Oops! We couldn't find the page you were looking for.", 404)
      else
        @write(data)

  pathname: ->
    unless @_pathname
      if @pathInfo.pathname is "/" or @pathInfo.pathname is ""
        @pathInfo.pathname = "index"
      unless /\..+$/.test @pathInfo.pathname
        @pathInfo.pathname += ".html"
      @_pathname = @pathInfo.pathname
    return @_pathname

port = 3000
ip = "127.0.0.1"

server = http.createServer (req, res) ->
  app = new Application(req, res)
  app.process()

server.listen(port, ip)

console.log "Server running at http://#{ip}:#{port}/"
```

Example: **(source: final/server.js)**

```
(function() {
  var Application, CoffeeScript, JavaScriptProcessor, Processor, PublicProcessor, fs,
➥http, ip, port, server, url,
    __hasProp = Object.prototype.hasOwnProperty,
    __extends = function(child, parent) { for (var key in parent) { if
(__hasProp.call(parent, key)) child[key] = parent[key]; } function ctor()
{ this.constructor = child; } ctor.prototype = parent.prototype; child.prototype =
new ctor; child.__super__ = parent.prototype; return child; };

  http = require('http');

  url = require('url');

  fs = require('fs');
```

```
CoffeeScript = require('coffee-script');

Application = (function() {

  function Application(req, res) {
    this.req = req;
    this.res = res;
    this.pathInfo = url.parse(this.req.url, true);
  }

  Application.prototype.process = function() {
    if (/^\/javascripts\//.test(this.pathInfo.pathname)) {
      return new JavaScriptProcessor(this.req, this.res, this.pathInfo).process();
    } else {
      return new PublicProcessor(this.req, this.res, this.pathInfo).process();
    }
  };

  return Application;

})();

Processor = (function() {
  function Processor(req, res, pathInfo) {
    this.req = req;
    this.res = res;
    this.pathInfo = pathInfo;
  }

  Processor.prototype.contentType = function() {
    throw new Error("must be implemented!");
  };

  Processor.prototype.process = function() {
    throw new Error("must be implemented!");
  };

  Processor.prototype.pathname = function() {
    return this.pathInfo.pathname;
  };

  Processor.prototype.write = function(data, status, headers) {
    if (status == null) status = 200;
    if (headers == null) headers = {};
    headers["Content-Type"] || (headers["Content-Type"] = this.contentType());
    headers["Content-Length"] || (headers["Content-Length"] =
➥Buffer.byteLength(data, "utf-8"));
```

Example: **(source: app.2/src/configuration.coffee)**

```
# Configure Express.js:
app.configure ->
  app.use(express.bodyParser())
  app.use(express.methodOverride())
  app.use(express.cookieParser())
  app.use(express.session(secret: 'd19e19fd62f62a216ecf7d7b1de434ad'))
  app.use(app.router)
  app.use(express.static(__dirname + '../public'))
  app.use(express.errorHandler(dumpExceptions: true, showStack: true))
  app.set('views', "#{__dirname}/views")
  app.set('view engine', 'ejs')
```

Let's create a new file, `src/views/index.ejs`. This file will be the landing page for our application when people visit the route we already defined. We'll make this page fairly simple and have it also say "Hello, World!"—but let's embed a little bit of dynamic content to make sure it works:

Example: **(source: app.2/src/views/index.ejs)**

```
<!DOCTYPE html>
<html>
  <head>
    <title>Todos</title>
  </head>
<body>
  <h1>Hello, World!</h1>
  <h2>The date/time is: <%= new Date() %></h2>
</body>
</html>
```

Finally, we need to update the `home_controller.coffee` file to use our new `index.ejs` file.

Example: **(source: app.2/src/controllers/home_controller.coffee)**

```
# Set up a routing for our homepage:
app.get '/', (req, res) ->
  res.render 'index', layout: false
```

All we had to do was get rid of the `send` call on the response object and replace it with a call to the `render` function, passing it the name of the template we wanted to use. We are also telling it to not look for a `layout` template.

> **Tip**
>
> It is *very* important to note that any dynamic content you put into an `ejs` template is to be written in JavaScript, *not* CoffeeScript. Trust me, that will bite you at some point. It has me! There are quite a few good CoffeeScript-based templating engines out there, but they require a bit more setup work. I recommend checking out Eco[4] and CoffeeKup.[5]

Fire up the server and you should see our new home page, complete with the current date and time.

Let's move on to the next step, setting up a database.

Setting Up MongoDB Using Mongoose

We need to be able to persist our todos for our application somewhere, and so we are going to use MongoDB.[6] MongoDB, also known simply as Mongo, is a popular NoSQL document object store. It's similar to a relational database in that you can store and retrieve data, but it's more fluid in that it doesn't require a traditional schema, meaning we can just start using it without writing a bunch of table creation scripts. That makes it a great choice for us because it means we don't have to jump through a lot of hoops just building tables and the like. We can simply start throwing todos into the store.

I'm going to make the assumption here that you have MongoDB installed. If you don't, feel free to go[7] to do that now and come back when you're done.

So what do we need to do to get Mongo up and running with our application? First, we need to install Mongoose,[8] a popular object relational mapping (ORM) framework for Node that works with Mongo. Mongoose is conveniently available as an NPM:

```
> npm install mongoose

mongoose@2.4.7 ./node_modules/mongoose
--- hooks@0.1.9
--- colors@0.5.1
--- mongodb@0.9.7-2-1
```

> **Tip**
>
> Technically, Mongoose isn't an ORM, because MongoDB isn't a relational database but rather a document store. However, the term ORM has become a bit overloaded these days to include tools such as Mongoose, so I'm going to run with it.

With Mongoose installed, we need to set it up for the application. This is incredibly easy to do. First create a file, `src/models/database.coffee`. The `src/models` directory is where we will put all the code that deals with our database.

Here's what that file should look like:

Example: **(source: app.3/src/models/database.coffee)**

```
# Configure Mongoose (MongoDB):
global.mongoose = require('mongoose')
global.Schema = mongoose.Schema
global.ObjectId = Schema.ObjectId
mongoose.connect("mongodb://localhost:27017/csbook-todos")
```

In that file we are first requiring Mongoose and then setting a few of its properties to the `global` object so that we can easily access them later from other parts of our code.

Last, in that file we are telling Mongoose where to find our Mongo server and which database it should use. This line may change on your system depending on how you have things set up.

All that is left to get Mongoose set up in our system is to require the `src/models/database.coffee` file we just created in our `app.coffee` file, like so:

Example: **(source: app.3/app.coffee)**

```
# Setup Express.js:
global.express = require('express')
global.app = app = express.createServer()
require("#{__dirname}/src/configuration")

# Set up the Database:
require("#{__dirname}/src/models/database")

# Set up a routing for our homepage:
require("#{__dirname}/src/controllers/home_controller")

# Start server:
app.listen(3000)
console.log("Express server listening on port %d in %s mode", app.address().port,
➥app.settings.env)
```

With Mongoose up and running, let's finish up this section by creating a `Todo` model. The `Todo` model doesn't have to be anything fancy. It should have a title, an ID, a state (so we know whether it's pending or completed), and a date so we know when it was created.

In Mongoose we create new models using the `model` function and passing it a new `Schema` object. That `Schema` object will tell Mongoose and Mongo what type of data we expect our `Todo` models to have.

Example: **(source: app.3/src/models/todo.coffee)**

```
# The Todo Mongoose model:
global.Todo = mongoose.model 'Todo', new Schema
  id: ObjectId
  title:
    type: String
    validate: /.+/
  state:
    type: String
    default: 'pending'
  created_at:
    type: Date
    default: Date.now
```

The `Schema` for our `Todo` model looks pretty much like we wanted it to. It's very self-describing. For the `state` and `created_at` properties, we defined some helpful default attributes. For the `title` property we set a very simple validation on it, insisting that it has at least one character in it before we save it.

> **Tip**
>
> Mongoose is capable of letting you write some pretty sophisticated validators. Check out the extensive documentation[9] for more information.

Finally, we need to update our `app.coffee` file to require the `Todo` model we just created.

Example: **(source: app.3/app.coffee)**

```
# Setup Express.js:
global.express = require('express')
global.app = app = express.createServer()
require("#{__dirname}/src/configuration")

# Set up the Database:
require("#{__dirname}/src/models/database")

# Set up a routing for our homepage:
require("#{__dirname}/src/controllers/home_controller")

# Start server:
app.listen(3000)
console.log("Express server listening on port %d in %s mode", app.address().port,
➥app.settings.env)
```

With that, the database and models are all set up ready to go to work. In the next section you'll see how we interact with the `Todo` model when we write the controller to handle the requests for our todos.

Writing the Todo API

All that is left on the server side of our todo application is to write an API to access our todo resources from the client side code we'll write in the next chapter. Let's start by adding a file to handle all the requests we expect for our API:

Example: **(source: app.4/src/controllers/todos_controller.coffee)**

```
# This 'controller' will handle the server requests
# for the Todo resource

# Get a list of the todos:
app.get '/api/todos', (req, res) ->
  res.json [{}]

# Create a new todo:
app.post '/api/todos', (req, res) ->
  res.json {}

# Get a specific todo:
app.get '/api/todos/:id', (req, res) ->
  res.json {}

# Update a specific todo:
app.put "/api/todos/:id", (req, res) ->
  res.json {}

# Destroy a specific todo:
app.delete '/api/todos/:id', (req, res) ->
  res.json {}
```

The first thing you should note is that for right now, we have stubbed out all the responses to API by rendering empty JSON[10] objects. We will add some substance to those responses in just a minute, but I would like to first talk a little bit about what we have so far and what it's doing.

Earlier in this chapter I mentioned how Express provides a function to map requests using each of the four HTTP verbs: `get`, `post`, `put`, and `delete`. In the `todos_controller.coffee` file we are using all those functions so that our API conforms to the REST[11] approach.

> **Tip**
>
> We could use just GET and POST requests, but to me that makes our API more confusing. The REST approach lets us better, and more clearly, define our intent in the API.

We are going to need to perform five actions on our todos.

The first action is getting a list of all of the todos in our database. That is what the first route we defined will be for.

The second action is to create a new todo. We will use the `post` function to do this.

The third action we will need is the capability to retrieve a specific todo from the database. Our third route mapping will be where we do this. Because we need to know which todo we want to pull from the database, we need to know the ID of that todo. Express lets us create mappings that have placeholders in them. We can then retrieve these placeholders inside of the callback function. Here we are doing that with the `:id` part of the path we mapped. We will be able to retrieve the value of `:id` later by using the `param` function off of the `req` object to which we have access. We will use this same technique again when we need to update or delete a todo.

The fourth action we need to handle is the updating of a todo. This will use the `put` function, which maps to the `PUT` http verb.

Our last mapping and action is to delete a specific todo.

All the mappings and actions are going to render out JSON as the response. Conveniently, Express offers a `json` method on the response to help us with that. Without the `json` method we would have to write our responses something like this:

```
res.send JSON.stringify({})
```

With stubs in place, you can test that things are working as expected by starting the application and going to `http://localhost:3000/api/todos`. You should see the following printed to the screen:

```
[{}]
```

That means it is hitting our API for listing all the todos successfully.

Querying with Mongoose

All that is left to do for this chapter, and before we move on to putting a nice front end on this bad boy, is flesh out each of the actions we've mapped for our API.

Finding All Todos

Let's start with getting all of the todos in the database:

Example: **(source: app.5/src/controllers/todos_controller.coffee)**

```
# This 'controller' will handle the server requests
# for the Todo resource

# Get a list of the todos:
app.get '/api/todos', (req, res) ->
  Todo.find {}, [], {sort: [["created_at", -1]]}, (err, @todos) =>
    if err?
      res.json(err, 500)
    else
      res.json @todos

# Create a new todo:
app.post '/api/todos', (req, res) ->
  res.json {}

# Get a specific todo:
app.get '/api/todos/:id', (req, res) ->
  res.json {}

# Update a specific todo:
app.put "/api/todos/:id", (req, res) ->
  res.json {}

# Destroy a specific todo:
app.delete '/api/todos/:id', (req, res) ->
  res.json {}
```

Mongoose provides a bunch of helpful and easy-to-use class-level functions for helping us find the exact records we want in the database. In our case, we want all the records in the database.

> **Tip**
>
> Mongoose has some incredible documentation. I highly recommend that you check out the Mongoose pages on finding documents[12] and on building complicated queries.[13]

To find all the records, we could simply call the `find` function and pass it a callback function that will be executed when the query returns or fails. For our application, we would like to add a sort so that our todos come back with the latest todo first and the oldest last. To do that, we must first pass in an object that contains the details of that sort. This is where it gets a little tricky. We can do this one of two ways: we can either break this into several lines, building up a query as we go and then executing that query, or we can do what we have here, which is pass in a few empty arguments before we pass in the argument containing the details of the sort. The first object would represent any clauses you would want to put on the query. In our case, we don't want to limit our results using a specific query. The second array is where you would specify any specific fields you want to retrieve. We want all the fields, so we'll leave this blank.

> **Tip**
>
> Why the nested arrays when defining the sort in our `find` call? That is actually a MongoDB-ism hard at work. If we wanted to sort by multiple fields, we would do something like `{sort: [["created_at", -1], ["updated_at", 1]]}`. The inner arrays are a group representing each sort we want to add. The first element of the array is the attribute name, and the second is the direction, `-1` for descending and `1` for ascending. In my opinion it could have been done a little nicer and cleaner, but it is what it is.

As I already mentioned, the callback function we pass into the `find` function will get executed regardless of whether the query was successful. This means that we must do our own error handling.

The callback function will be called with two arguments. The first argument will be an `Error` object, if there is an error, or `null` if there was no error. The second argument will represent the result of our query, in this case an array of `Todo` objects. If the query fails and there is an error, the second argument will be `null`.

Inside our callback function we should first check to see if there was an error. We can do so using the existential operator that CoffeeScript provides, aka `?`. Using the existential operator, we are checking to see if the `err` object is not `undefined` or `null`. If there was an error, we call the `json` function, passing it the error and the status code of `500`. This will let our front end respond appropriately to the error that occurred.

If there is no error, we can pass the list of todos we received from our query, `@todos`, into the `json` function, and Express will take care of the rest.

> **Tip**
>
> You might have noticed that we are using => when defining our callback function. We are doing that because we need to make sure that we have access to the `req` and `res` objects. All the Mongoose calls are asynchronous, which means the program could have moved on in execution before the callback function gets called, and it may no longer have access to the scope with the `req` and `res` objects.

Creating New Todos

Moving on, let's flesh out the creating of a new todo.

Example: **(source: app.6/src/controllers/todos_controller.coffee)**

```
# This 'controller' will handle the server requests
# for the Todo resource

# Get a list of the todos:
app.get '/api/todos', (req, res) ->
  Todo.find {}, [], {sort: [["created_at", -1]]}, (err, @todos) =>
    if err?
      res.json(err, 500)
    else
      res.json @todos

# Create a new todo:
app.post '/api/todos', (req, res) ->
  @todo = new Todo(req.param('todo'))
  @todo.save (err) =>
    if err?
      res.json(err, 500)
    else
      res.json @todo

# Get a specific todo:
app.get '/api/todos/:id', (req, res) ->
  res.json {}

# Update a specific todo:
app.put "/api/todos/:id", (req, res) ->
  res.json {}

# Destroy a specific todo:
app.delete '/api/todos/:id', (req, res) ->
  res.json {}
```

The code for creating a new todo is pretty simple. First, we instantiate a new instance of the `Todo` class and pass in an object that represents the values we want to set on our new todo. Where are we getting those values? We are getting them from the parameters that are sent with the `POST` request of the action we have mapped.

Express lets us retrieve parameters via its `param` function on the `req` object. We pass in the name of the parameter we want, and it will either return the value of that parameter or `null` if it does not exist.

In our action we are looking for the `todo` parameter, which we are assuming will be an object containing the key/value pairs necessary to create a new todo, something like this:

```
{
  todo: {
    title: "My Todo Title",
    state: "pending"
  }
}
```

To save our new todo, we call the `save` function that Mongoose provides and pass it a callback function. This function takes one argument that represents an error, should one have occurred. Our callback function has similar logic to the one we already saw when we were getting a list of todos. We first check to see if there is an error. If there is an error, we respond with the error and a status of `500`; if not, we send back the JSON of our new created todo.

> **Tip**
>
> Technically, if we were supporting the REST protocol exactly, we should return a status code of `201` ("successfully created") when we create a new todo. However, Express's default response status code of `200` ("success") is good enough for our purposes. I leave it up to you to try to implement the `201` status code.

Getting, Updating, and Destroying a Todo

The three remaining actions we need to have our todo API perform are all very similar in nature, so we can cover them all here fairly quickly.

Example: **(source: app.7/src/controllers/todos_controller.coffee)**

```
# This 'controller' will handle the server requests
# for the Todo resource

# Get a list of the todos:
app.get '/api/todos', (req, res) ->
  Todo.find {}, [], {sort: [["created_at", -1]]}, (err, @todos) =>
    if err?
      res.json(err, 500)
    else
      res.json @todos

# Create a new todo:
app.post '/api/todos', (req, res) ->
  @todo = new Todo(req.param('todo'))
  @todo.save (err) =>
    if err?
      res.json(err, 500)
    else
```

```
      res.json @todo

# Get a specific todo:
app.get '/api/todos/:id', (req, res) ->
  Todo.findById req.param('id'), (err, @todo) =>
    if err?
      res.json(err, 500)
    else
      res.json @todo

# Update a specific todo:
app.put "/api/todos/:id", (req, res) ->
  Todo.findById req.param('id'), (err, @todo) =>
    if err?
      res.json(err, 500)
    else
      @todo.set(req.param('todo'))
      @todo.save (err) =>
        if err?
          res.json(err, 500)
        else
          res.json @todo

# Destroy a specific todo:
app.delete '/api/todos/:id', (req, res) ->
  Todo.findById req.param('id'), (err, @todo) =>
    if err?
      res.json(err, 500)
    else
      @todo.remove()
      res.json @todo
```

The first thing we need to do with each of these actions is to find the specific todo we're looking for using the `id` parameter we mapped in the paths with the `:id` keyword. We can do this in Mongoose by using the `findById` class-level function and passing it the `id` parameter.

The `findById` function takes a callback function that receives two arguments. As always, the first argument is an error if one exists, and the second argument is the todo if one was found.

What we do with our found todo depends on which of the three actions we are looking at. For the action where we just want to show the todo, all we have to do is return the JSON of the todo.

For the action where we want to update the action, we can use the `set` function, passing it any attributes we want to update. This is not too dissimilar from when we created a new todo earlier.

Finally, for the action where we want to destroy the todo, we simply need to call the `remove` function on the todo to destroy it in the database.

Cleaning Up the Controller

In case you haven't noticed, our controller is rife with duplicated code. Because this is an example application, we could just leave it, but why not clean it up a bit? It will give us a chance to play with classes a bit more.

> **Tip**
>
> In reality, the clean-up code I'm about to show you might be overkill or could be even further refactored, but I think it's still fun to see how we could refactor it if we so desired.

To clean up our controller, we are going to create a few classes that will handle each of the actions we have mapped. We'll also use some inheritance to cut down on duplicated code, especially around the error-handling part of our actions where most of the code duplication is happening.

Let's start by building a base class, `Responder`, from which all our other classes will inherit. This class will handle our default and common functionality.

Example: **(source: app.8/src/controllers/responders/responder.coffee)**

```
class global.Responder

  respond: (@req, @res) =>
    @complete(null, {})

  complete: (err, result = {}) =>
    if err?
      @res.json(err, 500)
    else
      @res.json result
```

The first thing you should notice is that we are defining the `Responder` class on the `global` object. This will allow us to easily access it throughout the rest of our application.

Next up, we will add a default function called `respond`. This function will be what is passed to the mappings we define in our `todos_controller.coffee` file. The `respond` function will take in two arguments, the request object and the response object. We automatically assign those to the scope of the class, by prefixing them with `@`, so that we can have access to them in our functions.

The `respond` function will most likely be overridden by our subclasses, but just in case we will provide a default behavior. The default behavior we give it is to call the `complete` function.

The `complete` function is where we are wrapping up all that duplicated error handling and response logic we've been writing.

With our super class written, let's start writing our child classes that will handle each of the actions. Let's start with the class to handle the action where we get all of the todos.

Example: **(source: app.8/src/controllers/responders/index_responder.coffee)**

```
require "#{__dirname}/responder"

class Responder.Index extends Responder

  respond: (@req, @res) =>
    Todo.find {}, [], {sort: [["created_at", -1]]}, @complete
```

First, we need to require the `Responder` class we just wrote using the `require` function Node provides us.

When we define our class we could assign it to the `global` object, like we did with `Responder`, but it's good practice to try to namespace things and not put everything directly on the `global` object, so that's what we'll do here. We also need to make sure our `Responder.Index` class extends `Responder` using CoffeeScript's `extend` keyword.

> **Tip**
>
> In a real application, we would want to namespace the classes we build better so that it is clear they are dealing with the `Todo` resource. If we have multiple resources, it could prove problematic or confusing.

All that is left to do is to write a custom `respond` method. In that method we'll have the query we saw earlier for finding all of the todos. The big difference, compared to what we had already written, is that for our callback function we will pass in a reference to the `complete` function we wrote in the `Responder` super class.

Now let's build a class to handle the create new todos action.

Example: **(source: app.8/src/controllers/responders/create_responder.coffee)**

```
require "#{__dirname}/responder"

class Responder.Create extends Responder

  respond: (@req, @res) =>
    todo = new Todo(@req.param('todo'))
    todo.save(@complete)
```

The Responder.Create class is very similar to the Responder.Index class we just built. In the respond function, we are creating our new todo and passing the complete function as the callback function to the save call we are making.

Example: **(source: app.8/src/controllers/responders/show_responder.coffee)**

```
require "#{__dirname}/responder"

class Responder.Show extends Responder

  respond: (@req, @res) =>
    Todo.findById @req.param('id'), @complete
```

Again, the Responder.Show class is like the first two classes; we're just changing out the innards of the respond function. We will use the Responder.Show class as the super class for our final two classes that we will write. Let's take a look.

Example: **(source: app.8/src/controllers/responders/update_responder.coffee)**

```
require "#{__dirname}/show_responder"

class Responder.Update extends Responder.Show

  complete: (err, result = {}) =>
    if err?
      super
    else
      result.set(@req.param('todo'))
      result.save(super)
```

Because the action to update a todo also needs to find the todo in question, we can extend the Responder.Show class instead of the Responder class itself, because the Responder.Show class has all the functionality we need to find the todo.

In the Responder.Update class we are not going to write a new respond function, because we want to use the one we inherited from Responder.Show. Instead, we are going to write a custom complete function.

The first thing we need to do in our new complete function is to check the existence of an error. If there is an error, we call super, which will call the original complete function from the Responder class, and that will handle the error appropriately for us.

If there is no error, we can proceed with setting the attributes we want to update and then calling the save function. When we call the save function, we are going to pass in super, again the original complete function from the Responder class. This will handle any errors and respond with the appropriate JSON.

The class we need to build for the action to destroy a todo is very similar to the one we just built for updating the todo.

Example: **(source: app.8/src/controllers/responders/destroy_responder.coffee)**

```
require "#{__dirname}/show_responder"

class Responder.Destroy extends Responder.Show

  complete: (err, result = {}) =>
    unless err?
      result.remove()
    super
```

Again we are extending the `Responder.Show` class, and like the `Responder.Update` class, we are going to write a new `complete` function.

First, in the `complete` function, we need to check for any errors that may have arisen from trying to find the todo. If there are no errors, we call the `remove` function on the todo, which will destroy it in the database.

Finally, we call the `super` function to handle any errors and respond correctly.

All that is left now is to update our `todos_controller.coffee` to use the new classes we have built:

Example: **(source: app.8/src/controllers/todos_controller.coffee)**

```
# require all of our responders:
for name in ["index", "create", "show", "update", "destroy"]
  require("#{__dirname}/responders/#{name}_responder")

# This 'controller' will handle the server requests
# for the Todo resource

# Get a list of the todos:
app.get '/api/todos', new Responder.Index().respond

# Create a new todo:
app.post '/api/todos', new Responder.Create().respond

# Get a specific todo:
app.get '/api/todos/:id', new Responder.Show().respond

# Update a specific todo:
app.put "/api/todos/:id", new Responder.Update().respond

# Destroy a specific todo:
app.delete '/api/todos/:id', new Responder.Destroy().respond
```

At the top of the file, we need to require all the classes we have built.

> **Tip**
>
> We could have just written out the require statements for each file, because there are only a few of them, but I like to create an array and loop through it to build the require statements. It's cleaner, and to add another require just means typing a few characters into our array instead of copying and pasting a big line of code.

With the classes all required, we can pull out the original callback functions we had mapped for all the actions and replace them with a new instance of the appropriate class and the `respond` function for that class.

Now our `todos_controller.coffee` file is much cleaner, and we have extracted out all the common functionality for all our actions. This means that should we ever want to change the way we handle errors, or add other common functionality, we can do it all in one file.

Wrapping Up

In this chapter we built the server-side portion of an application to manage todos. We set up an Express application, added MongoDB support using Mongoose, and refactored it all into a nice clean backend.

In the next chapter we will take what we've built here and put a sexy[14] front end on it. We're going to get to play with jQuery to enable us to interact with our beautiful server-side code.

Notes

1. https://github.com/markbates/Programming-In-CoffeeScript
2. http://expressjs.com/
3. http://npmjs.org/
4. https://github.com/sstephenson/eco
5. http://coffeekup.org/
6. http://www.mongodb.org/
7. http://www.mongodb.org/
8. http://mongoosejs.com/
9. http://mongoosejs.com/docs/validation.html
10. http://www.json.org/
11. http://en.wikipedia.org/wiki/REST
12. http://mongoosejs.com/docs/finding-documents.html
13. http://mongoosejs.com/docs/query.html
14. Yes, I'm being a bit sarcastic here as anyone who knows me will tell you "sexy" front ends aren't my specialty.

11

Example: Todo List Part 2 (Client-side w/ jQuery)

In Chapter 10, "Example: Todo List Part 1 (Server-side)," we had just finished writing the server-side components needed for us to write a todo list application. In this chapter we will write a front end for that application that will run in a browser. We're going to do this using some pretty fun technology, such as Bootstrap[1] from Twitter[2] and jQuery.

Priming the HTML with Twitter Bootstrap

Let's start by setting up some basic styles and HTML for our application. To help get our CSS and styling off to a good start, we are going to use the Bootstrap project from Twitter. Bootstrap is a simple set of CSS and JavaScript files to help you, well, bootstrap your application. It gives you a simple grid to use to help align the elements on the page. It also provides some nice styling for forms, buttons, lists, and much more. I highly recommend that you check out the project for full details about what it can offer you, because we are using only a tiny portion of it for this application.

The first thing we need to do is update our `src/views/index.ejs` to use Bootstrap, as well as our own CSS, so we can make the few tweaks necessary for our application.

Example: **(source: app.1/src/views/index.ejs)**

```
<!DOCTYPE html>
<html>
  <head>
    <title>Todos</title>
    <link rel="stylesheet"
href="http://twitter.github.com/bootstrap/1.4.0/bootstrap.min.css">
    <%- css('/application') %>
```

```
  </head>
<body>

</body>
</html>
```

As you can see, we linked to the CSS file that Bootstrap offers us. We also have a rather unusual bit of dynamic code in there, a function called `css`, to which we are passing `/application`. That is how we will be adding our custom CSS, and later our CoffeeScript, into our application.

To do this we are going to use the `connect-assets` NPM module by Trevor Burnham.[3] This will provide a couple of hooks by which we automatically find our CSS and CoffeeScript files and add them into the HTML. In the case of CoffeeScript, it automatically converts them to JavaScript for us, saving us a step of compiling the files manually ourselves.

> **Tip**
>
> For those of you familiar with the asset-pipeline in Ruby on Rails, the `connect-assets` module attempts to mimic that in an Express application.

For `connect-assets` to find our assets, we need to place them in a folder called `assets` at the root of our application. So let's do that now, and while we're at it, let's place a little bit of CSS in there to help pretty up the HTML we're going to write.

Example: **(source: app.1/assets/application.css)**

```
#todos li {
  margin-bottom: 20px;
}

#todos li .todo_title {
  width: 800px;
}

#todos li .completed {
  text-decoration: line-through;
}

#todos #new_todo .todo_title{
  width: 758px;
}
```

Because this is not a book on CSS, I'm not going to explain the little CSS that we did there. If you are really curious, you can easily comment it out later and see how it affects the application.

Now we need to install the connect-assets module so that what we just wrote will work.

```
> npm install connect-assets

connect-assets@2.1.6 ./node_modules/connect-assets
__ connect-file-cache@0.2.4
__ underscore@1.1.7
__ mime@1.2.2
__ snockets@1.3.3
```

Finally, we need to tell Express to use the connect-assets module to serve up our assets. We can do that by adding a line to the end of the configuration.coffee file:

Example: **(source: app.1/src/configuration.coffee)**

```
# Configure Express.js:
app.configure ->
  app.use(express.bodyParser())
  app.use(express.methodOverride())
  app.use(express.cookieParser())
  app.use(express.session(secret: 'd19e19fd62f62a216ecf7d7b1de434ad'))
  app.use(app.router)
  app.use(express.static(__dirname + '../public'))
  app.use(express.errorHandler(dumpExceptions: true, showStack: true))
  app.set('views', "#{__dirname}/views")
  app.set('view engine', 'ejs')
  app.use(require('connect-assets')())
```

If we were to start up the application right now, we would be greeted by a rather dull, blank, white page on http://localhost:3000, which is what we want to see. If you see anything, something isn't right.

Let's finish up this section by adding a form so we can create a new Todo. This will prove especially useful because we don't have any todos in our database right now, and this will be a great way of getting some in there.

Example: **(source: app.2/src/views/index.ejs)**

```
<!DOCTYPE html>
<html>
  <head>
    <title>Todos</title>
    <link rel="stylesheet" href="http://twitter.github.com/bootstrap/1.4.0/bootstrap.
➥min.css">
    <%- css('/application') %>
  </head>
<body>
```

```
<div class="container">
  <h1>Todo List</h1>
  <ul id='todos' class='unstyled'>
    <li id='new_todo'>
      <div class="clearfix">
        <div class="input">
          <div class="input-prepend">
            <span class='add-on'>New Todo</span>
            <input class="xlarge todo_title" size="50" type="text"
➥placeholder="Enter your new Todo here..." />
          </div>
        </div>
      </div>
    </li>
  </ul>
</div>

</body>
</html>
```

Now if we were to start up our application and browse to it, we would see a nicely styled form in which to enter a new todo. That form doesn't do anything yet, but we'll take care of that in a minute. In case you were wondering where all those CSS classes came from in the HTML—they all come from Bootstrap, which we set up just a minute ago.

Interacting with jQuery

Now that we have a form, let's hook it up and see what happens. To do that let's start by using jQuery, that wonderful library that almost everyone on the Internet seems to love. To me there is no more powerful tool set in the JavaScript eco system than that of jQuery. Originally released in 2006 by John Resig,[4] jQuery is now used on 49% of the top 10,000[5] websites in the world and is currently one of the most popular JavaScript libraries available. jQuery is a JavaScript library that lets you write clean and concise code for manipulating the HTML DOM, executing AJAX requests, and handling events and simple animations. It does all this and is cross-platform, meaning it supports most major browsers and operating systems.

> **Tip**
>
> In the dark old days of the Web, developers had to write multiple versions of the same JavaScript. One version would work for Internet Explorer, another version would work in Netscape, and so on. Nowadays, jQuery lets us write our code once and trust that it will work the way it should on most modern browsers.

Adding jQuery to our application is simple; we just need to require it in our `index.ejs` file:

Example: **(source: app.3/src/views/index.ejs)**

```
<!DOCTYPE html>
<html>
  <head>
    <title>Todos</title>
    <script src="http://ajax.googleapis.com/ajax/libs/jquery/1.7.1/jquery.min.js"
➥type="text/javascript"></script>
    <%- js('/application') %>

    <link rel="stylesheet" href="http://twitter.github.com/bootstrap/1.4.0/
➥bootstrap.min.css">
    <%- css('/application') %>
  </head>
<body>

<div class="container">
  <h1>Todo List</h1>
  <ul id='todos' class='unstyled'>
    <li id='new_todo'>
      <div class="clearfix">
        <div class="input">
          <div class="input-prepend">
            <span class='add-on'>New Todo</span>
            <input class="xlarge todo_title" size="50" type="text"
➥placeholder="Enter your new Todo here..." />
          </div>
        </div>
      </div>
    </li>
  </ul>
</div>

</body>
</html>
```

> **Tip**
>
> In real-world applications, I tend to frown on linking to external libraries, like we have just done. It's possible that those libraries could get updated and introduce bugs in your application; or worse, the external reference could be removed or not available and then your application no longer works. I like to serve up local copies. However, just linking them here is easy for our purposes.

Hooking Up the New Todo Form

In addition to adding jQuery into our app, I used the `js` function provided by `connect-assets` to include an `application` file, which we can place into `assets/application.coffee`.

Example: **(source: app.3/assets/application.coffee)**

```
#= require_tree "jquery"
```

The `application.coffee` file is pretty small, and we're going to keep it that way. To help us do that, we are going to use a feature of `connect-assets` that lets us require other CoffeeScript or JavaScript files. In this case, we are requiring a directory called `jquery`. This means that every file we create under this directory will be required automatically for us.

In the `assets` folder, create a new folder called `jquery`, and within that folder create a new file called `new_todo_form.coffee`. It's in the `new_todo_form.coffee` file that we will place all the code that handles the new todo form we have in our HTML. Let's take a quick run at that code now.

Before we start writing the code to handle the new todo form, let's talk about what we want to happen. When a person types a todo into the form and presses the Enter key, we want to first test to make sure that the todo is valid, in that it has at least one non-whitespace character. If it's invalid, we want to raise an error letting the user know what the problem was. If the todo is valid, we want to post that data back to our API. If the response from the API is a success, we want to add the new todo to our list of todos on the page and reset the form. If the response from the server is an error, we want to show that message back to the user. Here's the code:

Example: **(source: app.3/assets/jquery/new_todo_form.coffee)**

```
$ ->
  # Focus the new todo form when the page loads:
  $('#new_todo .todo_title').focus()

  # Handle the keypress in the new todo form:
  $('#new_todo .todo_title').keypress (e) ->
    # we're only interested in the 'enter' key:
    if e.keyCode is 13
      todo = {title: $(e.target).val()}
      if !todo.title? or todo.title.trim() is ""
        alert "Title can't be blank"
      else
        request = $.post "/api/todos", todo: todo
        request.fail (response) =>
          message = JSON.parse(response.responseText).message
          alert message
```

```
request.done (todo) =>
  $('#new_todo').after("<li>#{JSON.stringify(todo)}</li>")
  $(e.target).val("")
```

The first thing we do after the page has loaded is focus the new todo form. This is a nice thing to do because it allows the user to start typing todos right away, without having to manually navigate to the form.

> **Tip**
>
> In jQuery you can pass a function into the `$` variable that aliases to `jQuery`, and everything in that function will be executed after the page is fully loaded. You can do this as many times as you need. Handy.

Next, we attach a function to the form that will get executed every time someone presses a key (event) in the form. This can get a little noisy, especially if we are looking for only one particular key, the Enter key. The Enter key has a numeric code of `13`, so using that we can look at the `keyCode` attribute of the event we receive from jQuery. If the key code is `13` we continue on; if we get something other than `13` we simply ignore the event.

Knowing that we are looking at the right event, we can continue. Next, we want to capture the value of the form. That will be the `title` attribute of the todo we are hoping to create. We then create an object that will represent all the data we want to send back to the server.

With the proposed `title` of the todo, we can now proceed to do some local validation of it. This is nice because it is faster, and therefore a nicer user experience, than posting it back to the server, waiting for the validations there to execute, and then coming back to the client with any errors.

> **Tip**
>
> There are a lot of ways to share validations across both the server and client side so you don't have to write them twice. If you find one that works for you, that's great. It's not always possible, though, to have validations that work both on the client and the server side the same way. A great example of this is username validation, which usually needs to hit a server to check for uniqueness. You can do that by using AJAX and hitting an API call, or you can validate that the username is not blank in the form and let the server side do the validation later.

Assuming the validations pass locally, we can proceed to posting the data back to the API. We create a new AJAX request using the `post` function that jQuery provides. We provide the url, `/api/todos`, and an object that represents the data we want to send. We assign the return value of the `post` function to a variable called `request`, which we can use in a minute to hang callbacks on when the request does certain things.

Tip

In jQuery 1.5 deferred objects were introduced. Before deferred objects, you would have to include any callbacks inside the original call to the `post`, or `ajax`, function when you originally call it. That was quite limiting. With deferred objects you can attach callbacks anytime, even after the request has finished processing. This makes it easier to write more isolated code that hangs on a request.

In our case, we want to add two callbacks to our request. The first callback function will be called if the request fails for any reason. The function will be passed a `response` object. Off that `response` object, we will need to get the `responseText`, which is JSON, parse it, extract the error message, and display it to the screen.

The second callback will be executed on successful completion of the request, in our case the creation of a new todo in the database. Because we haven't yet written a nice template for printing out our todos nicely, we'll print out the JSON representation of the todo inside of a `li` tag and append it to our list of todos just after the new todo form, so that the newest todos are always at the top.

If you fire up the application and try to create a new todo, you should see something similar to the following appear below the form:

```
{"title":"My New Todo","_id":"4efa82bdf65049000000001a","created_at":"2011-12-
➥28T02:45:17.992Z","state":"pending"}
```

Cleaning Up the Todo List with Underscore.js Templates

There are quite a few templating systems out there for JavaScript applications, and choosing the right one for your application is really a matter of taste. Because our needs here are quite simple, I'm going to make our choice of templating systems just as simple. We will use the templating system that ships with the library underscore.js.[6] Why did I choose this templating system over all the other ones out there? Simple, underscore.js is a dependency of the Backbone.js library we will be using later, so because we have to include it then as a dependency, we might as well use it now.

Tip

My personal favorite templating system is eco,[7] which lets you embed CoffeeScript in your templates. A couple of other popular templating systems include Handlebars,[8] Mustache,[9] and Jade.[10] The template plug-in[11] for jQuery was quite a popular choice for a while, but has been deprecated and is no longer under active development, so if you were planning on using that, I would strongly suggest you look elsewhere for your templating needs.

Let's update the `index.ejs` file to add in the dependency on underscore.js:

Example: **(source: app.4/src/views/index.ejs)**

```
<!DOCTYPE html>
<html>
  <head>
    <title>Todos</title>
    <script src="http://ajax.googleapis.com/ajax/libs/jquery/1.7.1/jquery.min.js"
➥type="text/javascript"></script>
    <script src="http://documentcloud.github.com/underscore/underscore-min.js"
➥type="text/javascript"></script>
    <%- js('/application') %>

    <link rel="stylesheet" href="http://twitter.github.com/bootstrap/1.4.0/
➥bootstrap.min.css">
    <%- css('/application') %>
  </head>
<body>

<div class="container">
  <h1>Todo List</h1>
  <ul id='todos' class='unstyled'>
    <li id='new_todo'>
      <div class="clearfix">
        <div class="input">
          <div class="input-prepend">
            <span class='add-on'>New Todo</span>
            <input class="xlarge todo_title" size="50" type="text"
➥placeholder="Enter your new Todo here..." />
          </div>
        </div>
      </div>
    </li>
  </ul>
</div>

</body>
</html>
```

That's one less thing we need to do later when we talk about Backbone.

Next let's create a new file, `assets/templates.coffee`, that will hold our templates for the application.

Example: **(source: app.4/assets/templates.coffee)**

```
# Change the syntax for underscore.js templates.
# The pattern is now {{some_var}} instead of <%= some_var %>
_.templateSettings =
  interpolate : /\{\{(.+?)\}\}/g

@Templates = {}

Templates.list_item_template = """
<div class="clearfix">
  <div class="input">
    <div class="input-prepend">
      <label class="add-on active"><input type="checkbox"
➥class="todo_state" /></label>
      <input class="xlarge todo_title" size="50" type="text" value="{{title}}" />
      <button class='btn danger'>X</button>
    </div>
  </div>
</div>
"""
```

The first thing we are going to do in this file is to change the default settings for how underscore.js interpolates dynamic data in the template. The reason for this is that I find `{{ }}` easier to type than <%= %>. This is also a popular convention among some of the other templating systems out there, so if you should want to port to one of them later it will be easier.

All that is left to do is define the template. To do this we are going to create a new `Templates` object and assign a property named `list_item_template` to the HTML template we want to use, using CoffeeScript's heredoc support that we learned about in Chapter 2, "The Basics."

The template is fairly simple; all we are going to dynamically push into the template is the title of the todo. We will update the state of the check box outside of the template. Let's create a new file, `todo_item.coffee`, under the `assets/jquery` folder. In this file we will create a function that lets us append a new todo to our list using the template we just created.

Example: **(source: app.4/assets/jquery/todo_item.coffee)**

```
@TodoApp ||= {}

TodoApp.appendTodo = (todo) ->
  li = $("<li>#{_.template(Templates.list_item_template)(todo)}</li>")
  $('#new_todo').after(li)
```

First, we create a new variable that is accessible outside of this file called `TodoApp`. By prepending the declaration of the variable `TodoApp` with `@`, we are telling CoffeeScript we want to attach that variable to the `this` object, which in this case is the `window` object in a browser. After it is attached to the `window` object, the `TodoApp` variable will be available to any scope that has access to the `window` scope.

Next we need to create a function that will take in a todo and print out to the screen using our template. When we required the underscore library, it gave us a variable named _ and off that variable is a function called `template`. Here we call that function, passing in the HTML template we want to use and the JSON representation of the todo we want to have access to in that template. The underscore library does the rest and returns back the appropriate HTML we want. We then append that HTML to our list of todos right after the new todo form.

Now let's update `new_todo_form.coffee` to use this new function when we create a new todo.

Example: **(source: app.4/assets/jquery/new_todo_form.coffee)**

```
$ ->
  # Focus the new todo form when the page loads:
  $('#new_todo .todo_title').focus()

  # Handle the keypress in the new todo form:
  $('#new_todo .todo_title').keypress (e) ->
    # we're only interested in the 'enter' key:
    if e.keyCode is 13
      todo = {title: $(e.target).val()}
      if !todo.title? or todo.title.trim() is ""
        alert "Title can't be blank"
      else
        request = $.post "/api/todos", todo: todo
        request.fail (response) =>
          message = JSON.parse(response.responseText).message
          alert message
        request.done (todo) =>
          TodoApp.appendTodo(todo)
          $(e.target).val("")
```

In the `request.done` callback function, we replace the line where we print out the JSON representation of the todo we got from the server with a call to the new `TodoApp.appendTodo` function.

Restart the application, add a new todo, and you should see it add a nicely styled todo to your list.

Listing Existing Todos

Now that we have a way of creating new todos in our database, and we have a way of printing out those new todos to our list when we create them, we need a way to display the todos that are already in the database when we load the page. Right now, if you were to add a few todos using our application and you reloaded the page, those todos would seem to have disappeared. In reality, they are safe and sound in our database, but because we haven't written any code to fetch them from our API and print them out, we don't see them. Fortunately, this is a relatively simple piece of code to write.

Example: **(source: app.5/assets/jquery/retrieve_existing_todos.coffee)**

```
$ ->
  request = $.get('/api/todos')
  request.done (todos) ->
    for todo in todos.reverse()
      TodoApp.appendTodo(todo)
```

First we need to wait until the page has been fully loaded before we retrieve the todos from the API. Then we create a new `request` that points to our API for retrieving the todos, and add a callback that will get executed when the response comes back with our todos. In that callback we are reversing the order of the todos and then passing them individually into the `appendTodo` function we wrote. Why are we reversing the order of the todos? The answer is as simple as it is annoying. The todos are actually coming back from the server in the correct order. However, the way our `appendTodo` function works is to append each todo at the top of the list, which would effectively place the todos in the wrong order on the page. We could change the way the API works, but it's behaving correctly; it's our client that isn't. We could write another function that places them in the right order, or add some sort of conditional in the `appendTodo` function, but at the end of the day this is probably the cleanest solution, and the least likely to cause issues.

If we were to reload our application now we should see all the existing todos that we have created in the database.

Updating Todos

With the ability to create new todos and to list our existing todos, it would stand to reason that we might want to make some changes to those todos at some point. In our application, we want to be able to update the `title` attribute of the todo as well as toggle the state of the todo.

We are going to do this by adding two functions. The first function will watch the check box and the text field associated with each todo. If there are changes to either of those, it will call the second function, which will send the updates back to the API.

Example: **(source: app.6/assets/jquery/watch_todo_for_changes.coffee)**

```
@TodoApp ||= {}

# Watch the todo for changes:
TodoApp.watchForChanges = (li, todo) ->
```

```
  # If the checkbox is checked/unchecked:
  $('.todo_state', li).click (e) =>
    TodoApp.updateTodo(li, todo)
  # If someone hits "enter" in the title field:
  $('.todo_title', li).keypress (e) =>
    if e.keyCode is 13
      TodoApp.updateTodo(li, todo)
```

The `watchForChanges` will do what its name implies—it will watch the specified `li` for the todo, and if the check box is checked/unchecked, or if the "enter" key is pressed in the title text field, the `updateTodo` function will be called. To make sure that the `watchForChanges` function gets called, we'll update the `appendTodo` function to call it when we append a new todo:

Example: **(source: app.6/assets/jquery/todo_item.coffee)**

```
@TodoApp ||= {}

TodoApp.appendTodo = (todo) ->
  li = $("<li>#{_.template(Templates.list_item_template)(todo)}</li>")
  $('#new_todo').after(li)
  TodoApp.watchForChanges(li, todo)
```

The todos are now being watched like a hawk. Let's write the `updateTodo` function so we can save those changes.

Example: **(source: app.6/assets/jquery/update_todo.coffee)**

```
@TodoApp ||= {}

# Update the todo:
TodoApp.updateTodo = (li, todo) ->
  todo.title = $('.todo_title', li).val()
  if !todo.title? or todo.title.trim() is ""
    alert "Title can't be blank"
  else
    if $('.todo_state', li).attr('checked')?
      todo.state = 'completed'
    else
      todo.state = 'pending'
    request = $.post "/api/todos/#{todo._id}",
      todo: todo
      _method: 'put'
    request.fail (response) =>
      message = JSON.parse(response.responseText).message
      alert message
```

The `updateTodo` function is similar to the code we wrote for creating a new todo. There are, however, a few important differences. First, we get the value of the title text field and do a simple validation on it to make sure it's not blank. If it passes the validation, we need to build the rest of the data we want to send back to the server. In this case we need to update the `state` attribute of the todo based on whether the check box is checked.

Next we create the request to the API. Because we want to update a specific todo, we have to make sure to include the ID of the todo as part of the API URL. Now, the more observant of you might have noticed that we are actually using `POST` to send this data to the server when, in fact, our API requires that it be sent via `PUT`. There are a couple of reasons for this. The first is that historically not all browsers support HTTP verbs beyond `GET` and `POST`; the same holds true of jQuery. To get around this limitation, a lot of frameworks, such as Express and Ruby on Rails, have taken to looking for a specially named parameter, `_method`. The frameworks will then consider the request to be of whatever type is set on that parameter. In our case we are sending along the value of `PUT` for the `_method` parameter, so Express will consider this not as a `POST` request, but rather a `PUT` request.

Finally we will look to see if there are error messages from the server because of our update. If there are errors, we display them; otherwise, we just let the users get on with their todo activities.

We do have a small problem here, however. If we were to mark a todo as `completed` and refresh the page, it would appear as though it was still pending because the check box wouldn't be checked and none of the `completed` styles would be applied to the todo to let the users know they've completed that task. Let's write a function that will update these styles as appropriate:

Example: **(source: app.7/assets/jquery/style_by_state.coffee)**

```
@TodoApp ||= {}

# Update the style based on the state:
TodoApp.styleByState = (li, todo) ->
  if todo.state is "completed"
    $('.todo_state', li).attr('checked', true)
    $('label.active', li).removeClass('active')
    $('.todo_title', li).addClass('completed').attr('disabled', true)
  else
    $('.todo_state', li).attr('checked', false)
    $('label', li).addClass('active')
    $('.todo_title', li).removeClass('completed').attr('disabled', false)
```

This function is very simple. When it is called, it will check the state of the todo, and if it's marked as `completed` it will apply the necessary CSS classes to the elements. If it is not, it will remove those styles. One of the nice things about jQuery is that it lets us write code like this, without having to first check to see if the element in question already has the CSS class.

If it already has the class, it ignores the request. The same goes for removing the class; if the element doesn't have the class in question applied to it, then it fails silently—just the behavior we were looking for.

All that is left to do now is call the `styleByState` function in the few places we need to make sure that we apply the correct styles. The first place we need to do that is in the `appendTodo` function. If an existing todo is passed into the `appendTodo` function, we want to make sure it gets styled appropriately.

Example: **(source: app.7/assets/jquery/todo_item.coffee)**

```
@TodoApp ||= {}

TodoApp.appendTodo = (todo) ->
  li = $("<li>#{_.template(Templates.list_item_template)(todo)}</li>")
  $('#new_todo').after(li)
  TodoApp.watchForChanges(li, todo)
  TodoApp.styleByState(li, todo)
```

The other place we need to make sure we update the classes associated with the todo is when a todo is updated. We can do that by adding a callback to the `request` object in the `updateTodo` function:

Example: **(source: app.7/assets/jquery/update_todo.coffee)**

```
@TodoApp ||= {}

# Update the todo:
TodoApp.updateTodo = (li, todo) ->
  todo.title = $('.todo_title', li).val()
  if !todo.title? or todo.title.trim() is ""
    alert "Title can't be blank"
  else
    if $('.todo_state', li).attr('checked')?
      todo.state = 'completed'
    else
      todo.state = 'pending'
    request = $.post "/api/todos/#{todo._id}",
      todo: todo
      _method: 'put'
    request.fail (response) =>
      message = JSON.parse(response.responseText).message
      alert message
    request.done (todo) ->
      TodoApp.styleByState(li, todo)
```

Deleting Todos

Our application is almost complete. All that is left is to hook up the `delete` button so users can delete their unwanted todos. At this point, this code should be pretty simple for you to write, but let's quickly look at it.

We will start by writing a `deleteTodo` function:

Example: **(source: final/assets/jquery/delete_todo.coffee)**

```
@TodoApp ||= {}

# Delete the todo:
TodoApp.deleteTodo = (li, todo) ->
  if confirm "Are you sure?"
    request = $.post "/api/todos/#{todo._id}", _method: 'delete'
    request.done =>
      li.remove()
```

The `deleteTodo` function makes a request back to the API using the `DELETE` HTTP verb, via the special `_method` parameter we discussed earlier. If the request to destroy the todo is successful, we remove the todo from the page—nice, clean, and simple.

Now we need to hook up the `delete` button and we are done. We can do this in the `watchForChanges` function we wrote earlier:

Example: **(source: final/assets/jquery/watch_todo_for_changes.coffee)**

```
@TodoApp ||= {}

# Watch the todo for changes:
TodoApp.watchForChanges = (li, todo) ->
  # If the checkbox is checked/unchecked:
  $('.todo_state', li).click (e) =>
    TodoApp.updateTodo(li, todo)
  # If someone hits "enter" in the title field:
  $('.todo_title', li).keypress (e) =>
    if e.keyCode is 13
      TodoApp.updateTodo(li, todo)
  $('button.danger', li).click (e) =>
    e.preventDefault()
    TodoApp.deleteTodo(li, todo)
```

That's it! Our application is now finished! Congratulations.

Wrapping Up

There you have it. We have used jQuery to write an interactive web client for our todo list application. It was pretty simple, and you can see how CoffeeScript can help us write some very nice looking jQuery.

The approach we took in this chapter, from a code "architecture" perspective, is that of what a lot of jQuery developers probably would have done. Write a bunch of functions, pass around some objects, and do what is necessary. We could have taken another approach to this application, which would have involved writing classes that managed each of the todos and more cleanly wrapped the HTML elements and their events to the todo itself.

So why didn't I show you the second approach? I did this for two reasons. The first I have already stated; the approach we have shown here is one that is common of someone writing plain old JavaScript and jQuery, so I wanted to give you a feel for what that would look like in CoffeeScript. The second reason I didn't write our code in the "class" style is because doing so would mean we would have reinvented the wheel that is Backbone.js.

Backbone.js is a simple framework that lets us write views that bind to elements of a page and associate those views with models, such as our todos, and have them easily listen to each other and respond to events accordingly. As a matter of fact, thinking about it, why don't we see Backbone in action? Turn the page to Chapter 12, "Example: Todo List Part 3 (Client-side w/ Backbone.js)" and let's get started!

By the way, if you are curious to see what the jQuery example would look like if we had written it using classes instead of the approach we took here, I happen to have it already written for you. Enjoy![12]

Notes

1. http://twitter.github.com/bootstrap/
2. http://twitter.com
3. https://github.com/trevorBurnham/connect-assets
4. http://en.wikipedia.org/wiki/John_Resig
5. http://en.wikipedia.org/wiki/Jquery
6. http://documentcloud.github.com/underscore
7. https://github.com/sstephenson/eco
8. http://www.handlebarsjs.com/
9. https://github.com/janl/mustache.js/
10. http://jade-lang.com/
11. https://github.com/jquery/jquery-tmpl
12. https://github.com/markbates/Programming-In-CoffeeScript/tree/master/todo2/alt-final

12

Example: Todo List Part 3 (Client-side w/ Backbone.js)

In Chapter 11, "Example: Todo List Part 2 (Client-side w/ jQuery)" we wrote a client-side front end for a todo list application using the jQuery library. At the end of that chapter I talked about how we could have written that code somewhat differently, but doing so would have meant that we basically rewrote the Backbone.js[1] framework. Because I'm not typically in favor of reinventing the wheel, I thought we could, instead, see what our application would look like if we used Backbone instead of jQuery to write our client-side code.

What Is Backbone.js?

Backbone is a client-side MVC[2] framework written in JavaScript by Jeremy Ashkenas,[3] the creator of a little language known as CoffeeScript.[4] Backbone helps us to write highly responsive client-side applications using JavaScript, or in our case, CoffeeScript.

Backbone has three separate parts. The first is the View layer. Views let us wrap up the rendering of elements on the screen and then watch those elements for changes and respond accordingly. Views can also listen for events on other objects and update themselves based on those events.

The second part of Backbone is models and collections. A model maps to a single instance of an object. In our case it would be a `Todo`. That model object can then communicate with a data store to persist itself. It can also contain other functions that can be helpful when dealing with an object, such as a function to concatenate a first and last name into a single string. A collection is what its name suggests. It is a collection of model objects, so in this application it would be a collection of `Todo` models. A collection in Backbone also has the capability to talk to a data store, such as our API.

Models and collections in Backbone also emit all sorts of events when different actions happen to those objects. For example, when a new model is added to a collection the collection triggers an `add` event. These events can be listened to by other objects, such as views. In the case of a view object, it might listen to a collection for an `add` event and when one is triggered, it will render the model to the screen in the appropriate way. We will see how this works in just a little bit.

The final part of Backbone is the router. Routers in Backbone let us listen to and respond to changes in the URL of the browser. When the URL changes and there is an appropriate mapping in the router, the code associated with that mapping will be executed. This is similar to what we did in our Express application when we built our API. We won't be using routers at all in this chapter, but that doesn't mean they aren't useful. Our particular application just doesn't have any need for them.

All that, of course, is a very quick overview of what Backbone is. We will go into a bit more detail throughout this chapter, but this chapter is not going to be a full tutorial on Backbone. We are just going to look into the parts of Backbone that are appropriate for our application.

Cleaning Up

Before we move on to rebuilding our application, we need to first do a bit of house cleaning in our application to make sure it is ready for us to start incorporating Backbone into it.

The first thing we can do to clean up our application is to delete the `assets/jquery` folder.

Second, we need to remove the reference to that directory from the `assets/application.coffee` file:

Example: **(source: app.1/assets/application.coffee)**

```
#= require "templates"
```

And we're done! If we were to restart our application now, we would be left with just the new todo form, and it would do nothing. Let's start to rebuild the application.

Setting Up Backbone.js

Getting Backbone installed into our application is fairly painless. It has only one dependency: underscore.js.[5] Despite there being only one "hard" dependency, Backbone is not very useful unless we give it a library to do DOM manipulation or AJAX persistence; this is where jQuery (or Zepto[6]) come in. Fortunately, we already have both jQuery and underscore.js in our `index.ejs` file, so all we need to do is add Backbone itself and we are basically done:

Example: **(source: app.1/src/views/index.ejs)**

```
<!DOCTYPE html>
<html>
  <head>
    <title>Todos</title>
```

```
    <script src="http://ajax.googleapis.com/ajax/libs/jquery/1.7.1/jquery.min.js"
➥type="text/javascript"></script>
    <script src="http://documentcloud.github.com/underscore/underscore-min.js"
➥type="text/javascript"></script>
    <script src="http://documentcloud.github.com/backbone/backbone-min.js"
➥type="text/javascript"></script>
    <%- js('/application') %>

    <link rel="stylesheet"
➥href="http://twitter.github.com/bootstrap/1.4.0/bootstrap.min.css">
    <%- css('/application') %>
  </head>
<body>

<div class="container">
  <h1>Todo List</h1>
  <ul id='todos' class='unstyled'>
    <li id='new_todo'>
      <div class="clearfix">
        <div class="input">
          <div class="input-prepend">
            <span class='add-on'>New Todo</span>
            <input class="xlarge todo_title" size="50" type="text" placeholder="Enter
➥your new Todo here..." />
          </div>
        </div>
      </div>
    </li>
  </ul>
</div>

</body>
</html>
```

That is all that is really needed to get Backbone installed into your application and up and running. I am, however, going to add one more file to our setup. I wasn't going to add this until we start writing our `Todo` model, but this seems like a good time to get all of the prep work out of the way.

When Backbone communicates with our API, by default it will want to send data like this:

```
{title: 'My New Todo'}
```

But, if you remember, our API is expecting our data to be namespaced like this:

```
todo: {title: 'My New Todo'}
```

To do this we are going to "borrow" a file from the Ruby gem, backbone-rails,[7] that will monkey patch Backbone to do this for us. So here is that file:

Example: **(source: app.2/assets/backbone_sync.js)**

```
// Taken from https://github.com/codebrew/backbone-rails.
// This namespaces the JSON sent back to the server under the model name.
// IE: {todo: {title: 'Foo'}}
(function() {
  var methodMap = {
    'create': 'POST',
    'update': 'PUT',
    'delete': 'DELETE',
    'read'  : 'GET'
  };

  var getUrl = function(object) {
    if (!(object && object.url)) return null;
    return _.isFunction(object.url) ? object.url() : object.url;
  };

  var urlError = function() {
    throw new Error("A 'url' property or function must be specified");
  };

  Backbone.sync = function(method, model, options) {
    var type = methodMap[method];

    // Default JSON-request options.
    var params = _.extend({
      type:         type,
      dataType:     'json',
      beforeSend: function( xhr ) {
        var token = $('meta[name="csrf-token"]').attr('content');
        if (token) xhr.setRequestHeader('X-CSRF-Token', token);

        model.trigger('sync:start');
      }
    }, options);

    if (!params.url) {
      params.url = getUrl(model) || urlError();
    }

    // Ensure that we have the appropriate request data.
    if (!params.data && model && (method == 'create' || method == 'update')) {
      params.contentType = 'application/json';
```

```
      var data = {}

      if(model.paramRoot) {
        data[model.paramRoot] = model.toJSON();
      } else {
        data = model.toJSON();
      }

      params.data = JSON.stringify(data)
    }

    // Don't process data on a non-GET request.
    if (params.type !== 'GET') {
      params.processData = false;
    }

    // Trigger the sync end event
    var complete = options.complete;
    options.complete = function(jqXHR, textStatus) {
      model.trigger('sync:end');
      if (complete) complete(jqXHR, textStatus);
    };

    // Make the request.
    return $.ajax(params);
  }

}).call(this);
```

I don't really expect you to understand just what it is doing, especially because we haven't gotten to talking about models yet, but believe me, it'll make our lives a little easier and nicer. So just accept that it is helping us and thank it for being there. To add it to our application, we should first place the code in a file under the `assets` directory called `backbone_sync.js` and then require the `backbone_sync.js` file in the `assets/application.coffee` file:

Example: **(source: app.2/assets/application.coffee)**

```
#= require "backbone_sync"
#= require "templates"
#= require_tree "models"
```

Now, with all of those necessary preliminaries out of the way we are ready to start writing some Backbone!

Writing our Todo Model and Collection

The first part of this application that we'll look at is the `Todo` model. This model will represent an individual todo that we get back from our API.

In the `assets` directory, let's create a new folder called `models`. In that folder we will put the `Todo` model as well as the `Todos` collection.

Example: **(source: app.2/assets/models/todo.coffee)**

```
# The Todo model for the Backbone client:
class @Todo extends Backbone.Model
  # namespace JSON under 'todo' see backbone_sync.js
  paramRoot: 'todo'

  # Build the url, appending _id if it exists:
  url: ->
    u = "/api/todos"
    u += "/#{@get("_id")}" unless @isNew()
    return u

  # The default Backbone isNew function looks for 'id',
  # Mongoose returns "_id", so we need to update it accordingly:
  isNew: ->
    !@get("_id")?
```

When writing a Backbone model, it is important that we extend the `Backbone.Model` class; otherwise, we won't get any of the functionality we expect of a Backbone-based model.

Because we are using `backbone_sync.js`, we need to set the name we want our data to be nested under when it is sent back to the server. We do that by setting `paramRoot` to `todo`.

Next, we need to tell Backbone what URL this model will use to talk to the API. We do this by creating a `url` function. Backbone will automatically look for this function later and tell it where our API is located. When we have a new `Todo` object, it won't have an ID associated with it, so we want to append it only if the object isn't new. The `isNew` function built in to Backbone will return true or false based on whether the object is "new" or not.

> **Tip**
>
> If you want to retrieve an attribute on a Backbone object, such as the `title` or `_id` attribute, you have to use the `get` function to do that. That is because all attributes on a Backbone model are stored in a variable called `attributes` to prevent any sort of clashing between the Backbone attributes and functions and your attributes.

The `isNew` function in Backbone does its magic by looking to see if the object has an `id` attribute. If it does, it considers the object not to be new. Unfortunately, MongoDB[8] does not return an `id` attribute, but rather an `_id` attribute. Because of this, we need to rewrite the `isNew` function to behave the way we want it to.

> **Tip**
>
> Like the `isNew` function, we had to write a custom `url` function because MongoDB uses `_id` instead of `id`. If we had an `_id` attribute, we could have set the `url` attribute (not function) equal to `/api/todos` in the `Todo` model, and Backbone would have automatically appended the `id` attribute to the `url` attribute for us. But, as it is, here we are.

With the `Todo` model written, let's write the associated collection, `Todos`. A collection, as we mentioned earlier, is a list, similar to an array, that holds many `Todo` models. In this application we will use the `Todos` initially to fetch all the existing todos from our API.

> **Tip**
>
> Personally, I find it a little annoying that I have to have a separate class to manage a collection of models, but it's a very small price to pay for the features and functionality you get from this. It's just something you learn to live with. As a side note, I usually place the collection class definition in the same file as the model definition. It makes it easier to find and change later. In this case, I have them separated because it makes it easier to show you the code.

The `Todos` collection class is going to be really simple:

Example: **(source: app.2/assets/models/todos.coffee)**

```
# The Todos collection for the Backbone client:
class @Todos extends Backbone.Collection
  model: Todo

  url: "/api/todos"
```

The `Todos` class needs to extend `Backbone.Collection` for the magic to happen. After that we just need to define two attributes of our collection.

The first is the `model` attribute, which we set to `Todo`. This tells the collection that when it fetches data from the server, or data is given to it, that data should be turned into `Todo` objects.

The second attribute is the `url` attribute. Because this is a collection, we don't have to concern ourselves with any IDs on the URL. So it's pretty straightforward.

With that, the `Todos` collection is completed.

Let's update the `assets/application.coffee` file to require the `models` directory we have created here:

Example: **(source: app.2/assets/application.coffee)**

```
#= require "backbone_sync"
#= require "templates"
#= require_tree "models"
```

If you're anything like me, you are probably eager to see this work in action. Okay, let's quickly use the `Todos` collection and the `Todo` model to fetch the existing todos from the API and print them out using the template we wrote in the previous chapter.

We can do this quite simply by adding a few lines to the `assets/application.coffee` file, like such:

Example: **(source: app.3/assets/application.coffee)**

```
#= require "backbone_sync"
#= require "templates"
#= require_tree "models"

$ ->
  template = _.template(Templates.list_item_template)
  todos = new Todos()
  todos.fetch
    success: ->
      todos.forEach (todo) ->
        $('#todos').append("<li>#{template(todo.toJSON())}</li>")
```

When the DOM is loaded, we will create a new instance of the template, so we can use it to render each todo out after we fetch them.

Next, we create a new instance of the `Todos` collection and assign it to a variable named `todos`.

With an instance of the `Todos` collection ready, we can call the `fetch` function. The `fetch` function will use the `url` attribute we set on the `Todos` collection to talk back to the server and fetch a list of todos for us. If the fetch is successful, it will call the `success` callback we passed into the `fetch` function.

The `success` callback, if executed, will call the `forEach` function on the `todos` object to iterate over the list of `Todo` models it retrieved from the server. We then render the template using each todo and write them to the screen.

The result of all this is that you should see your existing todos nicely printed to the screen when you reload your application. Don't expect to be able to update or destroy the todos yet. We'll get to that later. In the next section, we are going to write our first Backbone view to replace that display code we just wrote.

Listing Todos Using a View

The previous code we wrote works, but it can definitely be made a lot cleaner and more flexible. That's where `Backbone.View` classes come in. Let's replace what we've already written with a `Backbone.View` class to clean it up.

First create a `views` folder under the `assets` folder. That is where all the view files will live. In that file, let's create `todo_list_view.coffee` and fill it with the following:

Example: **(source: app.4/assets/views/todo_list_view.coffee)**

```
# The 'main' Backbone view of the application
class @TodoListView extends Backbone.View

  el: '#todos'

  initialize: ->
    @template = _.template(Templates.list_item_template)
    @collection.bind("reset", @render)
    @collection.fetch()

  render: =>
    @collection.forEach (todo) =>
      $(@el).append("<li>#{@template(todo.toJSON())}</li>")
```

So what is going on with this code? Great question. The first thing we do is create a new class, `TodoListView`, and have it extend `Backbone.View`. By extending the `Backbone.View` class we get access to some helpful functions and features that we'll be using throughout the rest of this chapter.

> **Tip**
>
> Notice that, like the `Todo` and `Todos` classes, we are defining the `TodoListView` class with a prefixed `@` symbol. The `@` will make sure the classes are available outside of the automatic wrapper function CoffeeScript writes around each `.coffee` file. If we didn't do this, we wouldn't have access to these classes outside of their respective `.coffee` files.

Next, we tell the view that the element on the page we want to associate this view with is the `#todos` element. We do this by setting the `el` attribute. If we didn't do this, Backbone would create a new `div` object for the `el` attribute, and you would be responsible for placing that element on the page yourself. We will see this in action in a little bit.

We move on next to the `initialize` function. The `initialize` function is a special function that will be called by `Backbone` after an instance of the view object has been initialized. You *definitely* do not want to write a `constructor` function in your view classes. This can potentially override all the rich chocolaty goodness that Backbone is trying to create for you. If you need to have things happen when the view is instantiated, the `initialize` function is definitely the way to go.

As it happens, we have a few things we do want to do when the `TodoListView` class is instantiated. In particular, we have a few things we want to do with the `@collection` object. Your first question should be, Where did that variable come from? Backbone has a few "magic" variables and attributes and `@collection` and `@model` are two of them. In a minute we will see that when we create an instance of the `TodoListView` class, we are going to pass it an object that contains a `collection` key that has a value of `new Todos()`. That will then get assigned to the `@collection` object, in the `TodoListView`, giving us access to the `Todos` collection. When we look at the necessary changes to the `application.coffee` file shortly, this should all become a bit clearer.

What do we need to do with the `@collection` object, also known as a `Todos` collection? First, we are going to call the `bind` function and tell it that whenever the collection triggers a `reset` event, we want to call the `@render` function in the `TodoListView` instance we have.

How does a collection object trigger a `reset` event? One of the ways, and probably the most common in Backbone, is through the `fetch` function. When called, the `fetch` function will get the full list of todos from the API, as we saw earlier. Because we need those todos, we call the `fetch` function as the last line of the `initialize` function. The calling of the `fetch` function will, in turn, trigger a `reset` event, which will then call the `@render` function.

The `@render` function is where we will print out the list of todos in the collection to the page. The `@render` function shouldn't look too different from the original code we had in `application.coffee` to render each todo on the screen. The big differences are that we are calling the `forEach` function directly on the `@collection` object, instead of through a `success` callback. The other difference is that we no longer have to refer to the `#todos` element directly; instead, we can use `@el` which will point there for us. Using `@el` instead of the name of the element directly is great should we ever have to refactor our code. We just change the value of `@el` and don't have to change the rest of the code base.

> **Tip**
>
> The `@render` function is declared using the => syntax instead of the -> so that when it is called after the `reset` event has been triggered, the `@render` function knows its context and has access to the rest of the class. If a -> was used, this code would result in an error similar to `TypeError: 'undefined' is not an object (evaluating 'this.collection.forEach')` because `@render` would not have access to the `@collection` object. If we really wanted to use the -> syntax, we would have to have manually bound the function ourselves in the `initialize` function by using the `bindAll` function in the Underscore library. `_.bindAll(@, "render")`. I would rather just use the => syntax.

All that is left now is to clean up the `application.coffee` file to use the new `TodoListView` class instead of our old code:

Example: **(source: app.4/assets/application.coffee)**

```
#= require "backbone_sync"
#= require "templates"
#= require_tree "models"
#= require_tree "views"

$ ->
  # Start Backbone.js App:
  new TodoListView(collection: new Todos())
```

As you can see, we had to first make sure we required the `views` directory so that it would pick up all the views we are going to write there. After that, when the page is loaded, all we have to do is create a new instance of the `TodoListView` class, passing it a new instance of the `Todos` collection. With that we are done with the `application.coffee` file for the rest of this chapter.

Creating New Todos

With our code to display existing todos to the screen working nicely, let's move on to hooking up our form so we can create new todos. To accomplish this, we need a view to manage the form and handle when people press the Enter key when typing their todos, so we can save them to the server and then display them to the screen.

The `NewTodoView` class we need should look like this:

Example: **(source: app.5/assets/views/new_todo_view.coffee)**

```
# The view to handle creating new Todos:
class @NewTodoView extends Backbone.View

  el: '#new_todo'

  events:
    'keypress .todo_title': 'handleKeypress'

  initialize: ->
    @collection.bind("add", @resetForm)
    @$('.todo_title').focus()

  handleKeypress: (e) =>
    if e.keyCode is 13
      @saveModel(e)

  resetForm: (todo) =>
    @$('.todo_title').val("")
```

```
saveModel: (e) =>
  e?.preventDefault()
  model = new Todo()
  model.save {title: @$('.todo_title').val()},
    success: =>
      @collection.add(model)
    error: (model, error) =>
      if error.responseText?
        error = JSON.parse(error.responseText)
      alert error.message
```

It's a bit longer than the `TodoListView` class we just wrote, but most of that is the `saveModel` function, which, by now, should be pretty old hat to you. However, we'll discuss it briefly in just a second.

The `TodoListView` needs to associate itself with the #new_todo element on the page, so again, we can set this via the `el` attribute.

Next, we have to tell the `NewTodoView` class to listen for certain events and respond to those events when they happen. Backbone lets us easily map those using the `events` object attribute. Mapping events using the `events` attributes is a little weird, though. The key for the event you want to create is a compound key. The first part is the event you are waiting for, `click`, `submit`, `keypress`, and so on, that is then followed by the CSS selector you want to watch for the event. The value of the mapping is the function you want to call when that event on that CSS selector happens. In our case, we are watching for a `keypress` event on the `.todo_title`, and when that happens, we want to call the `handleKeypress` function.

> **Tip**
>
> There are two important things to note about the `events` mapping in Backbone. The first is that the CSS selector is scoped to the `el` attribute you set. The second is that we pass in a string with the function name, not a reference to the function, like we do when binding to collections, as we saw earlier. I'm not sure about the reason for this mismatch, but that's just the way it is. This is something to look for if things aren't working quite as expected.

In the `initialize` function we want to bind the `resetForm` function to the `add` event on the `@collection` object, which we will pass in when we create the instance of the `NewTodoView` class. Later in the `saveModel` function, when we get an acknowledgement from the API that we have successfully created the new todo, we will add it to the `@collection`. That will trigger the `add` event, which will call the `resetForm` function. The `resetForm` function, as you can see, cleans up the form to its original state before the user typed in the todo.

Also in the `initialize` function, we want to set the `.todo_title` element in the form to have focus when the page loads. Here we can use a special function on the `Backbone.View` class, `@$`. The `@$` function lets us write jQuery CSS selectors that are already scoped to the `@el` element we are watching in the view. Without this special function, we would have to write something like `$('#new_todo .todo_title')` to get access to the same element.

The `handleKeypress` function should look pretty familiar to you. We are going to check that the key the user pressed is the Enter key; if it is, it will call the `@saveModel` function to do the heavy lifting of saving the model back to the API.

> **Tip**
>
> I could have saved the model directly in the `handleKeypress` function, but down the line if we ever wanted to add a `save` button, we can wire that button up directly to the `saveModel` function, using the `events` attribute, without having to duplicate any code.

The `saveModel` should mostly look like the other functions we've written that do something similar. First, we create a new instance of the `Todo` class. Then we collect a list of attributes, in this case just the `title`, and pass it to the save class along with a `success` callback and an `error` callback.

> **Tip**
>
> Why did I write `e?.preventDefault()` instead of `e.preventDefault()`? The reason is that sometimes there might be reasons why we would call this function and not pass in an `event` object. By using the existential operator in CoffeeScript, we can guarantee that the `preventDefault` function will be called only if there is an event passed into the function. It's a nice habit to get into.

The real magic, for us, happens in the `success` callback when the todo has been successfully saved to the database via the API. At that point we are going to call the `add` function on the `@collection` object and pass in the newly created todo. When we do so, the `resetForm` function will be called because we told the `@collection` to call that function when the `add` event is triggered.

If we were to fire up the application right now and try this, nothing would happen because we haven't created a new instance of the `NewTodoView` class yet. To do this, let's modify the `TodoListView` class a little bit to not only create the new `NewTodoView` instance, but also to handle when new todos are added to the `@collection` and display them properly to the page.

Example: **(source: app.5/assets/views/todo_list_view.coffee)**

```
# The 'main' Backbone view of the application
class @TodoListView extends Backbone.View

  el: '#todos'

  initialize: ->
    @template = _.template(Templates.list_item_template)
    @collection.bind("reset", @render)
    @collection.fetch()
    @collection.bind("add", @renderAdded)
    new NewTodoView(collection: @collection)
```

```
  render: =>
    @collection.forEach (todo) =>
      $(@el).append("<li>#{@template(todo.toJSON())}</li>")

  renderAdded: (todo) =>
    $("#new_todo").after("<li>#{@template(todo.toJSON())}</li>")
```

In the `initialize` function of the `TodoListView` class we added two new lines. The first new line adds another listener for the `add` event on the `@collection` object, this time telling it to trigger the `renderAdded` function in the `TodoListView` class.

The second line we added in the `initialize` function of the `TodoListView` class creates a new instance of the `NewTodoView` and passes it the `@collection` object.

The `renderAdded` function in the `TodoListView` class will be called when a new todo is added to the `@collection` object, being passed the newly minted todo. With that new todo in hand, we can easily add it to the list of todos being displayed on the page.

> **Tip**
>
> We could have written this code so that the `render` function did all the heavy lifting, and we wouldn't have needed a `renderAdded` function. There are a few reasons why I didn't do that. First, if we rerendered the whole list of todos, that's a lot more time consuming than just adding one more todo to the page. Second, we would have had to write a bit more logic in the `render` function to first clear out the list of todos already on the page, so we don't end up with duplicates.

A View per Todo

Our application has come a long way since we threw out all the jQuery code we wrote in Chapter 11, "Example: Todo List Part 2 (Client-side w/ jQuery)," but we're not there yet. We can create new todos and display them, along with existing todos to the page, but we can't edit or delete existing todos yet. Before we get to that, we need to do a little bit of clean up of the code we have already written. We are going to need a view to manage each of the todos on the page so we can watch them for changes, such as someone editing the title, marking it as "complete," or wanting to delete the todo.

For right now, let's update our code to use a new view, `TodoListItemView`, for each of the todos on the page. So let's create that class:

Example: **(source: app.6/assets/views/todo_list_item_view.coffee)**

```
# The view for each todo in the list:
class @TodoListItemView extends Backbone.View

  tagName: 'li'
```

```
  initialize: ->
    @template = _.template(Templates.list_item_template)
    @render()

  render: =>
    $(@el).html(@template(@model.toJSON()))
    if @model.get('state') is "completed"
      @$('.todo_state').attr('checked', true)
      @$('label.active').removeClass('active')
      @$('.todo_title').addClass('completed').attr('disabled', true)
    return @
```

The `TodoListItemView` class doesn't map to an existing element on the page, so we don't need to set the `el` attribute. By default, in a `Backbone.View` class the `el` will default to a `div` tag. However, in our case we want it to be an `li` tag. To set that we can set the `tagName` attribute.

In the `initialize` function in the `TodoListItemView` class, we are setting up a `@template` variable to hold the template we want to use when we render the todo out to the screen. After that, we call the `@render` function.

The `render` function will set the HTML of the `@el`, in this case an `li` element, to that of the template using the `@model` object. Where did `@model` come from? The `@model` object will be passed in when we instantiate new instances of the `TodoListItemView` class, as we'll see shortly.

After we render the template in the `render` function, we need to update the HTML to use the correct styling should the todo be marked as "completed."

Finally, the `render` function will return the instance of the `TodoListItemView` class. This is not necessary, but is somewhat of a convention in the Backbone world because it enables people to easily chain calls together on the object.

With the `TodoListItemView` class written, we can update the `TodoListView` to make use of it, and to eliminate the need for doing the template rendering there.

Example: **(source: app.6/assets/views/todo_list_view.coffee)**

```
# The 'main' Backbone view of the application
class @TodoListView extends Backbone.View

  el: '#todos'

  initialize: ->
    @collection.bind("reset", @render)
    @collection.fetch()
    @collection.bind("add", @renderAdded)
    new NewTodoView(collection: @collection)
```

```
  render: =>
    @collection.forEach (todo) =>
      $(@el).append(new TodoListItemView(model: todo).el)

  renderAdded: (todo) =>
    $("#new_todo").after(new TodoListItemView(model: todo).el)
```

In both the `render` and `renderAdded` functions of `TodoListView`, we are able to replace the HTML we had wrapping the templating in favor of creating a new instance of the `TodoListItemView` class and getting the `el` attribute on that class. Remember that the `el` attribute had its HTML defined in the `render` function of the `TodoListItemView` class.

Now when we restart our application, we should see all the todos nicely listed out, and any that had previously been marked as "complete" should now have the appropriate CSS styling applied to them.

Updating and Validating Models from Views

Now that we have a view, `TodoListItemView`, that is associated with each todo on the page, we have a nice central place to put logic to watch for changes on that todo and act appropriately. Let's start by watching for changes to the todo. There are two changes someone can make to the todo. They can edit the title or they can check or uncheck the check box, therefore changing the state of the todo. We will cover destroying the todo in the next section.

Example: **(source: app.7/assets/views/todo_list_item_view.coffee)**

```
# The view for each todo in the list:
class @TodoListItemView extends Backbone.View

  tagName: 'li'

  events:
    'keypress .todo_title': 'handleKeypress'
    'change .todo_state': 'saveModel'

  initialize: ->
    @template = _.template(Templates.list_item_template)
    @model.bind("change", @render)
    @model.bind("error", @modelSaveFailed)
    @render()

  render: =>
    $(@el).html(@template(@model.toJSON()))
    if @model.get('state') is "completed"
      @$('.todo_state').attr('checked', true)
```

```
    @$('label.active').removeClass('active')
    @$('.todo_title').addClass('completed').attr('disabled', true)
  return @

handleKeypress: (e) =>
  if e.keyCode is 13
    @saveModel(e)

saveModel: (e) =>
  e?.preventDefault()
  attrs = {title: @$('.todo_title').val()}
  if @$('.todo_state').attr('checked')?
    attrs.state = 'completed'
  else
    attrs.state = 'pending'
  @model.save attrs

modelSaveFailed: (model, error) =>
  if error.responseText?
    error = JSON.parse(error.responseText)
  alert error.message
  @$('.todo_title').val(@model.get('title'))
```

The first thing we need to do is to add a few events. The first is for when a `keypress` event happens on the `.todo_title` field. Just like in the `NewTodoView` class, we are going to call a `handleKeypress` function, which will check to see if the key pressed was Enter. If it is, the `saveModel` function will be called. We will also be looking for a `change` event on the `.todo_state` check box. Any change to the check box will result in the `saveModel` function being called directly.

In the `initialize` function we are going to tell the `@model` object that we are interested in two events. The first is the `change` event. If the model should change at all, we want to call the `render` function again to make sure that we are displaying the most recent version of the todo. This comes in handy when someone checks the check box to change the state of the todo and we need to add/remove CSS styles accordingly.

The other event we are listening to is the `error` event. This will get called if there are any errors when trying to save the todo to the API. If there are errors, we want to call the `modelSaveFailed` function, which will present any errors back to the user.

Finally, we need a `saveModel` function, because we already told Backbone to call it should someone try to update the todo. This function shouldn't need explaining by this point. Simply grab the appropriate attributes we want to update and pass them to the save function.

> **Tip**
>
> In the `NewTodoView` class, we are passing in `success` and `error` callbacks to the `saveModel` function, but in the `TodoListItemView` class we are not. The reason is that we are listening for events on the `@model` object that are going to, essentially, do that for us. We didn't use this approach in the `NewTodoView` class because we are constantly creating new `Todo` instances, so we would have to keep binding the events. It's just easier there to add the callbacks.

With all of this, we should be able to update the title and the state of the todo and have them persist back to the server and render appropriately when they've been updated.

Validation

Before we move off of updating the todos, let's add some simple, client-side validation to the `Todo` class so we don't have to keep going back to the server to validate the object. In particular, we are concerned with whether the `title` attribute is blank.

Because our `Todo` class inherits from `Backbone.Model`, we have access to a very simple validation system. The way it works is this: When the `save` function is called on a `Backbone.Model`, it checks to see if there is a function called `validate`. If the `validate` function exists, an object is passed into it that contains all the changed attributes. If the `validate` function returns a value other than `null`, the `save` function stops immediately and returns whatever value the `validate` function returned.

Let's add a `validate` function to the `Todo` model:

Example: **(source: app.7/assets/models/todo.coffee)**

```
# The Todo model for the Backbone client:
class @Todo extends Backbone.Model
  # namespace JSON under 'todo' see backbone_sync.js
  paramRoot: 'todo'

  # Build the url, appending _id if it exists:
  url: ->
    u = "/api/todos"
    u += "/#{@get("_id")}" unless @isNew()
    return u

  # The default Backbone isNew function looks for 'id',
  # Mongoose returns "_id", so we need to update it accordingly:
  isNew: ->
    !@get("_id")?
```

```
  # Validate the model before saving:
  validate: (attrs) ->
    if !attrs.title? or attrs.title.trim() is ""
      return message: "Title can't be blank"
```

As you can see, it's pretty simple. We check to make sure that not only is there a `title` attribute but that it is also not a blank string. If it doesn't exist, or it is blank, we return an object that contains the key `message` that has a value of `"Title can't be blank"`.

That's it! Try it out. If you enter a blank value for the title of either an existing todo or a new todo, you should be presented with an alert that reads "Title can't be blank." All the code up to this point has been written to handle the `validate` method right out of the box. There was nothing more we needed to add.

Deleting Models from Views

All that is left to do now is to hook up the Delete button, and our application will be complete. This is incredibly easy. We need to update the `TodoListItemView` and tell it to listen for a click on the button, and then have it call the appropriate function to destroy the todo and remove it from the page.

Example: **(source: final/assets/views/todo_list_item_view.coffee)**

```
# The view for each todo in the list:
class @TodoListItemView extends Backbone.View

  tagName: 'li'

  events:
    'keypress .todo_title': 'handleKeypress'
    'change .todo_state': 'saveModel'
    'click .danger': 'destroy'

  initialize: ->
    @template = _.template(Templates.list_item_template)
    @model.bind("change", @render)
    @model.bind("error", @modelSaveFailed)
    @render()

  render: =>
    $(@el).html(@template(@model.toJSON()))
    if @model.get('state') is "completed"
      @$('.todo_state').attr('checked', true)
```

```
      @$('label.active').removeClass('active')
      @$('.todo_title').addClass('completed').attr('disabled', true)
    return @

  handleKeypress: (e) =>
    if e.keyCode is 13
      @saveModel(e)

  saveModel: (e) =>
    e?.preventDefault()
    attrs = {title: @$('.todo_title').val()}
    if @$('.todo_state').attr('checked')?
      attrs.state = 'completed'
    else
      attrs.state = 'pending'
    @model.save attrs

  modelSaveFailed: (model, error) =>
    if error.responseText?
      error = JSON.parse(error.responseText)
    alert error.message
    @$('.todo_title').val(@model.get('title'))

  destroy: (e) =>
    e?.preventDefault()
    if confirm "Are you sure you want to destroy this todo?"
      @model.destroy
        success: =>
          $(@el).remove()
```

With another addition to the `events` attribute, we just need to write a `destroy` function that will destroy the todo through the API and remove it from the page when it's done. That's exactly what the `destroy` function we wrote here does. Before we call the `destroy` function on the `Todo` model, another built-in Backbone function, we are going to be polite and ask the users if they are sure they really want to destroy the todo.

When the todo is successfully destroyed from the server, we use jQuery and its `remove` function to remove the `@el` for the todo from the page. With that, the application is done!

> **Tip**
>
> There are a few events we can listen for when a model is destroyed. For example, on the collection we could have listened for the `destroy` event and then rerendered the list of todos. I didn't do this for the same reasons I didn't rerender the list of todos when a new one was added. It's just nice to know that you can listen for those events, should you need them.

Wrapping Up

In this chapter we ripped out the jQuery we wrote in Chapter 11, "Example: Todo List Part 2 (Client-side w/ jQuery)," and replaced it with the Backbone.js framework. This seems like a great place to remind you that should you want to download the code from this chapter, as well as the code from Chapter 11 to see how they compare, you can find all the code from this book on Github.com.[9]

We learned about Backbone's models and collections. Then we learned how to use views and events to manage the elements on our page and how they interact with each other.

This chapter just scratches the surface of what Backbone.js has to offer in terms of writing highly responsive, well-organized front ends for your applications. I encourage you to seek out some of the great tutorials, blog posts, and screencasts on Backbone to learn more about it.

Notes

1. http://documentcloud.github.com/backbone/
2. http://en.wikipedia.org/wiki/Model–view–controller
3. https://github.com/jashkenas/
4. Seriously, I'm not just plugging Backbone in this chapter because Jeremy also wrote CoffeeScript. I really do love it and use it all the time.
5. http://documentcloud.github.com/underscore
6. http://zeptojs.com
7. https://github.com/codebrew/backbone-rails
8. http://www.mongodb.org/
9. https://github.com/markbates/Programming-In-CoffeeScript

Index

@ alias, 51-52

=> (fat arrow), 154-156

\ (back slashes), 5

/ (forward slashes), 76

A

adding

compilers to browsers, 6-7

form to client-side todo list application, 242-247

jQuery to client-side todo list application, 240-241

views to todo list application, 268-273

aliases, 46-47

@ alias, 51-52

and alias, 49-50

Boolean aliases, 50-51

not alias, 48-49

or alias, 49-50

and alias, 49-50

anonymous wrapper function, 20-22

APIs, writing todo API, 225-226

app server

building with Node.js, 199-213

testing with Node.js, 214-215

arguments, 70-72
default arguments, 72-75
splats, 75-79
arithmetic operators, 33-35
arrays, 81-90
destructing assignment, 86-90
iterating, 105-106
slicing, 92-94
swapping assignment, 85-86
testing inclusion, 83-84
values
injecting, 95-96
replacing, 94-95
Ashkenas, Jeremy, 255
assignment operators, 35-39
asynchronous programming, 151-154
attributes, retrieving from objects, 101-103

B

back slashes (\), 5
Backbone, 255-256
configuring for todo list application, 256-259
todo model, writing, 256-259
todos
creating, 265-268
listing with view, 263-265
bare flag, 9-10
beforeEach function, 181-187
binding, 151-158
block comments, 30
Boolean aliases, 50-51
Bootstrap, building client-side todo list application, 237-240
browsers, in-browser compilation, 6-7
build task (Cake), 167
building
objects, 96-101
todo list application
client-side, 237-252
controller, cleaning up, 232-236
Express, setting up, 218-222
MongoDB, setting up, 222-225
server-side, 217
todo API, writing, 225-226
by keyword, 106-107

C

Cake, 161
tasks
invoking, 167-169
options, 163-167
running, 163
writing, 162-163
Cakefiles, 161
calling functions, 68-70
classes
defining, 123-124
extending, 137-145
inheritance, 137-145
scope, 127-137
class-level functions, 145-150
clean task (Cake), 167
cleaning up todo list application controller, 232-236
client-side todo list application, building, 237-252
closing REPL, 5

code, not repeating, 68

coffee command, 8-9

CoffeeScript, declaring variables, 19-20

collections

arrays

destructing assignment, 86-90

injecting values, 95-96

iterating, 105-106

replacing values, 94-95

slicing, 92-94

swapping assignment, 85-86

testing inclusion, 83-84

ranges, reverse ranges, 91-92

command-line compilation, 7-8

comments, 29-30

block comments, 30

inline comments, 29-30

comparison operators, 39-42

compile flag, 7-8

compiling

command-line compilation, 7-8

in-browser compilation, 6-7

comprehensions, 116-118

concatenation, forward slashes (/), 76

conditional statements

if statement, 53-54

if/else if statement, 56-58

if/else statement, 54-56

inline conditionals, 60

switch case statements, 60-63

unless statement, 58-60

configuring

Backbone for todo list application, 256-259

Jasmine, 172-175

constructor function, 126-127

creating objects, 96-101

custom matchers (Jasmine), defining, 187-190

D

declaring variables

in CoffeeScript, 19-20

in JavaScript, 18-19

default arguments, 72-75

defining

Cake tasks, 162-163

classes, 123-124

functions, 68-70

arguments, 70-72

default arguments, 72-75

parentheses, 72

matchers (Jasmine), 187-190

regular expressions, 31

deleting

models from views (todo list application), 273-274

todos in client-side todo list application, 252

"describe" block (Jasmine), writing, 175

destructing assignment, 86-90

do keyword, 119-120

dot notation, 101

E

executing CoffeeScript files, 11

existential operator, 43-46

Express, building todo list application, 218-222

extended regular expressions, 31
extending classes, 137-145

F

fat arrow (=>), 154-156
flags
- bare flag, 9-10
- compile flag, 7-8
- output flag, 9
- print flag, 10
- watch flag, 10-11

for loops
- by keyword, 106-107
- when keyword, 107, 109-110

form, adding to client-side todo list application, 242-247
function keyword, 16
functions, 65-68
- anonymous wrapper function, 20-22
- arguments, 70-72
  - default arguments, 72-75
  - splats, 75-79
- beforeEach, 181-187
- binding, 151-158
- class-level, 145-150
- constructor, 126-127
- defining, 68-70, 125-126
- overriding, 142-145
- prototype functions, 110, 150-151

G-H

Hello World program, Node.js, 195-197
heredocs, 28-29
HTML files in-browser compilation, 6-7

I

if statement, 53-54
if/else if statement, 56-58
if/else statement, 54-56
in-browser compilation, 6-7
inheritance, 137-145
injecting array values, 95-96
inline comments, 29-30
inline conditionals, 60
installing
- Jasmine, 172
- Node.js, 194-195

interpolation, string interpolation, 23-25
iterating arrays, 105-106

J-K

Jasmine
- "describe" block, writing, 175
- installing, 172
- matchers, defining, 187-190
- setting up, 172-175
- testing with, 175-176
  - beforeEach function, 181-187
- unit testing, 176-181

JavaScript
Backbone, 255-256
todo model, writing, 256-259
todos, listing with a view, 263-265
Node.js, 193-194
app server, building, 199-213
app server, testing, 214-215
Hello World program, 195-197
installing, 194-195
streaming APIs, writing, 197-199
variables, declaring, 18-19
jQuery, adding to client-side todo list application, 240-241
keywords, var, 19

L

listing existing todos in todo list application, 247-248
literal strings, 25-28
long options, 163
loops
comprehensions, 116-118
do keyword, 119-120
for loops
by keyword, 106-107
when keyword, 107, 109-110
until loops, 114-115
while loops, 113-114

M-N

MongoDB, setting up, 222-225
Mongoose, finding todos in todo list application, 227-228
new keyword, 124
Node.js, 193-194
app server
building, 199-213
testing, 214-215
Hello World program, 195-197
installing, 194-195
streaming APIs, writing, 197-199
NPM (Node Package Management), 193
Express, setting up, 218-222

O

objects
attributes, retrieving, 101-103
building, 96-101
destructing assignment, 103-105
iterating, 108-113
operators
aliases, 46-47
@ alias, 51-52
and alias, 49-50
Boolean aliases, 50-51
not alias, 48-49
or alias, 49-50
arithmetic operators, 33-35
assignment operators, 35-39
comparison operators, 39-42
existential operator, 43-46
string operators, 42-43
options for Cake tasks, 163-167
or alias, 49-50
output flag, 9
overriding functions, 142-145

P

parentheses, 16-17
- comprehensions, 117
- functions, calling, 72

print flag, 10
prototype function, 110
prototype functions, 150-151

Q-R

querying todo list application, 227-228
quitting REPL, 5

ranges, 90-96
- reverse ranges, 91-92

regular expressions, extended regular expressions, 31
REPL, 3-5
- \ (back slashes), 5
- Node.js, 194
- quitting, 5

replacing array values, 94-95
retrieving attributes from objects, 101-103
reverse ranges, 91-92
running Cake tasks, 163

S

scope in classes, 127-137
servers (Node.js), creating, 195-197
server-side, building todo list application, 217
setting up Jasmine, 172-175
short options, 163
significant whitespace, 14-16
slicing arrays, 92-94
splats, 75-79
streaming APIs, writing with Node.js, 197-199
string interpolation, 23-25
string operators, 42-43
strings
- heredocs, 28-29
- literal strings, 25-28

switch case statements, 60-63
synchronous programming, 151
syntax
- function keyword, 16
- parentheses, 16-17
- ranges, 90
- significant whitespace, 14-16

T

tasks
- Cake
  - invoking, 167-169
  - options, 163-167
  - running, 163
  - writing, 162-163

TDD (test-driven development), 171
terminating REPL, 5
testing
- with Jasmine, 175-176
  - beforeEach function, 181-187
  - matchers, defining, 187-190
- TDD, 171
- unit testing, 176-181

testing inclusion, Node.js app server, 214-215

todo list application
- Backbone
  - configuring, 256-259
  - todos, creating, 265-268
  - todos, listing with a view, 263-265
- client-side
  - building, 237-252
  - exisiting todos, listing, 247-248
  - form, creating, 242-247
  - jQuery, adding, 240-241
  - todos, deleting, 252
  - todos, updating, 248-251
- controller, cleaning up, 232-236
- server-side
  - building, 217
- todo API, writing, 225-226
- todos
  - creating, 228-230
  - finding, 227-228
  - updating, 230-232
- views
  - adding, 268-273
  - deleting models from, 273-274

todo list application, building
- Express, setting up, 218-222
- MongoDB, setting up, 222-225

Twitter Bootstrap
- todo list application
  - client-side, building, 237-240

U

unit testing with Jasmine, 176-181

unless statement, 58-60

until loops, 114-115

updating
- todo list application, 230-232
- todos in client-side todo list application, 248-251

V

var keyword, 19

variables, declaring
- in CoffeeScript, 19-20
- in JavaScript, 18-19

views
- adding to todo list application, 268-273
- models, deleting from (todo list application), 273-274

W-X-Y-Z

watch flag, 10-11

when keyword, 109-110

while loops, 113-114

writing
- Cake tasks, 162-163
- "describe" block (Jasmine), 175
- todo API, 225-226
- todo model with Backbone, 256-259